Literary Lives

General Editor: **Richard Dutton**, Professor of English, Lancaster University

This series offers stimulating accounts of the literary careers of the most admired and influential English-language authors. Volumes follow the outline of the writers' working lives, not in the spirit of traditional biography, but aiming to trace the professional, publishing and social contexts which shaped their writing.

Published titles include:

Gary Waller
EDMUND SPENSER

Linda Wagner-Martin
SYLVIA PLATH

Cedric Watts
JOSEPH CONRAD

John Williams
MARY SHELLEY
WILLIAM WORDSWORTH

Tom Winnifrith and Edward Chitham
CHARLOTTE AND EMILY BRONTË

John Worthen
D. H. LAWRENCE

David Wykes
EVELYN WAUGH

Literary Lives
Series Standing Order ISBN 0–333–71486–5
(*outside North America only*)

You can receive future titles in this series as they are published by placing a standing order. Please contact your bookseller or, in case of difficulty, write to us at the address below with your name and address, the title of the series and the ISBN quoted above.

Customer Services Department, Macmillan Distribution Ltd, Houndmills, Basingstoke, Hampshire RG21 6XS, England

Mary Shelley

A Literary Life

John Williams
Reader in Literary Studies
University of Greenwich

First published in Great Britain 2000 by
MACMILLAN PRESS LTD
Houndmills, Basingstoke, Hampshire RG21 6XS and London
Companies and representatives throughout the world

A catalogue record for this book is available from the British Library.

ISBN 0–333–69830–4 hardcover
ISBN 0–333–69831–2 paperback

First published in the United States of America 2000 by
ST. MARTIN'S PRESS, INC.,
Scholarly and Reference Division,
175 Fifth Avenue, New York, N.Y. 10010

ISBN 0–312–22832–5

Library of Congress Cataloging-in-Publication Data
Williams, John, 1946–
Mary Shelley : a literary life / John Williams.
p.   cm. — (Literary lives)
Includes bibliographical references (p.   ) and index.
ISBN 0–312–22832–5 (cloth)
1. Shelley, Mary Wollstonecraft, 1797–1851.   2. Women authors,
English—19th century—Biography.   I. Title.   II. Series: Literary
lives (New York, N.Y.)
PR5398.W55   1999
823'.7—dc21
[B]   99–40596
                                                         CIP

© John Williams 2000

This book is printed on paper suitable for recycling and made from fully managed and sustained forest sources.

10   9   8   7   6   5   4   3   2   1
09   08   07   06   05   04   03   02   01   00

Printed and bound in Great Britain by
Antony Rowe Ltd, Chippenham, Wiltshire

In memory of
Valerie Pitt

Contents

Note on Abbreviations and Texts

Abbreviations

F: *Frankenstein; or The Modern Prometheus*, Mary Shelley, ed. J. Paul Hunter, Norton Critical Edition (New York and London 1996).

FN: *Falkner*, Mary Shelley, 3 vols (London 1837).

J: *The Journals of Mary Shelley 1814-1844*, ed. Paula R. Feldman and Diana Scott-Kilvert, 2 vols (Oxford 1987).

Quotations from the *Journals* omit the detailed textual markings used to indicate corrections and alterations in the manuscript.

L: *Lodore*, Mary Shelley, ed. Lisa Vargo (Ontario 1997).

L I, II, II: *The Letters of Mary Wollstonecraft Shelley*, ed. Betty T. Bennett, 3 vols (Baltimore 1980-88).

References to the *Letters* give volume, date and page unless any of that information is already present in the text.

LM: *The Last Man*, Mary Shelley, ed. Morton D. Paley (Oxford 1994).

M: *Matilda*, Mary Shelley, ed. Janet Todd (London 1992).

References to *Matilda* in the text adopt Mary Shelley's original spelling, 'Mathilda'.

P: *The Fortunes of Perkin Warbeck: a Romance*, Mary Shelley, 3 vols (London 1830).

PW: *Shelley: Complete Poetical Works*, ed. Thomas Hutchinson, corrected by G. M. Matthews (Oxford 1971).

The abbreviated form PW is reserved for Chapter 8 where Mary Shelley's Notes to her 1839 edition of Percy Shelley's poems are discussed. The text referred to is the Oxford University Press *Complete Poetical Works*, based on Thomas Hutchinson's edition of 1905.

R: *Rambles in Germany and Italy, in 1840, 1842, and 1843*, 2 vols, Mary Shelley (London 1844).

S: *Essays, Letters from Abroad, Translations and Fragments*, Percy Bysshe Shelley, edited by Mrs Shelley, 2 vols (London 1852).

V: *Valperga*, Mary Shelley, ed. Stuart Curran (Oxford 1997).

Texts

Mary Shelley's novels: *The Novels and Selected Works of Mary Shelley*, edited by Nora Crook, with Pamela Clemit and Betty T. Bennett, published in 8 volumes by Pickering and Chatto was published in 1997; it is available only as a set, and therefore remains well beyond the purchasing power of most individuals. This book has used modern affordable scholarly editions of the novels where possible (*Frankenstein, Valperga, The Last Man, Mathilda* and *Lodore*), and continues to use the first editions of *Perkin Warbeck* and *Falkner*. When referring to first editions, volume numbers are given before page numbers. This is also the case with *Rambles in Germany and Italy*.

1
Introduction

> ... she would have been eminent among her sex at any time, in any circumstances, and would, it cannot be doubted, have achieved greater personal fame than she actually did but for the fact that she became, at a very early age, the wife of Shelley.
>
> (Mrs Julian Marshall, 1889)[1]

The events of Mary Shelley's life from the time of her birth in 1797 to the death of her husband, Percy Bysshe Shelley, in 1822, have been exhaustively researched and written up over many years. The same is true of the novel she wrote and published during that time, *Frankenstein, or The Modern Prometheus*. More recently, however, attention has increasingly turned to the study of Shelley's literary output as a whole; this includes seven novels, numerous short stories, literary biography and criticism, and travel-writing. In addition to her published work, information to be found in Shelley's letters and her *Journals* have helped to bring together the threads of her public and private life in ever greater detail from the time of Percy Shelley's death to that of her own in 1851.

In 1972 William Walling produced a book on Mary Shelley for Twayne's English Authors series. Walling discussed Shelley's first three published novels, *Frankenstein* (1818), *Valperga* (1823), and *The Last Man* (1826) in some detail. The rest of her output was dealt with in two of the book's six chapters. Two biographies followed; Jane Dunn published *Moon in Eclipse* in 1978, and in 1987 Muriel Spark's *Mary Shelley: a Biography* appeared.[2] Though both writers sought to free Mary Shelley from the fate of being considered an appendage to the life and work of Percy Shelley, both still tended to concentrate on the

1

early period of her life and work. Emily Sunstein's *Mary Shelley: Romance and Reality*, published in 1989,[3] was indicative of a steadily growing interest in relocating Mary Shelley within the literary canon, and in 1993, Audrey A. Fisch, Anne K. Mellor and Esther H. Schor published a book intended to signal the fact that students of Mary Shelley had joined the major players in the literary criticism game. *The Other Mary Shelley* claimed that it was appropriate to discuss Mary Shelley as 'an astute, informed, literate, self-conscious, and above all courageous critic of culture'.[4] The 'other Mary Shelley' was the one who could manage very well without Percy, and who had a great deal more going for her besides *Frankenstein*.

Three years later, Twayne brought out a new Mary Shelley volume, this time by Johanna M. Smith.[5] Smith could still claim to be doing something relatively unusual. 'Until quite recently', she explains, 'a book on Mary Shelley would have justified itself by reference to her husband, Percy Shelley, and to her novel *Frankenstein*.' She describes her critical position as 'consistently feminist and Marxist', which is to say that she shares her methodology with the majority of her immediate predecessors. She explains that her theoretical agenda is best served by avoiding a biographical approach; she prefers to work 'by genre in order to emphasise the breadth of [Shelley's] writing'. The consequences of this are important.

Firstly, by replacing the biographical chronology with genre groupings Smith marginalises the importance of issues and events in the life of the writer. She does the biography in Chapter 1, then proceeds to group Shelley's work as 'Plays and Poems', 'Science Fiction', 'Historical Fiction', 'Domestic-Sentimental Fiction', 'Literary Biography and Criticism', and 'Travel Narratives'. It is a refreshingly new perspective, not least because no one can study Shelley for long without becoming aware of how powerfully inhibiting are the people who gather round her in any biographically organised account: her mother and father, her step-sister Claire, her lover and husband, her father-in-law, her husband's first wife, whose suicide in 1816 was never far from her mind, and the remnants of the Shelley/Byron circle who continued to monitor her progress as novelist, editor and potential biographer of Percy Shelley after 1822. It is good to see Shelley's person and her work rescued (by whatever means) from what frequently becomes a wearyingly disagreeable company of men and women capable of making her life a misery.

Smith does not deny the place which an awareness of the biography must have in any satisfactory reading of Shelley's work, but she sees it as something that can all too easily get in the way of appreciating Shelley's engagement with 'contemporary questions and issues' in her writing, and occluding 'the continuing interest in political questions and gender issues that salts her work'. *Mary Shelley Revisited* is therefore structured in accordance with a genre-specific way of looking at writing. A further justification for such a plan is that it challenges the 'invidious distinction between "major" and "minor" works' that otherwise invariably takes place. Removing the chronological framework, and refusing to be concerned with 'major/minor' literary distinctions has drawbacks as well as benefits, however. There will inevitably be questions about Shelley's work that do not get asked, and issues around the production of her work that fail to be raised.

The 'literary life' format adopted here reintroduces a chronological framework. But this does not require a rigorous, year-by-year reading of Shelley. The second chapter of this book – concerned with childhood – works its way back into Shelley's early years from a point of crisis in 1819, when she was 22. A chronologically based approach should not assume that the biography explains the writing, nor should it exercise overall control of the critical processes at work. That said, studying Shelley's writing as the product of a 'literary life' has much to offer by way of adding to existing Mary Shelley criticism; one important consequence is to appreciate the extent to which Shelley's work after 1822 was dominated by her determination to proceed with one major project, the editing of her husband's poetry and prose into a definitive collected edition, to be accompanied by a biography that would silence his many detractors, and establish him as the leading poetic genius of the age. What goes on in the novels, articles, reviews, short stories and biographies as the years pass, is intricately bound up with Mary's continuing struggle – against considerable odds – to sustain the Percy Shelley project.

The chronological approach also requires that a writer's work be judged in accordance with the extent to which it displays a process of development from early work into maturity. There is very little space for qualitative assessment of Shelley's writing within the structure and methodology of Smith's book. One of the most positive aspects of a 'literary life' format is that it extends the scope of the study of a writer's personal literary life towards a contextual concern with the literary life of the country (or countries) within which the work is produced. The reading public's verdict on the writer (gauged from reviews, sales figures, and in some cases – as with Shelley – from contemporary novels by other writers, where there is evidence of an overt response to her work) is best studied as part of an historical process, where it becomes possible to argue that a writer is either following the fashion of the day, or in some way contributing towards the creation of it. The literary life of Mary Shelley therefore explores the work of her contemporaries in more detail than the genre-based study. The context is established not so much by genre with reference to her own writing – though that remains important – as by the existence of other writers and their readers, writers like Godwin, Wollstonecraft, Inchbald, Brockden Brown, Disraeli, Bulwer-Lytton, Catherine Gore and Charles Dickens. When Mary Shelley begins to contribute to Dionysius Lardner's biographical anthologies in the mid-1830s, a study of the literary life of Mary Shelley engages not just with her contributions: it concerns itself with the phenomenon of Lardner's project as part of the larger literary life of England, the study of which begins to define and assess Shelley's contribution to it. The work of other contributors to the volumes Shelley was responsible for will be considered, as will other books in the series where Shelley had no involvement. It is also helpful to consider Lardner's background, to discover what his extraordinary career illustrates in relation to early-nineteenth-century political and scholarly activity.

With this in mind, it is time to remind ourselves of the fact that when Shelley scholars of the late nineteenth and early twentieth centuries turned once more to a reading of the novels and short stories Shelley produced after *Frankenstein*, they found material that failed to interest or enthral them in the way the voices of Dickens, Gaskell or George Eliot had done. Shelley was worthy, but undeniably second-rate; a follower of fashion rather than an innovator. Florence Marshall, in her *Life and Letters* of Mary Shelley (1889) was in no doubt of the explanation; Mary had been taken over by Percy Shelley in her teens, and in consequence was never allowed to mature as her own person.[6] In 1938, Sylva Norman delivered a verdict on Shelley's fiction that remained unchallenged until well into the 1970s. Walling effectively endorsed it in 1972, while the later, more positive scholarship of Sunstein, Mellor, Fisch, Schor, Smith (and many more) has simply not felt the need to address it. Norman first established the context:

> The early nineteenth century favoured melancholy.... Its drama must be tragic, its lyrics despairing, its lengthy novels stuffed out with disasters and bespattered with the bleeding fragments of warm hearts.

Then she placed Mary Shelley:

> Genuine imaginative fertility was denied her.... Plot, in both
> novel and short story, was an initial bugbear that had to be
> overcome by a desperate search into memory or history.[7]

And there, in Norman's final phrase, lies a pointer to the debate to
which the literary life must inevitably return. Given that Shelley's
ideas are important and interesting, when it comes to execution, how
are we to assess the extent, nature and the consequences of autobiographical penetration into her fiction? Norman's verdict will no
longer do, but despite fresh insights from recent scholarship, there
remains little discussion of the impact of Shelley's compulsion to
write autobiographically on her fiction, her biography, and on her
work editing Percy Shelley's poetry and prose from 1822 to 1839.

It had originally been the intention to plan this book by presenting
Mary Shelley from a variety of viewpoints, all of which are to be found
repeatedly reinforced in accounts of her work from her own time to
the present. There was to have been a section on Shelley as 'the
daughter of William Godwin and Mary Wollstonecraft', a section on
her as 'the partner of Percy Shelley', and one on 'the widow of Shelley'
and another on 'the editor of Shelley', and of course there was a
section to be written on 'the author of *Frankenstein*'. In practice such
a scheme proved impractical, though vestiges of it are still discernible
in the chapter headings. It remains important to be aware of the fact
that Shelley's literary life generally appears as a life lived in the service
of someone or something else: this might include the ideals of her
parents, the reputation of her husband, or the persona she acquired
not as an author, but very specifically as 'the author of *Frankenstein*'.
It is important to appreciate that Shelley cannot always be liberated
from these restrictions; the fact that she willingly submitted herself to
the task of restoring Percy Shelley to the reading public as one of
England's greatest poets must inevitably contextualise our assessment
of her as an author in her own right. Equally problematic in writing
this particular literary life is the extent to which the life we uncover
(particularly as we read her own account of it in the *Journals* and
letters) elides with the romantic fiction of her time; here again,
Shelley was initiating the process herself, offering the reader her own
life lived out in the manner prescribed by the Romantic myth she
was involved (with Percy Shelley, Byron and others) in creating. Not
only will she do this to herself, but biographers and critics – not

surprisingly, given the drama and tragedy that seems to mark so much of her time with Percy Shelley – have frequently ended up writing her life in similar terms. This too, then, is a theme that runs throughout this book, reminding us that a major preoccupation of all Mary Shelley's fiction was to explore the relationship between life and ideas, between reality and fiction, between the radically idealist, rationalist tradition in which she had been brought up, and the world of heartrending dilemmas and tragic loss in which she lived for 54 years.

2
Parents

'the dark speck of life to come'[1]

Mary Shelley's life was inescapably literary. Both her parents lived by writing. In the case of her mother, Mary Wollstonecraft, her death in childbirth meant that Mary could only ever know her by repute. She might only hope to hear her voice through her writings, and through what others wrote about her, in particular through the *Memoir* that her father, William Godwin, published in 1798. Mary Godwin grew up in a house where literary celebrities met regularly to discuss and read their work; the child's experience was of life lived at every turn through books, writing them, selling them, reading them, discussing them; and she herself seemed destined to live a life that followed the course of the kind of romantic fiction that was so popular with her generation. It is small wonder that when Thomas Jefferson Hogg set about writing up the whirlwind romance between his friend Percy Bysshe Shelley and the teenage Mary Godwin, he did so as though it were just that, a chapter from a novel. Fact or fiction, Hogg did the job so well that it has since become virtually impossible to think of it in any other way.[2]

In his 'Memoir' of Shelley (1858–60), Thomas Love Peacock could think of no better way of putting it. He begins:

> Mr. Hogg saw Mary Godwin for the first time on the first day of Lord Cochrane's trial. This was the 8th. of June, 1814. He went with Shelley to Mr. Godwin's.

From a solidly factual prologue, Peacock moves directly to quote Hogg's seductive prose:

> We entered a room on the first floor. – William Godwin was
> not at home. – A thrilling voice called 'Shelley!' A thrilling
> voice answered 'Mary!' And he darted out of the room like an
> arrow from the bow of the far-shooting king.

It is irresistible, and by the time the late-twentieth-century biographer
appears, all need to attribute has melted away:

> the quick, unmistakable sound of his footsteps darting up the
> stairs at the back of the shop and the sudden low call – Mary!
> He spoke to her with a directness and intensity which was so
> new to her, and yet she instantly recognised it as love.[3]

Mary Godwin was destined to lead a literary life in a variety of guises,
not least as the fictionalised tragic heroine of her own story.

In the summer of 1819 Mary Shelley began work on her second novel,
Mathilda. The author was 22, and was pregnant with her fourth child.
In June 1819 her son William had died of malaria; in September of the
previous year her daughter Clara had died from fever. She had married
Percy Shelley in December 1816, an event only made possible by the
death of Shelley's first wife, Harriet, who had committed suicide.
Harriet had borne Shelley two children; her pregnant body had been
fished out of the Serpentine on 10 December 1816; Percy and Mary's
wedding took place just 20 days later. Two months before this, Mary
Shelley's half-sister, Fanny (the daughter of Mary Wollstonecraft) had
committed suicide. In February 1815, some seven months after her
elopement with Shelley, Mary had given birth prematurely to a baby
girl, also named Clara, who died within a month.

The tenor of a life retold must inevitably rest to a significant degree
on the selection of events, and how they are then narrated. If *Mathilda*
is anything to go by, in August 1819, Mary Shelley's own narrative of
her life was dominated by a sense of irreparable loss and despair; her
depression was the culmination of just 22 years that from the outset
had delivered a dislocated domestic life, and with Percy Shelley had
continued to foster a nomadic, Bohemian, hand-to-mouth existence.
It may have been August 1819 in Leghorn, but for Mary Shelley 'it is
winter and the sun has already set':

> I am alone ... the blight of misfortune has passed over me and
> withered me; I know that I am about to die and I feel happy
> – joyous. – I feel my pulse; it beats fast: I place my thin hand
> on my cheek; it burns: there is a slight, quick spirit within me
> that is now emitting its last sparks. I shall never see the snows
> of another winter.... (M 151)

Shelley was not so completely prostrated by grief that she could not
channel it into fiction, however. She had enough spirit left to build a
sustained narrative around her despair, and to review her own situation by dramatising it in the 'literary' life of her tragic heroine,
Mathilda.

There are four events in Mary Shelley's life that figure in all the
biographies as seminal: the tragic death in childbirth of her mother;
her own elopement with Percy Shelley; the publication of *Frankenstein*
in 1818; and the devastating events of July 1822, when Percy Shelley
was drowned. Arguably, however, the moment when Mary Shelley sits
down and begins to review her life through the writing of *Mathilda* is
every bit as important. Percy Shelley's death notwithstanding, it is
hard to imagine her at a much lower ebb:

> We went from England comparatively prosperous & happy –
> I should return broken hearted & miserable – I never know
> one moments ease from the wretchedness and despair that
> possesses me – (L. I p.101)

That was how she described the situation to Marianne Hunt in June
1819; in her *Journal* for August of that year she noted cryptically, 'I
begin my journal on Shelley's birthday – We have lived five years
together & if all the events of the five years were blotted out I might
be happy ...'(J 293).

The feeling that Percy Shelley was at least in part to blame for what
had happened lurks within these comments, and with good reason;
but far worse was a persistent voice whispering that she had only
herself to blame. And then there was a further blight upon her young
life. It becomes very clear from *Mathilda* that in addition to mourning
the loss of her children, Mary was not only struggling with the fact
that she could no longer give her husband the love she once had, she
was mourning the loss of a father. Despite Godwin's anger over her
elopement, Mary continued to idolise him and never failed to support
him when it came to his constant requests for money, money the

Shelleys rarely if ever had. Now, clearly persuaded that his own needs far outweighed the significance of his daughter's loss and the consequent state of her health, he wrote to her:

> I had thought you to be ranked among those noble spirits that do honour to our nature. Oh! what a falling off is here!... you have lost a child; and all the rest of the world, all that is beautiful, and all that has a claim upon your kindness, is nothing, because a child of three years old is dead![4]

Percy Shelley wrote in despair to Leigh Hunt, 'he heaps on her misery, still misery'. A year later, with Mary's fourth child safely born, but the relationship between husband and wife no less strained, Godwin's persistence prompted Shelley to write a magnificent letter of sustained, despairing rage to his father-in-law. 'Your letters', he wrote, 'from their style and spirit ... never fail to produce an appalling effect on her frame...'.[5]

Mathilda is evidence of Mary Shelley's perception of herself not just as a tragic outcast, cut off from those she most loved (husband and father as well as children), but also as an individual who actively brings disaster upon those who would befriend her. Matthew Lewis had named the *femme fatale* of his Gothic novel *The Monk* (1796) Matilda; it was a book the Shelleys knew well. Percy had used the name for the villainess in his Gothic tale of 1810, *Zastrozzi*. In both cases Matilda is the willing agent of evil. Mary never lost a sense of guilt over Harriet's death, and at every new tragedy in her own life she called to mind the fate of the woman she had replaced in Shelley's life and reflected on her part in it, reflecting also no doubt on how she might be brought to account for it. 'Poor Harriet,' she wrote in her *Journal* of 1839, 'to whose sad fate I attribute so many of my own heavy sorrows as the atonement claimed by fate for her death' (J 560).

This is 'literary' evidence culled from a life saturated in literary activity; it is how Mary Shelley herself worked and survived, turning to the creation of fiction to review her own sorry state. But as with all fiction, the interpretation of it will vary. For example, both Godwin's response to his daughter's depression, and his reaction to the manuscript of *Mathilda* which Mary sent him, have been subject to very different readings. Godwin received the manuscript in 1820, expressed his distaste and refused to set about finding a publisher for it. Anne K. Mellor comments, 'Probably he perceived, beneath the surface story of incest, his daughter's portrait of his own equally horrendous failure as a loving, supportive parent'.[6] Yet Peter H. Marshall suggests that when Godwin 'quietly put the manuscript back in the drawer' he was acting in Mary's best interests; on the subject of the correspondence between Godwin and Mary at the time of William's death, he writes, '... he sincerely sympathised but character- istically called her to stoicism: 'it is only persons of a very ordinary sort, and of a pusillanimous disposition, that sink long under a calamity of this nature"'.[7] Marshall's book has been subject to much adverse criticism over the years, and unconvincing as his judgement is, we should at least note that his selection of a quote which offers a slightly milder example of Godwin's insensitivity is also a quote that other commentators have tended to exclude from their accounts.

What this present narrative depicts is a Mary Shelley whose literary life had scarcely begun in 1819, but who nevertheless already contem- plates its termination. The author has come to believe that she is both inadequate as a seriously creative writer, and personally responsible to a considerable degree for the catastrophic failure of her domestic life. She will have reflected bitterly on the fact that she had been born with the label of great promise hung about her neck; how could she not prove to be a remarkable person with such notable, if not notorious parents? Her father had been ready to remind her of this: 'I had thought you to be ranked among those noble spirits who do honour to our nature. Oh! What a falling off is here!' Godwin took it as an insult if this daughter of his turned out to be anything other than a 'noble spirit'. With such a lineage she could not afford to be anything (or anyone) else. She was destined to perpetuate a personality cult that had started when her mother and father had attracted the attention of journalists who reported their commitment to the revolutionary poli- tics and feminist polemics of the 1790s.

To understand the depths of despair into which Mary was cast in 1819, we need therefore to reflect on the circumstances of her birth, and in doing so remember just how charged those circumstances were with literary assumptions. Mary's birth – heralded by many as a portentous event because her parents were who they were – may equally well be perceived as directing her into the blind alley she was forced to admit had imprisoned and defeated her by 1819.

Mary Shelley's life began in circumstances which sound as though they might have originated in a work of contemporary popular fiction: 'My mother died a few weeks after I was born; and I lost my father when I was very young...'.[8] It is a recurring motif, being repeated here by Maria Edgeworth in her novel *Ennui* (1809). It may be that the father is the first to go, 'The father of Mademoiselle Monique C———— was a farmer, and died three months before the birth of his child', but in such cases the mother can usually be relied upon to follow before too long:

> It seemed as if this respectable woman had, after the death of her husband, only supported life for the sake of her infant family, from whom she was snatched by death.[9]

That was Helen Maria Williams relating a story told to her by friends in *Letters written in France* (1790). One way or another, the fate of the daughter of Mary Wollstonecraft was being written and rewritten to a point where the reality was in danger of being elbowed out completely:

> The fruit of this unhappy union was a daughter. Her mother died shortly after her birth. Her father was careless of her destiny. She was consigned to the care of a hireling....[10]

The opening of Charles Brockden Brown's novel *Edgar Huntly* (1799) is not an exact description of Mary Godwin's circumstances, but given the way her father saw fit to deal with his daughter's behaviour as a teenager, it is not so very from the truth.

It should always be borne in mind that the writer of any 'literary life' must construct a narrative of some sort, and though the outcome may be expected to look very different from what Edgeworth, Williams or Brockden Brown produced, the process by which those narratives come into being may not always be as far apart as we might assume. Edgeworth, Williams and Brockden Brown were all to become required reading for the daughter of Mary Wollstonecraft; they were all, in a sense, 'sources' for Mary Shelley as she wrote her own life into her various literary works, even as the self-consciously literary performances of Hogg and Peacock (and others) were in their time to become sources for later biographers.

Mary Godwin was born on 30 August, 1797. 'The period from the birth of the child till about eight o'clock the next morning', wrote

Godwin, 'was a period full of alarm and peril.' The placenta had not come away with the birth, and the infection that resulted from its removal meant that within two weeks Mary Wollstonecraft was dead. The circumstances and the crude unhygienic methods of attempting to rectify the situation were not exceptional. The spotlight falls where it does because in this instance the players are from the world of letters, the curtain is therefore pulled back to allow our imagination the opportunity to participate in the drama. William Godwin, 'in the very gulph of despair', was awoken at 6 o'clock on the morning of 10 September; Mary Wollstonecraft 'expired at twenty minutes before eight'.[11]

Godwin's account of his wife's death in his *Memoirs of the Author of 'The Rights of Women'* (published in 1798) avoids for the most part the rhetoric of the popular sentimental narrative; we sense the depths of his despair primarily because of his tendency to understatement. The fact remains, however, that one means of coping with bereavement was to remove the situation to a world of fiction, using well-trodden clichés and truisms to effect the release of emotions that lay beyond naming. For Godwin, writing the *Memoirs* constituted a therapeutic exercise (whether or not he recognised the fact) practised extensively by Mary Wollstonecraft herself; and their daughter Mary was to continue in the same vein. These were all literary lives, for ever exploring paths which led from actual existence into fiction, fable and dream, and out again.

William Godwin's route to this indeterminate territory between literature and life was very different from that of Mary Wollstonecraft. Raised in a strictly Calvinist home where love and affection were in short supply, Godwin made his way into the stimulating world of intellectual religious dissent and radical journalism, adopting in due course the atheistic view that conduct was determined (and thus to be understood) by the operation of scientific laws. His great purpose, the realisation in society of political justice through rational means, would be hindered, not helped, by the intervention of the emotions; unless, that is, the rationalist could intervene objectively to channel love, hate and ambition into the creation of a greater good for society. At 40 years of age, this son of relentless Enlightenment reason fell deeply in love with Mary Wollstonecraft. Within 18 months of his new life beginning, the woman lay dead, and he was faced with the responsibility of looking after their daughter, and of caring for Fanny, Mary's child by Gilbert Imlay, born in 1794.

In Mary Wollstonecraft's case, the spring of 1796 seemed to mark an end to years of emotional trauma suffered in the course of an unhappy childhood, and an adult life spent in a luckless quest for fulfilment in a string of personal relationships. Many of these experiences had entered the world of fiction through her two novels, *Mary* (written in 1789) and *Maria* (uncompleted at her death, and published by Godwin with the *Memoirs* in 1798). Her daughter's novel *Mathilda* was in fact partly at least a reworking of another of her mother's unfinished autobiographical fictions, 'The Cave of Fancy'; thus fiction and reality became inextricably interwoven across the generations, with Godwin – who recognised fiction as a powerful vehicle for the spread of rational ideas – looking somewhat perplexedly on.

It must never therefore be forgotten that Mary Godwin had been born into a world where identity, thought and action were defined by a never-ending programme of reading and composition, and that foremost in that programme was the reading of books authored by her father and mother.

Mary Wollstonecraft's personality was emotional and volatile, very different from the received notion of the man she eventually married, the calculated rationalist author of her *Memoirs*. In that book Godwin is ready enough to reveal himself as the distracted lover, grasping at straws as his wife's condition steadily deteriorates, but he manages to do so with a degree of objectivity very much in keeping with his rationalist philosophy. Far from being unattractive, however, there is an engaging ingenuousness in the attempt he makes to summarise his wife's qualities at the end of the book:

> We had cultivated our powers...in different directions; I chiefly in an attempt at logical and metaphysical distinction.... I did not possess, in the degree of some other men, an intuitive perception of intellectual beauty.... What I wanted in this respect, Mary possessed, in a degree superior to any other person I ever knew.... She adopted one opinion, and rejected another, spontaneously, by a sort of tact, and the force of cultivated imagination; and yet, though perhaps, in the strict sense of the term, she reasoned little, it is surprising what a degree of soundness is to be found in her determinations.[12]

The William Godwin we are not allowed to find in the *Memoirs* surfaces in fictional form two years later with the publication of *St. Leon* in 1799. The central figure of this novel sets his commitment to learning, power and wealth above that of his domestic life, and his consequent neglect of his wife is directly linked to her physical decline and eventual death in childbirth. Some 15 years later the Count de St Leon was to be an important model for Mary Shelley's Victor Frankenstein; for Godwin St Leon provided a means of giving vent to grief and guilt he could not otherwise describe:

> There is nothing in the vast variety of objects which this wretched world presents to our view so dreadful and distress-ing as the sight of one we have loved, but who is now no more.... Within that petty frame resided for years all that we worship, for there resided all that we know and can conceive of excellence.... It remains no longer, but to mock my sense and scoff at my sorrow, to rend my bosom with a woe, complicated, matchless and inexpressible.... Let me recollect all that Marguerite was as she lived ... for that is a divine and celestial madness: but let me not recollect her as I saw her on the bier, lest I become raving and blaspheme.[13]

As she read the novel, discovering in St Leon a man doomed since his wife's death to remain a stranger to his daughters, Mary Shelley cannot fail to have recognised an autobiographical strand to the plot. She continued in the same vein with her own fiction; whatever else *Frankenstein* may be about, it is certainly about fathers and mothers (or creators) who are tragically absent when they are most needed.

Understanding the opening pages of Mary Shelley's literary life clearly involves understanding the way in which it was variously being written immediately before and after her birth. To do this it is neces-sary to consider further the contrasting lives led by her mother and father up to the time of her birth.

By the mid-1790s, William Godwin had become the acknowledged intellectual leader of political radicalism in England. He was single, and seemingly his only commitment was to the abstract cause of polit-ical justice. Mary Wollstonecraft, already famous as the author of *A Vindication of the Rights of Women* (1792), was, by way of contrast, moving from an unresolved affair with the painter Henry Fuseli (she was 29, he was 47) to residence in Paris in the dangerous revolution-ary year of 1792. There she lived with her new lover, Gilbert Imlay;

she gave birth to Fanny, and as the relationship with Imlay deterio-
rated, eventually sought half-heartedly to take her own life.[14] She then
travelled to Sweden on Imlay's behalf, following this by a further
attempt at suicide. It is a life that without much difficulty can be made
to read like an amalgam of the most sentimental and tearfully melodramatic fictions of the period; Rousseau's *La Nouvelle Héloise* (1761)
and Goethe's phenomenally successful *The Sorrows of Young Werther*
(1774) may seem like chapters of the same book. Wollstonecraft's own
fictions reproduce this popular format, while also incorporating the
commonsense teachings of her *Vindications of the Rights of Women*.

Godwin's life up to 1797 can also be written to read very much like
his own publications. *Political Justice*, published in 1793, became the
bible of radical political theory; the novel *Caleb Williams* of 1794 was
a psychological crime novel of pursuit written to spread the rationalist maxims of *Political Justice* to a wider audience. He was not,
however, considered dangerous enough to prosecute, and had always
maintained a discreet distance between himself and the London
Corresponding Society, a radical association the government sought
to exterminate in 1794 through the prosecution of its leading
members. Eight hundred warrants had been drawn up against other
reformers, 300 of which had already been signed pending the successful outcome of the 1794 trials. In response to this, Godwin
anonymously published his *Cursory Strictures on the Charges Delivered
by Lord Chief Justice Eyre to the Grand Jury*. The *Cursory Strictures* were
hastily rebutted, Godwin duly producing a withering riposte. Though
his intervention was by no means necessarily the one decisive factor
in demolishing the government's case against the LCS, it was clearly
of great significance, and it confirmed his prominence in the dangerous world of political activism. But ironically this was the moment
that also marked the beginning of Godwin's gradual slide toward relative obscurity.

Encouraged by their success, the radicals – led by John Thelwall –
looked to press home their advantage by launching a series of mass
meetings aimed at pressuring the government into conceding
demands based firmly on the radical teachings of *Political Justice*. But
although Thelwall may have been preaching the matter of *Political
Justice*, he was not practising the methods recommended by its author.
Godwin now denounced both sides, deploring in particular Thelwall's
rabble-rousing tactics. Like so many others at this time, he was beginning to reassess the optimism with which he had viewed the first
stirrings of radical change in France and England, a process which was

reflected in his revised 1795 edition of *Political Justice*. In many respects these were halcyon days, when a degree of notoriety justifiably encouraged Godwin to anticipate his continuing success as an author of both philosophy and fiction; lionised by the liberal wing of London society, he enjoyed fame at home and abroad, and was now being discreetly pursued by several women who clearly believed him a worthwhile catch.

Despite the triumph of the 1794 acquittals, however, the political tide had turned, and not even Godwin's skill could prevent the passage of two emergency bills through Parliament (the so-called 'gagging acts' of 1796) designed to suppress political meetings and seditious publications. Doubts about the likelihood of rational debate giving rise to the triumph of reason began to emerge, and although the man who met Mary Wollstonecraft in 1796 still enjoyed a considerable reputation, the father of Mary one year later was already having to come to terms with the prospect of financial difficulties in the near future. Godwin's detractors were swift to point out that his marriage to Wollstonecraft constituted a climb down from the couple's much-publicised detestation of the marriage contract; it was a gift to loyalist commentators for whom *Political Justice* epitomised the doctrine of political sedition and sexual licence. Mary Wollstonecraft presented them with a stereotypical image of the disreputable, immoral harridan only to be expected in a woman dabbling in radical politics and feminist polemics.

It is hard to imagine a less inauspicious time for Mary Godwin to be born. Within a year of Wollstonecraft's death, the *European Magazine* claimed that Godwin's *Memoir* would be read 'with disgust by every female who has pretensions to delicacy; with detestation by everyone attached to the interests of religion and morality; and with indignation by anyone who might feel any regard for the unhappy woman, whose frailties should have been buried in oblivion'.[15] While the child's mother was being vilified, her father – though still respected by many – was being attacked and ridiculed by many more, and if not that, easily forgotten. Percy Shelley would no doubt have come looking for Godwin well before 1812 had he realised – which he probably didn't – that he was still alive.[16]

Mary Wollstonecraft and Godwin shared common intellectual roots, that of progressive dissent. Wollstonecraft's engagement with radical political thinking was contextualised early on by the difficulties that beset her own attempts to become educated as a child and a young woman. She first published her views on the subject in 1787, when with the encouragement of liberals and reformers living in Newington Green where she ran a school, she wrote *Thoughts on the Education of Daughters*. Her father was a spendthrift, liable to brutality; her mother, according to Godwin, was 'the first, and most submissive of his subjects'.[17] After Mrs Wollstonecraft's death in 1780, it fell to Mary to support her father, her brother and her sisters with what money she could earn through writing and teaching. In her teens she had a close friendship with Fanny Blood, and when Fanny moved to Portugal to marry, subsequently becoming pregnant and seriously ill, Mary left Newington to nurse her. Fanny's death, along with that of her newly born child, ended what had often been a difficult but always a deeply felt relationship.

Mary drew on this experience for *Mary* (1788), where the heroine travels to Lisbon with her consumptive friend Anne, who dies, leaving Mary to make her way sadly home:

> In England then landed the forlorn wanderer.... she saw vulgarity, dirt, and vice – her soul sickened.... Forgetting her own griefs, she gave the world a much indebted tear; mourned for a world in ruins.[18]

The school in Newington was in disarray, so she travelled to Ireland to become a governess in the household of Lord and Lady Kingsborough. A year later she returned to England, and, with the help of Newington Green friends, became involved in the world of radical publishing in London. She lodged with the printer Joseph Johnson, and fell in love with Henry Fuseli the painter. In 1790 she published *A Vindication of the Rights of Men*, following this with *A Vindication of the Rights of Women* in 1792; in both books she argued on a rational basis for women's liberation from the feminine stereotype of docility in the face of male dominance. Claire Tomalin has described Wollstonecraft at this time as 'an enthusiast' with more reason to express 'contempt than enthusiasm':

> her most remarkable trait was still that she had refused to learn the techniques whereby women in her situation usually attempted to make life tolerable for themselves: flattery, docility, resignation to the will of man, or God, or their social superiors, or all three.[19]

When her scheme for a *ménage à trois* between herself, Fuseli, and his wife failed to win approval, she had moved to Paris with Gilbert Imlay, and in 1792 witnessed the onset of one of the most violent phases of the Revolution, the 'Terror'. Her return to London in the spring of 1795 followed her discovery that Imlay's commitment to her in no way matched hers to him.

Imlay had been making his money by trading between Gothenburg and Le Havre, a venture which required breaking the English wartime blockade. In the course of this it seems that a Norwegian captain in Imlay's employ had double-crossed him, commandeering a cargo worth some £3500. Since the whole business was at best semi-legal, Imlay had to move with great care in his attempt to retrieve his losses. In a bizarre coda to his relationship with Mary, he arranged for her (with Fanny and a nurse in tow) to go to Norway and Sweden and negotiate on his behalf for the return of his property. Her account of this trip (excluding the business aspects) was published in January 1796 as *A Short Residence in Sweden*. It was a text her daughter read repeatedly.

Wollstonecraft returned to London in 1795 to find Imlay living with another woman; once more she attempted suicide, throwing herself into the Thames from Putney Bridge. She was rescued, and subsequently met William Godwin in the spring of 1796, by which time Godwin had read and been impressed by *A Short Residence*. The book revealed the intellectually penetrating author of *A Vindication of the Rights of Women* as also a melancholy, sentimental traveller, sharply perceptive, but equally attuned to the imaginative influence of nature on her troubled soul:

> I enquired for a walk, and mounting near two hundred steps made round a rock, walked up and down for about a hundred yards, viewing the sea, to which I quickly descended by steps that cheated the declivity. The ocean, and these tremendous bulwarks, enclosed me on every side. I felt the confinement, and wished for wings to reach still loftier cliffs, whose slippery sides no foot was so hardy as to tread; yet what was it to see? – only a boundless waste of water – not a glimpse of smiling nature – not a patch of lively green to relieve the aching sight, or vary the objects of meditation.[20]

What transpired was a relationship of deeply emotional commitment managed in a determinedly rational way. Initially the couple retained their respective homes, Wollstonecraft at Judd Place, Godwin in Charlton Street. Both considered the institution of marriage at best an irrelevance, and at worst for the woman an unjust contract of enslavement; but when Mary became pregnant a compromise was judged unavoidable, and the couple married on 29 March 1797. They then moved to a new house in Somers Town, The Polygon, while Godwin rented a room nearby in which to work. Love and cohabitation modified Godwin's rationalism significantly, and *Political Justice* was revised accordingly. The first edition included a fable in which the house of a great educator, Archbishop Fénelon, catches fire. There is time to save only one person, and the choice is between Fénelon and his chambermaid. Justice, where sentimentality is ousted by rationality, sacrifices the chambermaid, even 'had she been my wife, my mother or my benefactor'. In the 1796 and 1798 editions, the age of chivalry proves not to be dead for Godwin after all. In a somewhat disreputable manoeuvre the chambermaid becomes a valet, and the story – though retaining its commitment to rational impartiality – looks increasingly out of place as the tone elsewhere softened even more to reflect Godwin's recognition of his love for Mary as a person rather than as an indispensable educator.[21]

Two notorious literary figures, celebrated in the public mind as radically subversive thinkers, the man who preaches immorality, the woman who practises it; two people who in fact could hardly be more contrasting in temperament, both of whom are considered by their detractors now to have sold out by submitting to a formal marriage; these two, William Godwin and Mary Wollstonecraft, produce a child, Mary.

It was an inauspicious moment to be born.

The world of Mary Godwin's father had been turned upside-down, first with the arrival of Mary Wollstonecraft, then with the brutality of her departure from it. Mary grew up with a famous father who was even then becoming a struggling author turned bookseller, a man out of place in a London that wished to put its radical past firmly behind it. It was not just her mother who had died. She grew up with an emotionally reserved father whose life revolved around writing and intellectual debate, and various bookish schemes to raise money, and – from 1801 – with a stepmother with two children of her own. Mary had, along with her stepsister Fanny, a busy, but not an overly loving home. Indeed, she spent a good deal of time away from it, dispatched to Scotland by her father in 1812 to stay with a family he hardly knew (and Mary not at all), returning after six months, but leaving again in June 1813, to return finally in the spring of 1814. She was sent because Godwin had decided that this would be best for all of them, and most certainly beneficial for his daughter's education. For Mary it must have seemed – as she suffered the lonely, interminable sea-voyage up the east coast of England to Dundee – tantamount to paternal rejection. In 1819, writing *Mathilda*, the Dundee exile is incorporated into her novel as the setting within which Mary Shelley reflected on a life blighted by the unrequited love of a father.

Her life, as we see her on the eve of her first meeting with Percy Shelley (she is just back from Scotland), has already been measured out for her in the chapters of innumerable sentimental novels, of philosophical and educational tracts, in the increasing tendency of the world to ridicule – or simply forget – her father, the twice-married scorner of marriage, and in scurrilous attacks on the mother she never knew, the loving parent upon whose portrait she gazes in the Skinner Street house, wondering the while at the fatal consequences of her birth, at the consequences of her father's subsequent marriage to Mary Jane Clairmont, and at what her future might be.

To the intellectuals who continued to come to the house and talk, to recite poetry, to reflect on times past and on battles won and lost, she was the daughter of genius, of whom great things were expected. Though her schooling remained minimal, it was assumed that she would write; she would follow a literary life in the footsteps of her parents; she would be exceptional. Unlike Fanny, however, who had yet to learn that she had no living parent, she had every reason to believe that she ought to feel that she belonged; but to whom, and to what? She grew to loathe her stepmother, while her father was evidently at a loss as to how to proceed with her as a father. It was one thing to find herself in the presence of literary giants, Godwin himself, Sheridan, Thomas Moore, Lamb, Southey, all passing through the living-room; Samuel Taylor Coleridge would sit there reading from *The Ancient Mariner*, a poem destined to live with Mary for the rest of her life; but what was she to do with it all? The circumstances of her birth meant that there was precious little space left for her to grow up in. Mary Godwin's parentage rendered her a literary composition, but the final chapters of that particular tale were already being written. Where was her own first chapter to begin, and who was to write it? She might at least take some comfort from the passionate longing for self-fulfilment she found in her mother's writing. She herself would in due course seek to emulate the kind of descriptive writing that distinguished *A Short Residence in Sweden*, she too would want to stretch out her hand to eternity, yearning towards 'the dark speck of life to come':

> Reaching the cascade...my soul was hurried by the falls into a new train of reflections. The impetuous dashing of the rebounding torrent from the dark cavities which mocked the exploring eye, produced an equal activity in my mind: my thoughts darted from earth to heaven, and I asked myself why I was chained to life and its misery. Still the tumultuous emotions this sublime object excited, were pleasurable; and, viewing it, my soul rose, with renewed dignity, above its cares – grasping at immortality – it seemed as impossible to stop the current of my thoughts, as of the always varying, still the same, torrent before me – I stretched out my hand to eternity, bounding over the dark speck of life to come.[22]

3
Early Years, 1797–1814

Although she herself later described it as a 'common-place affair', Mary Shelley's childhood was, by any standards, an eventful one;[1] to an outside observer it may have appeared a happy and even privileged one. Aaron Burr, a former vice-president of the United States who took to visiting the Godwins when Mary was 14, described her and her half-sisters Fanny and Jane as cheerful company, cared for by Mary's stepmother, 'a sensible, amiable woman...a charming lady'. Jane remembered a family where everyone relished having to work hard 'learning and studying ... we all took the liveliest interest in the great questions of the day – common topics, gossiping, scandal, found no entrance in our circle'.[2] Jane (or Claire Clairmont as she had decided to call herself) was 70 years old when she wrote that, so it should perhaps be treated with some circumspection as evidence. Other sources suggest that life at Skinner Street was by no means all a matter of 'learning and studying'; there could be fun and games too. Most important is the fact that the children were being brought up in a household where books provided not only pleasure, nor were they just a means of personal improvement, they were also the source of the family income. Reading and writing – serious application to the literary life – was in every respect an integral part of the children's world.

Given that all literary production will have its roots to some degree in the experiences of childhood, and that in the case of the intellectual, bookish world of William Godwin's daughter those roots will have drawn heavily on literary nourishment, this chapter will consider the extent to which the fiction she read had its part to play in influencing how she saw herself. What Aaron Burr saw, or thought he saw, when he visited the home of the great philosopher, and what Jane Clairmont chose to remember some sixty years on, or the way for that matter in which Mary herself chose to describe her childhood, may not always be with hindsight what appears to be of most significance when it comes to analysing this particular literary life in the making. For example, Mary's brief reference to her childhood in the 'Introduction' to the 1831 edition of *Frankenstein* is of less value for its reference to pleasurable day-dreaming, writing stories, and time spent in 'the pleasant region' of Scotland, than for her reference there to herself as 'the daughter of two persons of distinguished literary celebrity'(F 169). This was how people habitually appeared to have thought of her, and no doubt it will have been reflected in the way they tended to speak to her. She may well have wondered at times if she existed as anything other than a medium for her parents. It was in all probability this issue of identity that prompted her to recall that, despite indulging in day-dreams, 'I did not make myself the heroine of my tales.... I could not figure to myself that romantic woes or wonderful events would ever be my lot ...' (F 169). Thoughts of 'romantic woes' and 'wonderful events' were fed by her reading in the popular fiction of the day, and it was her particular sense of exclusion – from both this fictional world and from a family that had sent her off to live in Scotland – that lies at the heart of the development of her literary life.

Mary Godwin spent her childhood negotiating a tortuous path through a complex pattern of fraught familial relationships, learning from an early age about the treacherous vagaries of domestic politics in an oddly assembled family that had always threatened fragmentation. In 1814, of course, fragmentation on a spectacular scale was precisely what took place, and Tolstoy's opening gambit for *Anna Karenin* could hardly be more appropriately applied than here: 'All happy families are alike but an unhappy family is unhappy after its own fashion.'[3]

In 1801, four years after Mary Wollstonecraft's death, William Godwin married Mary Jane Clairmont, a widow with two children, Charles aged 18, and his half-sister , Clara Mary Jane, aged 13. Godwin and his new wife produced a son in 1803, William.

With the exception of Aaron Burr, the second Mrs Godwin has had a consistently bad press. Richard Holmes envisages 'a widow with a powerful and determined personality... it was a practical rather than a romantic match.'[4] The arrival of Mary Jane would have been understandably hard for friends to come to terms with after the departure of Mary Wollstonecraft. Mary Jane clearly was a practical woman, energetic and able; and the way in which she alienated visitors to the Skinner Street home suggests she had no hesitation in staking her claim and speaking her mind. Coming from a man understood to be patient and mild-mannered almost to a fault, 'gentle hearted' Charles Lamb's indictment has always made it difficult to sympathise with the woman he called 'That damned infernal bitch Mrs. Godwin'.[5]

A major stumbling-block would have been Mary Jane's religious and political affiliations. She was a Roman Catholic and a Royalist who spoke excellent French, was widely travelled, and maintained close contacts with the French émigré community in London. No one really knew who she was before she moved into the house next-door to Godwin in 1801. Speculation remains that she arrived with the specific aim of entrapping the widowed philosopher into matrimony.[6] She had lived in France with her family as a girl, then travelled to Spain to be with her brother at the time of the Revolution. The father of Charles was apparently Karl Gaulis, a Swiss. Mary Jane claimed that both her children were by Gaulis, but it has since been suggested that Jane's father was the member of a French émigré family called de Vial. Abandoned by her second lover in Bristol, Mary Jane ended up in a debtor's prison, was released with the aid of charity money, and when Godwin came in view (so the story goes) she knew what to do. She had marketable literary ability to offer, and her contribution to the bookshop business the Godwins launched in Hanway Street in 1805 was crucial to its survival. It became known as the 'City French and Juvenile Library', and when the family moved from Somers Town to 42 Skinner Street in 1807, the ground floor was fitted out as the shop.

Mary Jane could not have been more different from the volatile, manic depressive Mary Wollstonecraft. She was a shrewd, determined and ambitious woman, ready to take on and manage a strange family:

> Charles Clairmont was the half-brother of Jane Clairmont who was the half-sister of William Godwin Junior who was the half-brother of Mary Godwin who was the half-sister of Fanny Imlay. Four of the five had either Godwin or Mary Jane as a natural parent, but no two of them had the same father and the same mother.[7]

She knew only too well with whom she would always be compared, and with this in mind her reputation for petty animosity, her use of curiously unnecessary, manipulative lies or half-truths, and her lack of sensitivity might just be seen to pale before the prospect of quizzically raised eyebrows of Godwin's intellectual visitors, all of whom had no small opinion of their own importance, none of whom were willing to read on after the exquisite chapter of Godwin and Wollstonecraft had been brought to its dramatic conclusion. Mary Jane belonged to the army of jobbing women writers who lived by their trade in essays, tales, translations, novels and journalism. What she made of the literary stars who occasionally gathered at Skinner Street we can only imagine; they must have struck her as 'precious' to say the least, and she developed the conviction that strategies were needed if she was to retain a hold on her stake in the family. Perhaps most significantly, she was utterly representative of the literary world in which her daughter was growing up.

By the end of the eighteenth century, the literary culture of England had become to a high degree feminised. Thousands of women were publishing poetry and novels, and seeing their plays performed. Since the middle of the century, the so-called Blue Stockings, economically independent intellectual women, had been exerting a steadily strengthening influence on the cultural evolution of society. Women like Elizabeth Montagu (1720–1800) wrote, criticised, translated and debated in the same arena (and with minimal rancour) as the men. In 1798 Richard Polwhele unenthusiastically observed that:

> At the present day, indeed, our literary women are so numerous, that their judges, waiving all complementary civilities, decide upon their merits with the same rigid impartiality as it seems right to exercise towards the men. The tribunal of criticism is no longer charmed into complacence by the blushes of modest apprehension ....[8]

As Mary Godwin grew up, therefore, the prospect of her developing a similar career to that of her father and both her mothers will have suggested itself as an entirely predictable aspiration.

The coming of the French Revolution in 1789 brought with it the development of a significantly radicalised group of women writers alongside those like Montagu who essentially complemented existing middle-class cultural aspirations. Novels by women had in many cases already started to steer the course of the genre towards a critical re-examination of the position of women in families. In *Mary* (1787) Wollstonecraft criticised male repression of female individuality, female acceptance of that situation, and the disruptive consequences within the family:

> Her father always exclaimed against female acquirements, and was glad that his wife's indolence and ill health made her not trouble herself about them.... [He] was very tyrannical and passionate; indeed so very easily irritated when inebriated, that Mary was continually in dread lest he should frighten her mother to death.[9]

Women were active in two of the most potentially subversive of genres, journalism and educational literature. In her *Letters written in France*, Williams reminds her readers that it was as frequently the women as the men who understood the 'absurdity' of 'aristocratical rights':

> But let me do justice to the ladies of France. The number of those who have murmured at the loss of rank, bears a very small proportion to those who have acted with a spirit of distinguished patriotism; who, with those generous affections which belong to the female heart, have gloried in sacrificing titles, fortune, and even the personal ornaments, so dear to female vanity, for the common cause.... The women have certainly had a considerable share in the French revolution....[10]

There is a similarly subversive emphasis in Wollstonecraft's *An Historical and Moral View of the Origin and Progress of the French Revolution and the Effect it has Produced in Europe* (1794). Wollstonecraft argues that if we can appreciate how women have been oppressed in the past, and should now be liberated, we will effectively have conceded the justice of the revolutionary cause in France.[11] Richard Polwhele named Wollstonecraft as the leader of a group of women – including Helen Maria Williams, Mary Robinson and Mary Hays – who deserved to be castigated as *The Unsex'd Females*, intent on overturning the God-given roles of male and female in human society:

> See, Wollstonecraft, whom no decorum checks,
> Arise, the intrepid champion of her sex;
> O'er humbled man assert the sovereign claim,
> And slight the timid blush of virgin fame.

Polwhele is interesting partly because he clearly feels able to assume tacit agreement with his ideal of the perfect woman. 'Miss Wollstonecraft,' he comments, 'seriously laments the neglect of all muscular exercises at our female Boarding-schools'; he then proceeds to reflect on what she considers appropriate to the intellectual content of the curriculum, confident that the thought of girls studying botany will horrify us. 'I have', he tells us, 'several times, seen boys and girls botanising together'; and we can guess that he has 'muscular exercises' rather than plant-collecting in mind. 'I cannot but think', he concludes, 'that the Hand of Providence is visible, in her life, her death, and in the Memoirs themselves [referring to Godwin]. As she was given up to her "heart's lusts," and let "to follow her own imaginations," that the fallacy of her doctrines and the effects of an irreligious conduct, might be manifested to the world ...'.[12]

Radical women writers in this period were paradoxically advantaged by their disenfranchisement, a situation that placed them in a political limbo from which they could claim a disinterestedness that enabled them to survive the worst of the anti-Jacobin backlash.[13] Their response to the political scene was to continue to reflect above all on the evidence of domestic dislocation, as in the work of Charlotte Smith (1746–1806), Lady Morgan (otherwise Sydney Owenson 1776–1859), Mary Robinson (1758–1800) and Mary Hays (1760–1843), all of whom in various ways focused on the dispossessed and marginalised:

> 'What have I done?' cried I passionately, in a voice interrupted by sobs, 'that I must be exiled from your presence?... I shall not long survive when banished from you!'[14]

Outbursts of this kind were relatively commonplace; this comes from Mary Hays's fictional autobiography *The Victim of Prejudice* (1799), where her critique of the subjection of women is linked to a powerful attack on the British class system in general.

In Owenson's *Woman, or Ida of Athens* (1809), Ida is a child of nature, free from all pretence; her story illustrates the point we saw being made earlier by Wollstonecraft in her *Historical and Moral View ... of the French Revolution*. Ida is 'lovely, tender, gentle', but she is also 'a woman of strong mind'; we don't know if she studied botany or indulged in 'muscular exercises' at school, but her feminine honesty dramatically undermines the defensive structures of male privilege, instigating a revolution in the domestic life of her English lover, a revolution that threatens to spread more widely through the social order.[15] In *Desmond*, Charlotte Smith's novel of 1792, the story is built upon essentially the same foundations. Smith supplied a Preface that insists on the political implications of her tale:

> To those however who still cherish the idea of our having a *natural* enemy in the French Nation, and that they are still more *naturally* our foes, because they have dared to be freemen, I can only say that against the phalanx of prejudice kept in constant pay ... the slight skirmishing of a novel writer can have no effect.[16]

Her ironic self-deprecation must in part rest on our knowledge of the fact that she is both a mere novelist and a mere woman. *Desmond* shows aristocratic tyranny worn down by an artless heroine who tends, as Smith herself does, to deny any subversive intention; she is simply being herself. Her oppressors treat her 'like an insignificant child'.[17] All the greater is the shock when their cruel world of unmerited privilege crumbles around them.

Wollstonecraft, Hays, Smith, Morgan and Robinson, along with Elizabeth Hamilton and Letitia Landon, were novelists with whom the young Mary Godwin could identify, learning the use of Gothic to inculcate an atmosphere of oppression, and the language of sensibility to elicit sympathy. Like most readers she will have used her reading of fiction to help her come to terms with her actual circumstances; and when it came to writing, the dislocation of her domestic life was to be relentlessly ploughed back into her own texts. The scene was more than ably set, for example, by Mary Robinson's fictional autobiography, *Perdita* (published in 1801). She is doomed to struggle and despair by the very nature of the place in which she was born:

> On this spot was built a private house.... the west side was bounded by the Cathedral, and the back was supported by the antient cloisters of St. Augustine's monastery. A spot more calculated to inspire the soul with mournful meditation can scarcely be found amidst the monuments of antiquity.
>
> In this venerable mansion there was one chamber whose dismal and singular constructure left no doubt of its having been a part of the original monastery. It was supported by the mouldering arches of the cloisters; dark, Gothic, and opening on the minster sanctuary, not only by casement windows that

> shed a dim mid-day gloom, but by a narrow winding stair-
> case, at the foot of which an iron-spiked door led to the long
> gloomy path of cloister solitude....
>
> In this awe-inspiring habitation...during a tempestuous
> night, on the twenty-seventh of November 1758, I first
> opened my eyes to this world of duplicity and sorrow.[18]

Gothic fiction is being employed to enhance the 'factual' autobiography. In the room next door, we would not be surprised to find Victor
Frankenstein already busily polishing his electrodes and swilling out
his test-tubes.

As Charlotte Smith's *Desmond* has illustrated, work of this kind
embodies a critique of society that could by no means remain exclusively concerned with the enslavement of women within society. But
grounded as they were in the male-oriented school of Enlightenment
'Common Sense' philosophy, the way forward for these women
writers (and for not a few men besides) was by no means clear.
Frankenstein was in due course to articulate a profound uneasiness
with the intellectual tradition that had fuelled so much late-eighteenth-century radical political thinking.

Where Mary Godwin's education was concerned, we might reasonably expect to see it being taken systematically in hand early on.
Wollstonecraft had put the case with celebrated clarity: 'women
cannot be confined to merely domestic pursuits, for they will not fulfil
family duties, unless their minds take a wider range'.[19] And Godwin
clearly did have high expectations from the first that his daughter
would, in some way, live the life of the new woman that
Wollstonecraft had envisaged, achieving fame in public life. He wrote
hopefully of her 'considerable talent' when she was 15, and we have
already seen the extraordinary way in which he attempted to counter
her depression in 1819: 'I had thought you to be ranked among those
noble spirits that do honour to our nature'.[20] Mary did not, however,
receive the education that might have been expected; the explanation
for this may in part lie with the teaching careers of both her parents.
What really drew both Wollstonecraft and Godwin to education was
its relevance to the issue of social and political reform. Their main
concern was with the dissemination of ideas; in that respect the class-
room was an obvious place to start, but so also was the book-shop.

Godwin had had a strict Calvinist upbringing as a Sandemanian,
possibly the bleakest version of Christianity to be had in England at
the time. His shyness and apparent coldness as an adult must to some

degree be put down to the long-term psychological damage done to him in consequence at home, at school, and as a private pupil of the Rev. Samuel Newton in Norwich. After returning briefly as an usher to his village school at Hindolveston in Norfolk when he was 14 years old, his mother sent him to the dissenting academy at Hoxton, where at last he experienced an enlightened educational regime designed to inculcate progressive, liberal views. He left Hoxton in 1778.

His intention of opening a seminary at Epsom in 1783 came to nothing primarily because, it seems, nobody came. Prior to this he had exhibited a disturbing willingness to emulate the perverted piety of his Sandemanian elders, but Epsom was intended to change all that and his prospectus amounted to a manifesto proclaiming that any religious commitment was counterproductive to the progress of political liberty.[21] Godwin saw teaching as a somewhat demeaning 'business'; his task was to campaign on behalf of enlightened education. When discussing his wife's career he therefore wrote:

> No person was ever better formed for the business of education; if it be not a sort of absurdity to speak of a person formed for an inferior object, who is in possession of talents, in the fullest degree adequate to something on a more important and comprehensive scale.[22]

It is hardly surprising that Godwin's daughter stood to gain little practical help from a man who considered teaching an 'inferior object'.

Education was for both Godwin and Wollstonecraft essentially a literary activity designed to promote an enlightened view of society for adults and children. Mary Wollstonecraft's *Original Stories from Real Life*, written for Joseph Johnson in 1788, was typical of the direction being taken by men and women writers adopting a liberal educational agenda. It followed the established, didactic format of Thomas Day's *Sandford and Merton*, the first volume of which appeared in 1783. Wollstonecraft's stories emphasise 'real life', and depict women as capable of sound common sense; in the *Vindication* she argues that an institutional education is the right of children of both sexes. Kept at home in the company of men and women, she writes, damage will be done by bringing the children on 'too hastily'.[23]

So much for the theory. When it came to the education of Fanny, Mary and Jane, their fate lay primarily in the hands of Mary Jane Clairmont. Godwin was by no means entirely absent from the decision-making, but in Mary's case he seems to have encountered considerable difficulties in deciding how to act. He offered guidance in her reading routine, and further evidence of his tutoring exists in the similarity between his neatly ordered handwriting and that of his daughter (so different from Wollstonecraft's slanted, flowing style); but for the most part his energies were primarily engaged in refereeing a contest between the clashing temperaments of Mary and Mary Jane; little time was left to ensure that Mary's intellectual abilities received the stimulation they merited.

When, in 1812, Godwin was asked about the extent to which his daughters had been educated in accordance with the principles laid down by his first wife, his response was revealing:

> They are neither of them brought up with an exclusive attention to the system and ideas of their mother.... in 1801 I married a second time.... Neither Mrs. Godwin nor I have leisure enough for reducing novel theories of education to practice....[24]

Drawn into giving advice to William Cole in 1802 'respecting the books I think best adapted for the education of female children from the age of two to twelve', we can see that he paid little attention to immediate practicalities, resting primarily on a belief in allowing the child to develop at its own speed, taking care the while to provide ample stimulation for the imagination. Not until 12 years of age would he introduce 'some smattering of geography, history, and the other sciences'.[25] In the event, it is hardly surprising that Mary Godwin's education should have been piecemeal and disjointed.

After Wollstonecraft's death, Godwin appointed Louisa Jones as both housekeeper and governess. Mary and Fanny seem to have been lovingly cared for, and Jones probably used Wollstonecraft's *Ten Lessons* (written initially for Fanny) as a primer with the girls. In 1798 she wrote to Godwin (away in Bath on a business trip) about the girls' progress:

> Fanny's progress in reading astonishes as much as it pleases me. all the little words come as freely from her as from a much older child & she spells pig, boy, cat, box, boy, without seeing them when asked.... Sister Mary goes on very well indeed, has left off her cap today and looks like a little cherub....[26]

Jones was forced to leave the household in 1800 when Mary was just 3. She had become involved with George Dyson, one of Godwin's admirers. Godwin disapproved, and she went. Responsibility for the family when Godwin was away from home then fell on James Marshall until Godwin remarried.

Mary showed early signs of considerable intellectual ability, and it is from the letter to William Cole quoted earlier that we learn of Godwin encouraging and advising her on her reading, 'it is the train of reading I have mentioned which I should principally depend upon for generating an active mind and a warm heart'. Inevitably, Mary began to write herself, and in the Introduction to the 1831 edition of *Frankenstein* she tells us that 'As a child I scribbled; and my favourite passtime during the hours given me for recreation was to "write stories"' (F 169). Writing, we should note, has only the status of a 'passtime', and the idiosyncratic punctuation in many of her letters suggests that (before Shelley) she was never formally tutored in composition.

Until recently it was assumed that her first literary success came in 1808 with an adaptation of a satirical poem by Charles Dibdin, called 'Mounseer Nongtongpaw'. We now know that this was not her work. This discovery exposes the fact that in later years neither Mary nor her father ever saw any reason to correct the false impression. There may well have seemed little point; but the fact remains that here was a fictional chapter in Mary Godwin's life that accorded with everyone's expectations of her, and as such it was allowed to remain on the record, duly entering the biographical record. She did, however, attempt to write lectures on current affairs which were duly delivered to the family by her younger brother William. If Mary ever aspired to the post of lecturer herself, her father would probably not have approved. All the evidence suggests that Godwin was increasingly drawn into the distasteful business of attempting to curb and control his daughter's spirit as her dislike for her stepmother steadily grew. The shade of Mary Wollstonecraft notwithstanding, therefore, there was no formal education for Mary Godwin beyond the ministrations of Mr Benson, who instructed the children in singing and reading music for half an hour a week. With the two boys, it was an entirely different story.

Charles was sent to Charterhouse School. In 1811 Godwin sent him Anthony Collins's book on rationalism, including an injunction not to let Mary have a sight of it. William also went to Charterhouse, then to Dr Burney's school at Greenwich, and then on to a school at

Woodford. He received further private tutoring in mathematics. The decision was also taken to send Jane Clairmont to boarding school at Margate for six months, and then to a school in Walham Green when she was 14 in 1812. No such opportunity was to come Mary Godwin's way. Much later, Mary's daughter-in-law, Lady Jane Shelley, was to recall Mary telling her of the animosity of her step-mother, 'Jane might be well educated ... but Mary could stay at home and mend the stockings.'[27]

The evidence relating to what went on during these formative years is primarily anecdotal, but it is certain that Mary came to loath her stepmother, holding her responsible for the fact that a close relation-ship was never allowed to develop between her and her father. She saw herself as the victimised daughter of Mary Wollstonecraft, set aside by a stepmother who felt threatened by the presence of them both. She did not have far to read in her mother's *Short Residence in Sweden* before finding a persona with whom she could instantly identify:

> How frequently has melancholy and even misanthropy taken possession of me, when the world has disgusted me, and friends have proved unkind. I have then considered myself as a particle broken off from the grand mass of mankind.[28]

At the age of 13 Mary began to be ill with what sound like problems – in part at least – of a psychosomatic order. Her mother took her for a health-cure to Ramsgate, where she lodged with Miss Petman for six months. She was suffering from a wasting condition of her arm and hand, accompanied by a skin infection. Mary Jane remained at Ramsgate until her stepdaughter looked set to recover. We know that Miss Petman ran a 'Ladies School', but we know also that the situation was not exploited to further the child's education. A letter written by Godwin to his wife at this time provides us with a clue to the nature of the vexed situation in the Godwin household; he instructs Mary Jane to 'tell Mary that in spite of unfavourable appearances, I have still faith that she will become a wise, & what is more a good & happy woman'.[29] From this is it difficult not to conclude that by 1810 this precocious girl – reading avidly as ever – had significantly overstepped the mark. She may well have rounded on her stepmother, and her mood-swings will have started to become too reminiscent of her dead mother for her father to bear; certainly he found himself more at ease with the passive, orphaned Fanny, than he was ever to be with his own daughter. On her return at Christmas-time, 1811, Mary's presence once more swiftly became a problem, and almost before she knew it she had again been banished.

In September 1809, Godwin wrote to David Booth thanking him for introducing him to William Baxter, 'I dare swear he is an honest man; & he is no fool.'[30] William Baxter of Dundee remained an acquaintance rather than a friend, but Godwin wrote to him in May 1812 asking if Mary might board with the family for a few months. The letter he wrote to Baxter the day after he dispatched his 14-year-old daughter by ship for Scotland indicates just how fraught the domestic situation had become: 'I am quite confounded to think how much trouble I am bringing on you & your family, & to what a degree I may be said to have taken you in...'. While praising Mary's 'talents' without specifying them, and admitting to his own shortcomings as a father, Godwin returns to the theme of Mary as a problem child: 'I tremble for the trouble I may be bringing on you in this visit.' He knew he had to break the destructive tangle of strategies, schemes, dreams, shifting alliances and skirmishing at Skinner Street, and his remedy was desperate indeed; sending the girl away to live with people who were virtually strangers. No wonder Godwin 'trembles' at the thought of being responsible for introducing Mary into the Baxter household: 'I do not desire that she be treated with extraordinary attention, or that any of your family should put themselves out of their way on her account.' But his concern that the Baxters should not spoil her eventually gives way to regret at what he has been responsible for: 'sending her, on board a ship, with not a single face around her that she had ever seen till that morning... she is extremely subject to sea-sickness, & the voyage will not improbably last nearly a week...'.[31]

To the mind of a young girl reading popular fiction, this scenario of rejection and despair will have doubtless found its literary parallels. In Wollstonecraft's *Maria* the heroine is unjustly incarcerated in a mental asylum. In just two years' time, Mary was to make her bid for freedom from Skinner Street and the woman who sought to control her life there; in *Maria*, the wardress Jemima grudgingly allows her victim brief clandestine walks in the prison-grounds:

> Maria wished to pass the threshold of her prison, yet, when by chance she met the eye of rage glaring on her, yet unfaithful to its office, she shrunk back with more horror and affright, than if she had stumbled over a mangled corpse.[32]

Mary Hays also used the imagery of incarceration to describe a life that Mary Godwin could readily identify with, as her ship battled its way up the east coast of England:

> A child of misfortune, a wretched outcast from my fellow-beings, driven with ignominy from social intercourse, cut off from human sympathy.... If, as I have been taught to believe, a Being existeth who searcheth the heart, and judgeth not as man judgeth, to Him I make my last appeal from the injustice and barbarity of society.[33]

Although we do not know what novels Mary was reading in her adolescence, they will certainly have included the works of her mother, and doubtless those of writers known personally to the family, as Mary Hays was.

None of Godwin's fears for the impact of Mary's arrival on the Baxter family were realised. They lived in open countryside on the Tay estuary, the source, as we have already seen, for an idyllic interlude in the life of the heroine of *Mathilda*. The account she gives of it in her 1831 Preface to *Frankenstein* suggests a memory of mixed impressions. It was 'the eyry of freedom, and the pleasant region where unheeded I could commune with the creatures of my fancy'; but equally it was a very long way from home: 'my habitual residence was on the blank and dreary northern shores of the Tay'. In *Mathilda* the Tay is exchanged for the shores of Loch Lomond:

> My greatest pleasure was the enjoyment of a serene sky amidst these verdant woods: yet I loved all the changes of Nature; and rain, and storm, and beautiful clouds of heaven brought their delights with them. (M 158)

Mary no doubt benefited from her removal from London; but it will also have been a difficult time for her emotionally. Finding new friends will have helped, and she got on well with the Baxter daughters, Christie and Isabella. The problem with Mary's arm seemed also to be improved by the trip. The Baxters offered Mary a model for what was to become a central motif throughout her fiction, a happily integrated, stable family unit. She was destined soon to abandon Skinner Street for an equally unbalanced, chaotic lifestyle with Percy Shelley, but she would be for ever striving to bring to it what she most desired, domestic order and security. Her literary life was to evolve around the process of writing through the problems and issues that seemed to stand in the way of her achieving this goal for herself and for those she loved.

By the time Mary returned from Scotland in November 1812, Godwin had been approached by a disciple of his younger self. Percy Shelley was looking for a kindred spirit in his crusade against political injustice and religious intolerance. Out of patience with radicals of an earlier generation who had failed to keep the faith, he had discovered where to find the author of *Political Justice*. The first edition of *Political Justice* was a seminal text in the development of his political creed, and he therefore wrote to its author. Godwin – interested in both Shelley's ideas and in what he took to be the young man's access to funds – encouraged him to visit. The day following Mary's return from Dundee she saw Shelley, his wife Harriet, and Harriet's sister, when they came to dinner; and the more she discovered about him, the more interesting he cannot fail to have become.

Shelley was 20 years old, his wife was 17. He had rescued her from what he took to be the tyranny and religious bigotry of her father the year before. He had already published two Gothic romances, *St. Irvyne* and *Zastrozzi*. Reading Godwin's *Political Justice* had confirmed him in the opinion that the first step on the way to comprehensive reform was to purge society of all religion. The pamphlet he had written with his friend, Thomas Jefferson Hogg, *The Necessity of Atheism,* had failed to achieve this end, though it did get the pair of them expelled from Oxford University in 1811. In the same year he eloped with Harriet, and the pair of them – armed with copies of *The Necessity of Atheism* – travelled to Ireland to wage war on Roman Catholicism. From there they moved to Wales and joined William Madoc's socialist community at Tremadoc and Portmadoc. Shelley was now preparing to write his atheistical manifesto into the lengthy notes he planned for his poem, *Queen Mab* (1812–13):

> The same means that have supported every other popular belief, have supported Christianity. War, imprisonment, assassination, and falsehood.... The blood shed by the votaries of the God of mercy and peace, since the establishment of his religion, would probably suffice to drown all other sectaries now on the habitable globe.[34]

For Mary Godwin, the humanitarian force of Shelley's arguments, bringing to life the beliefs of a father now increasingly remote from her, began to become a part of her life. She was, however, destined to return to Scotland for a second time before meeting him properly.

In March 1814 Mary left Dundee for the last time. In the meantime, Harriet had given birth to a daughter, Eliza Ianthe, and the marriage was beginning to founder. Harriet was no longer the ardent disciple she had been, and her new domestic duties only served to make matters worse. There were aspects of Shelley's complex personality involved in the crisis that Mary Godwin as yet knew nothing of; in 1814 she was primarily aware of the way he brought life and liberty into a household where she felt stifled and neglected. Shelley appeared to step straight out of popular romance, playing the part of the hapless, forlorn lover to this newly found mistress of his fate:

> Upon my heart your accents sweet
> Of peace and pity fell like dew
> On flowers half dead, thy lips did meet
> Mine tremblingly, thy dark eyes threw
> Their soft persuasion on my brain,
> Turning to bliss its wayward pain.[35]

These lines are from a four-verse poem now accepted as written by Shelley to Mary Godwin in 1814. Though she may well not have seen it then, it illustrates how their moods must have matched. Shelley was incarcerated in an unhappy marriage, Mary was locked into the Skinner Street *ménage* with her father almost as distant from her there as he had been in Scotland; meanwhile, the keys of her prison continued to dangle from the waist of her stepmother. Both were fated 'To curse that life which is the cage/ Of fettered grief that dares not groan,/ Hiding from many a careless eye/ The scornèd load of agony'.[36] Both viewed their situation from an intensely 'literary' standpoint, and when the crisis came to a head, the plans that were laid might as easily have been the draft of a Gothic romance; though the events that followed had their existence in a disconcertingly real world.

Shelley called regularly at Skinner Street from spring into early summer, and the couple's relationship deepened as they developed a routine of regular visits to Mary Wollstonecraft's grave in St Pancras churchyard, Jane Clairmont acting as chaperone. Godwin discovered what was afoot in July, and at once forbade Mary to meet Shelley. Shelley proceeded to play the drama out with due regard to the literary precedents in such cases. Mary Jane was to recall a dishevelled young man proposing a suicide pact with Mary (laudanum for her, a bullet for him) if Godwin did not consent to their union.[37] Godwin called his bluff and sought to confine Mary and Jane to the house. Both Godwin and Mary Jane had reasons for playing their parts. Godwin will have seen his daughter heading off down the same unhappy road as his first wife; Mary Jane too knew all about untrustworthy men, and the present situation seemed likely to involve her own daughter Jane every bit as much as Mary. In the event, with laudanum and firearms set aside, plans were laid to flee London for the continent. On 18 July 1814, taking a willing Jane Clairmont with them, Percy and Mary set out for France. An already fragmented family was devastated, and an irate Mrs Godwin set off in hot pursuit, finally catching up with the young lovers in Calais. She managed to speak to her daughter, but Jane was persuaded to stay with Shelley and Mary, an early example of the way Shelley was able to influence and manipulate her.

It was a part of their plan that Shelley would take Mary's creative talent in hand and coach her to become a successful writer. In the event, though something of the sort took place, it was hardly the straightforward process dreamt of by the young exiles in 1814. Anne K. Mellor draws particular attention to the symbolic fate of Mary's early writings, left behind in a box in Paris when the party set off for Switzerland:

> Mary's first impulse ... was to establish her own literary credentials ... and to assume a role as [Shelley's] intellectual companion and equal.... No sooner is that voice uttered than it is lost, considered not worth taking along, even though Percy carefully carried with him the books he wished to read.[38]

Though Mary's literary life had got off to a less-than-satisfactory start, she remembered the moment later as essentially one where fact was dressed as enchanting fiction: 'Every inconvenience was hailed as a new chapter in the romance of our travels ... it was acting a novel, being an incarnate romance.'[39] In the summer of 1814 all that mattered was the dramatic narrative of escape from parental intransigence to a life of freedom, where the central figures were borne on by a selfless love for each other, and their shared belief in the right of their fellow-creatures to liberty from the slavery of custom and outmoded tradition.

At the centre of it all was an earnest, unpredictable, egotistical young idealist possessed of remarkable poetic gifts; beside him was an even younger, idealistic, impressionable girl starved of parental affection, and determined to emulate her father and mother in their intellectual and literary lives, while she also craved a stable domestic life. Alongside them stood an intelligent, excitable girl, physically more robust than her half-sister, ready for the great adventure and not a little in love with the great poet herself. Mary Godwin's literary life was destined to be framed to a significant degree by her subsequent analysis, through the medium of fiction, of the story that began to unfold as this unlikely trio began to make its way across France. It began with a syntactically ill-disciplined *Journal* entry for 11 August 1814:

> not with standing the entreaties of the people who eagerly desired us to stay all night we continued our Route to *trois maisons* 3 long leagues farther on an unfrequented road & which in many places was hardly perceptible from the surrounding waste – (J 12)

Manifestly, Mary Godwin still had a long way to travel.

4
The Author of *Frankenstein*, 1814–20

Looking back to England from France – imagining, perhaps, with some satisfaction, the back view of her furious stepmother returning to London without her – Mary may have reflected on how Shelley had come to her like the rejuvenated form of her father, wanting her company and more than ready to promote her education. She will have discovered that Shelley was living the life of an exile, suffering oppression at the hand of a tyrannical, politically unregenerate father, while no longer being understood or appreciated by his wife. Mary's schooling began now in earnest as Shelley poured forth envenomed attacks on the pride and power of the aristocracy, the evils of Christianity, and extolled the rational political opinions to be found in Godwin's writings. There will have been optimistic talk of the loan Shelley was negotiating, and how it would free himself and Godwin to continue the struggle for political justice in partnership.

When it came to her future with Shelley, there was no reason why his existing marriage need stand in their way. It was Godwin himself who had written:

> The abolition of the present system of marriage appears to involve no evils. We are apt to represent that abolition to ourselves as the harbinger of brutal lust and depravity. But it really happens, in this, as in other cases, that the positive laws that are made to restrain our vices irritate and multiply them.[1]

Shelley had endorsed this view in his Notes to *Queen Mab*:

> A husband and wife ought to continue united so long as they love each other: any law which should bind them to cohabi-

tation for one moment after the decay of their affection, would be a most intolerable tyranny....[2]

Mary Godwin had been born into a culture of exclusivity where the reactionary mores of an unreformed, unjust society were to be given no credence; Shelley's arrival and his subsequent treatment of her will have reaffirmed this belief. Her father's straightened circumstances were evidence of the fate of a visionary reformer marginalised by a hostile political establishment. She was now an exile within an exiled group whose destiny it was to refashion the world, and it was not difficult for her to find herself personified in innumerable fictional heroines, women invariably outcast and abandoned, whose lives were transformed by the entrance of an appropriately enigmatic stranger:

> My natural Sensibility had already been greatly affected by the sufferings of the unfortunate Stranger and no sooner did I first behold him, than I felt that on him the happiness or Misery of my future life must depend.

These are the words of Laura, the heroine of Jane Austen's youthful parody of Romantic fiction, *Love and Freindship* (c.1790). Though Mary Godwin will not have known this text, it is a masterly compendium of the genre. She would not have been surprised to discover that Laura's 'Stranger' is the victim of an unsuitable marriage arranged by his father, a man 'seduced by the false glare of Fortune and the Deluding Pomp of Title.'[3]

Though belonging to an ancient aristocratic family, Percy Shelley's branch of it was a minor one. The family fortune had come about through two advantageous elopements on the part of Percy's grandfather, Sir Bysshe. Sir Bysshe's son Timothy, as staid in temper as his father was eccentric, set about adding an aura of respectability to their recently acquired affluence. Timothy's eldest son, however, turned out to be an alarming throwback to his grandfather, rebelling against the regime that his father had established on their estate at Field Place, in Sussex. From early on, therefore, Shelley set his life on a course that was to take him – and whoever happened to be with him – into exile.

Rebellion at home led to rebellion against the political and religious establishment. Alongside this Shelley developed an interest in science, an activity which every true son of the Enlightenment believed held the key to the demystification of creation, an important rationally grounded adjunct to the achievement of fundamental reform in society. Shelley's enthusiasm for 'science' began while he was still at Syon House Academy where he went, aged 10, in 1802. His friend Thomas Jefferson Hogg was later to describe his rooms at Oxford as 'his laboratory'; Shelley was 'the alchemist in his study, the wizard in his cave'.[4] The radical political views to which Shelley aspired were informed by a century of scientific advances; Godwin was foremost among those who believed that empirical argument possessed the power needed to topple a corrupt political system. But Shelley was equally drawn to an idea of science as the route to a very different kind of power, that of magic, necromancy and the occult. Political implications here were provided by numerous histories of the operations of secret societies across Europe, pledged to undermine the political *status quo*. Gothic literature is shot through with accounts of Freemasonry in its more exotic forms; Shelley seized enthusiastically upon a literature of subversion which explored the power to be derived from secrecy, and a literature committed to transgression. It is in Ingolstadt, home of the Illuminati, a particularly sinister offshoot of Masonry, that Enlightenment science and Gothic magic most famously meet, mingle, and produce a monster; it is here that Mary Godwin located Victor Frankenstein's laboratory.

When Shelley arrived at New College from Eton in 1810, he brought with him – literally – the eclectic baggage of a rebel:

> Into this stronghold of royalist tradition and prejudice, Shelley unloaded trunkloads of French philosophy, German horror novels, his solar microscope and several crates of chemical and electronic equipment.[5]

Shelley's journey into exile continued with his expulsion from Oxford in 1811. His father's attempt to bring him back to Field Place and private tutoring was met with his son's announcement that when he came of age in three years' time, he would resign his claim to the family inheritance. Family, school and university life all fuelled Shelley's pathological detestation of authoritarianism, and Harriet Westbrook was an early recipient of his iconoclastic idealism. He had little difficulty convincing her that she was the victim of repression both at home and at school, and in 1811 the couple eloped to Scotland. Harriet was 16. There then ensued a nomadic life dedicated to the cause of political reform. The Shelleys went twice to Ireland, then to Wales, ending up back in London in the spring of 1813. Here he published his first long poem, *Queen Mab*. In the course of celebrating Harriet's liberation, the poem, with its notes, unleashed a powerful Godwinian salvo against the political establishment and the institutions that upheld it; marriage and Christianity in particular were exposed as the tools of superstition and enslavement against which the liberated soul of Ianthe stood 'Instinct with inexpressible beauty and grace'.[6] Ianthe was the name given to Harriet in the poem, and to their first child, born in June 1813.

The fact that Shelley was endeavouring to lead a life inspired by the pursuit of Godwinian principles in no way dampened his enthusiasm for the cloak-and-dagger exclusivity he tended to associate with the cause. Shelley had been an outcast and exile for almost as long as he could remember, and his life was dominated by his attempts to establish a politically enlightened, exclusive circle around himself, a community of Godwinian illuminati who would expect to see the world progressively won over to their superior vision of humanity. The Tremadoc venture which Shelley had discovered and joined in 1812 was framed within just such a concept of the enlightened radical commune. Following Shelley's and Harriet's subversive activities in Ireland in the spring of 1812 (in the course of which they were reported to the Home Secretary, Lord Sidmouth) Shelley attempted to establish a commune of his own in Lynmouth, suggesting that Godwin might send Fanny down to join them. The offer was declined. Both the communitarian ideal and its attendant nomadic lifestyle were by this time stretching Harriet's relationship to Shelley to near breaking-point.

Shelley's first meeting with Mary Godwin in 1814 followed a further spell at Tremadoc; his determination to establish a commune remained unabated and became an integral part of the young couple's determination to elope. In Mary he found a disciple who already spoke his language, and when she heard of his plan to establish a radical community abroad, an élite shorn of the bigotry that both of them detested, she will have felt herself to have been on familiar ground. Twenty-five years later, when she was writing the Preface to her edition of his prose works, Mary continued to claim that Shelley's commitment to a 'spirit of domestic peace and general brotherhood founded on love' provided the key to an understanding of his personality (S vi & ix). The community they envisaged in 1814 was made all the more attractive by the fact that it would bring Mary's father back to her, while liberating her from the intolerable domination of her stepmother. It was to be a community dedicated to the task of giving literary expression to the participants' radical ideas; Mary's consequent commitment to a shared literary life effectively set the seal on the way in which her career as a writer was to evolve.

Having taken on the Shelleyan political agenda, she exchanged one small, domestically fraught circle for an equally fraught, even smaller circle that professed a radically enlightened rejection of eighteenth-century political and social systems and institutions. From here she progressively wrote her way towards her own perception of that agenda as she travelled, lived, and increasingly suffered with the Shelley entourage. By projecting herself into her fiction, she was able to explore the virtues of individuals threatened with exclusion because they sought the power to construct an alternative society, as against the virtues of those who sought to maintain the kind of harmonious, loving relationships within society that had always eluded her.

When the renegade trio of Shelley, Mary Godwin and Jane Clairmont left Skinner Street, it was as founder-members of a radical community planning to settle in Uri, on the shores of Lake Lucerne. They were happy to believe that in due course enlightened friends and relations would arrive to swell their numbers. In the event, they were to spend just six weeks on the continent.

Having arrived in Paris, Shelley managed to raise sufficient money to continue their journey towards Switzerland across a country devastated by the Napoleonic wars. The ass they had bought was eventually exchanged for the speedier option of a *voiture*, and the depressing sequence of ruined villages eventually gave way to the first signs of Alpine scenery. They arrived at Lucerne on 23 August, but after only three days they decided to return to England by the cheapest – and swiftest – route. This meant using river transport as far as Bonn, and then travelling overland to Rotterdam. They landed at Gravesend on Tuesday, 13 September.

Writing in 1889, Mrs Julian Marshall was in no doubt about the damaging consequences of the situation Mary Godwin had got herself into:

> it is a general truth that from the moment one mind is penetrated by the influence of another, its own native power over other minds has gone, and for ever. And Mary parted with the power at sixteen, before she knew what it was to have it.[7]

Arguably, she spent the rest of her life struggling to discover that power; but aged 16 and footloose in Europe, this was not an issue; it was a great adventure, and the literary part of that adventure began with the discipline of compiling a journal. Characteristically, it was initially to be a journal shared with Percy, and the composition of it was accompanied by a demanding programme of reading. Whatever else was to happen to the Shelley coterie, be it trailing haphazardly – as now – across France, being pursued by debt-collectors across London, messing about in boats on Lake Geneva, or battling with difficult pregnancies and suicidal depression, the one thing they none of them ceased to do at any time was read. They read Godwin, Wollstonecraft, Wordsworth, Southey, Milton, Voltaire, Brockden Brown, Cicero, Petronius, Suetonius, Radcliffe, Scott, Barruel, Rousseau, Goethe, Ovid; the list is endless, the appetite was insatiable; it was how the 'community' worked. It had been Godwin's way, Wollstonecraft's way, it was a keystone of the dissenting educational tradition; now more than ever it became the Shelleys' way.

The *Journal* acted as a primer through which Mary might learn to channel the radical intentions of the group into creative literary activity; Jane likewise undertook a similar exercise. The melodramatic description of the company's flight with which Shelley opened the *Journal* illustrates the particular prose medium being employed to do the job:

> I watched until the lightning & the stars became pale. At length it was 4. I believed it not possible that we should succeed: still there appeared to lurk some danger even in certainty. I went. I saw her. She came to me.... (J 6)

It is a romantic fiction. Shelley, like Godwin before him, was attempting to imagine a future that could not be predicated on the recent past. His literary life consisted of ransacking books, the product of both earlier and contemporary creative imaginations, to find hints and suggestions that pointed towards the nature of a supposed 'reality' in the present. These fragments were then used in conjunction with his own imagination to aid him in the representation of an unknown future. Mary was soon to describe Victor Frankenstein constructing his creature (frequently read as a metaphor for the future) in a similar way, stitching it together from bits and pieces, from stray fragments. It was the function of the *Journal* to document the transformation of what necessarily begins as fiction into fact. In the event, this particular attempt to establish a community was to founder; in the event, of course, Frankenstein's creature also failed to turn out quite as planned.

From the point at which Shelley passed the pen to Mary on 11 August, the *Journal* became increasingly her affair. By the time they were hastening back to England, both Mary and Jane were also planning to write novels. 'Mary begins *Hate*', wrote Shelley, '& gives S. the greater pleasure' (J 24). After two days back in London, Mary's entry (using the third-person style as though she is her own character) confirms her commitment to the literary life as a central principle in the pursuit of their ideal:

> Mary reads the Excursion all day & reads the history of Margaret to PBS. He reads part of Caleb Williams to us.
> Friday 16
> Read the Excursion & Madoc …
> Saturday 17
> M Read Madoc all morning. PBS. Out on business – He reads the curse of Kehama to us in the evening…. (J 25–7)

Seldom can the term 'literary life' have been more appropriate than in the case of Mary Godwin's apprenticeship. Even Shelley's choice of Uri as the home for his commune was probably inspired by Godwin's novel *Fleetwood* (1805). Uri is one of the places where Fleetwood, disillusioned by the materialism of the modern world, seeks solace in a community of sympathetic friends. As they travelled towards their goal in 1814, they were reading Barruel's *History of Jacobinism* which, though it was a reactionary attack on the politics of the French Revolution, was also a mine of information about Masonic secret societies. Tacitus was also prescribed reading, specifically his account of the siege of Jerusalem; Shelley, Mary and Jane saw themselves as a community under siege. A compelling reason for the careful study of Wordsworth's latest work (*The Excursion*) was because here was a poet of Godwin's generation, at one time notorious as a 'Jacobin' coterie poet, who now reflected at length on the virtues of life lived by people in isolated communities.

In a book acquired in Paris, de Lisle's *Le Vieux de la Montaigne* of 1799, Shelley discovered the story of a sect of Ismaeli extremists of the eleventh century, the Assassins. Here Shelley believed was a source he could use to produce a Gothic tale to educate his readers into new and enlightened ways of thinking. De Lisle's Assassins were fanatical opponents of the tyrannical powers of church and state. Shelley transformed them into proto-Godwinians:

> They esteemed the human understanding to be the paramount rule of human conduct ... Attached from principle to peace and hating the pleasures and the customs of the degenerate mass of mankind, this unostentatious community of good and happy men fled to the solitudes of Lebanon. (S 150–1)

Shelley's Assassins evolve into a peace-loving people devoted to pleasure and beauty. But they are challenged by the arrival of a mysterious visitor. What would Shelley and his group do if newcomers turned out to be disruptive? His way of finding out was to imagine the situation within a fiction.

Shelley did not write beyond the fourth chapter of *The Assassins*. What we have indicates his concern for how a small group of people who have risen to a degree of civilisation superior to those around them should respond when the rest of the world turns up on the doorstep. The 1814 *Journal* makes it very clear that Shelley, Mary and Jane saw themselves as engaged in writing the first chapters of a revolutionary social experiment; scenic moments were appreciated, but these were travellers with a mission. The devastated land through which they travelled only confirmed this, and though the contempt which Mary expressed for her German travelling companions on their homeward journey seems extreme, we need to appreciate that she was viewing them in much the same way that she had been taught to view the rest of the world since childhood. Hers is an immature report on how it looks to a junior member of Godwin's intellectual, radical circle who now aspire to set up home in the happy valley inhabited by Shelley's Assassins:

> our only wish was to absolutely annihilate such uncleansable animals.... Twere easier for god to make entirely new men than attempt to purify such monsters as these. (J 20–1)

This is, of course, a passage where with hindsight we can be tempted to see already the seeds of Mary's first novel. Frankenstein will set out 'to make entirely new men' in his attempt to purify the 'monsters' that his fellow human beings have become, but with disastrous results. In due course, as she began to emerge from beneath the shadow of the poet she unreservedly worshipped in 1814, Mary's writing and reading became part of a process by which she was able to question what both her father, and then her lover, had attempted to make of her. The evidence of *Frankenstein* suggests that when she read that *Journal* entry again after nearly two years had elapsed, she may well have done so with some embarrassment. We can be sure that she reread it because in 1817, with *Frankenstein* halfway through its two-year period of gestation, the 1814 adventure was written up in travelogue form for the press. There was certainly no shortage of incident and observation to draw on. There had been the sightseeing in Paris, and then Shelley's twisted ankle which had meant that he, rather than his companions, had ended up using the ass on the first part of the journey. Rewriting the *Journal* provided Mary with the opportunity to work up her picturesque style; where in 1814 Percy had noted 'Piny mountains & barren rocks, & scenes of verdure surpassing imagination', Mary was to write: 'the horned moon hung in the light of sunset, that threw a glow of unusual depth and redness over the piny mountains and the dark deep valleys they enclosed…'.[8] There was also the opportunity to rehearse the democratic enthusiasm that entering Switzerland occasioned; the sublime scenery was more than matched by the inspirational heroism of William Tell's fight against tyranny.

In addition to revising and extending the text of the *Journal*, the *History of a Six Weeks' Tour* included the edited text of two letters by Percy, and two by Mary describing details of their subsequent travels on the continent in 1816. Shelley also added his poem *Mont Blanc* (1816) to the volume. The contents of Mary Godwin's first published book, therefore, illustrates the way her literary life was envisaged as a joint venture with Shelley, though of course it could not conclude with a description of the community they had intended to create. The intention was to produce a marketable blend of traveller's tales, relatively muted political opinion, landscape description and personal reflection.

When the three travellers turned for home in August 1814, they left Lucerne without paying their bills. Lack of money was to be the controlling factor in their lives from their return to London in September 1814 until May the following year, when Shelley finally learned he was to get an annuity of £1000 following his grandfather's

. four months earlier. The situation then eased, but the problems
no means disappeared. Shelley's suggestion to Harriet that she
.night now consider joining his household as a 'sister' met with
outraged rejection. Where the Godwins were concerned, Shelley was
to be considered disinterestedly as an acceptable source of funds, but
in every other respect he was denounced as a monster who had stolen
Mary and Jane from the family, ruining their reputations in consequence. In the event, Shelley managed to get some money out of
Harriet, but by October the bailiffs were closing in. From their initial
lodgings in Margaret Street, they moved to 5, Church Terrace, St
Pancras. Harriet was pregnant with Shelley's second child; Mary was
now also pregnant. Thomas Jefferson Hogg, who might have been
expected to give support, was out of town, and in the event it was an
old friend, Thomas Love Peacock, who gave the three outcasts help
and encouragement.

Peacock had first met Shelley in 1812. Privately educated, largely
self-taught, he shared Shelley's atheistical views, and knew only too
well what it was to be short of money. He swiftly took on the role of
go-between, as Shelley attempted to avoid the imminent threat of
debtors' prison. The couple were reduced to a life of clandestine
meetings while, with Peacock's help, a loan was negotiated with the
bookseller, Thomas Hookham. Mary was now also having to
confront the fact that Shelley's mission to radicalise Jane had
resulted in a close emotional relationship between the pair of them.
Aged 16, Jane registered an increasingly ambiguous presence in the
triangular relationship. She had been reading *King Lear* while abroad,
and wrote in her *Journal*, '"What shall poor Cordelia do – Love and
be silent" – Oh this is true – Real love will never show itself to the
eye of broad day – '.[9] Shelley was now spending an increasing
amount of time with her when he wasn't hiding from the bailiffs in
Peacock's mother's house, leaving Mary to cope with what was
becoming a difficult, debilitating pregnancy. The great adventure
seemed to have collapsed in ruins; Mary remained estranged from
her father, and deeply hurt by the way he continued to insist that
Shelley should honour his earlier promises of financial help. Her
response was to cling ever more desperately to Percy and to stoke up
her hatred of her stepmother: 'she plagues my father out of his life',
she wrote to Percy in October, 'why will not Godwin follow the
obvious bent of his affections & be reconciled to us... do you not
hate her my love' (L I 3). In the meantime there was still no shortage
of plans for the future: 'discuss the possibility of converting & liber-

ating two heiresses', Shelley jotted down in September 1814 (he could well have been serious); '...talk in the evening of our running away scheme', Mary noted; the following day there was 'talk of the west of Ireland plan' (J 30). But the reality was that nobody in this commune was going anywhere.

Ever since their departure for the continent, it had been apparent that Shelley was not only an adept at inducing a state of high nervous tension in himself, he was also able to take Jane with him, and he not infrequently did so, much to Mary's evident disapproval. It was just such an excursion into emotional excess that now finally overflowed into a night of disturbingly paranormal experiences in early October. Shelley's account in the *Journal* includes the information that it was in the course of the night that he told Jane of Mary's pregnancy. Although we have only a series of highly subjective accounts to work from, there can be little doubt that these events mark a crisis in the relationship between Jane and Shelley, channelled into a series of hysterical encounters through the night. Jane wanted Shelley, but when she discovered that the best she could hope for was to share him with Mary, 'her horror & agony increased even to the most dreadful convulsions. She shrieked and writhed on the floor' (J 33). Shelley recognised Mary's right to his attention, but was loath to lose the intimacy he had cultivated in his other pupil. Mary's entry in the *Journal* for the following day sums the situation up with characteristic candour: 'Read Political Justice. We walk out – when we return Shelley talks with Jane and I read Wrongs of women...' (J 33).

Mary Godwin had ended up living a life surrounded by the paraphernalia that accompanied Shelleyan radicalism: his belief in the commune as a social unit, his penchant for cloak-and-dagger secrecy, and his fascination for magic and the occult. But there seemed now little promise of ushering in a new age to make the effort (including childbearing) worthwhile. At least with the Hookham loan it became possible for them to move to more comfortable lodgings in Nelson Square, Blackfriars. With the return to London of Hogg, however, Shelley persisted in his determination to dissolve the traditional pairing arrangements within the circle. Although Mary resisted the initial pressure on her to adopt Hogg as a partner while Shelley continued to concern himself more with Jane, she did in due course come to rely on Hogg for emotional support. This clearly becomes the case when in March 1815 her baby, born prematurely on 22 February, died. She wrote to him at once:

> My dearest Hogg my baby is dead – will you come to see me
> as soon as you can – I wish to see you.... Will you come – you
> are so calm a creature & Shelley is afraid of a fever from the
> milk – for I am no longer a mother now.... (L I 10)

After the child's death, Shelley was prompted to take Mary away from
London to Salt Hill, near Windsor, for a short holiday. From here she
corresponded with Hogg in a way that suggests they were lovers; but
beyond the playfulness lies a determination to break with life in
London, to get rid of Jane, and to rebuild her relationship with the
partner of her original choice.

Shelley was also under pressure from the Godwins to give up Jane.
They were quick to let him know that both Fanny and Jane's chances
of finding teaching posts were seriously compromised by the scandal
of the poet's *ménage-à-trois*. The Godwins were unwilling to have their
errant daughter return home, and Jane certainly did not wish it. With
no doubt a genuine concern for Fanny's situation, and acting as a
catalyst on all parties concerned, Jane agreed to move into lodgings at
Lynmouth. As a further gesture of her continuing independence from
Skinner Street, it was at this time that she decided to rechristen herself
with the more romantic name of Claire Clairmont.

From Salt Hill, Shelley and Mary returned to London at the end of
April, taking up lodgings in Bloomsbury. Then, still in pursuit of their
ideal community, they were off again, this time on a tour of the West
Country. They ended up eventually in Torquay, where Mary remained
while Shelley continued to travel, eventually renting a house near
Peacock at Bishopsgate, on the edge of Windsor Great Park. They
moved there in August 1815. On her own in Torquay, Mary – not
surprisingly – feared the worst. She was pregnant again, and, for all
she knew, Shelley had once more sought out Claire. The nightmare of
being in love, being dependent, and being alone, living on the edge of
complete rejection having risked all on their great experiment, wrung
from her letters pleading with Shelley to return, or to let her come to
him. In due course such experiences were to become an indelible part
of the fabric of her novels. For a significant amount of the time he
spent away from Mary, Shelley had in fact been seeking medical
advice in London for a serious abdominal complaint, and for the onset
of symptoms of consumption. His decision to settle into a relatively
more ordered way of life came about largely as a consequence of the
realisation that he might otherwise become very ill indeed. A time of
reflection on what he had achieved, and on what he might expect of

the future became the theme of his poem *Alastor*, written at Bishopsgate in the autumn of 1815.

In the Preface to *Alastor* Shelley contemplates his own imminent death in the belief that it is to be brought about by his failure to achieve the ideal way of life he has sought. Any suggestion that he might have been in some way misguided is denied. His early death marks him off as a 'luminary', distinct from 'Those who love not their fellow-beings, live unfruitful lives, and prepare for their old age a miserable grave.'[10] While we might recognise here something of Mary's tone of scorn in the 1814 *Journal* when she contemplated the lesser mortals she had been forced to travel home with on the Rhine, we should perhaps question whether, a year later, preparing for the birth of her second child, she will have seen Shelley as an entirely blameless victim of an unregenerate world, 'a youth of uncorrupted feelings and adventurous genius'. The Preface also expresses a preoccupation he shared with Mary over the evils of injustice, betrayal and rejection; they were mutually committed to the pursuit of perfection, and shared a sense of frustration at the 'selfish, blind, and torpid ... unforseeing multitudes who constitute, together with their own, the lasting misery and loneliness of the world'.[11] But, as her literary life reveals, Mary's analysis of those preoccupations becomes progressively distinct from that of her husband.

In January 1816, Mary Godwin gave birth to a son, William. By March of that year, Claire (now 18) had managed to get herself pregnant by Lord Byron as well as out to Bishopsgate and back into Skinner Street. Byron had a great deal more to contend with at this time than Claire's attentions; when he departed for the continent in April, he left behind him an estranged wife, Annabella, and the woman he loved, his half-sister Augusta. Claire had been at best a *divertissement*; worth the effort if for no other reason than that she had brought the daughter of Godwin to meet him, and – according to Claire – Mary had been favourably surprised: 'She perpetually exclaims, "How mild he is! How gentle! So different from what I expected."'[12]

Claire's plan to follow Byron to Switzerland seemed to suit everyone. Mary – as yet kept in ignorance of Claire's pregnancy – believed that the climate would suit Shelley's condition, while Byron himself certainly constituted an attraction. For Shelley, the prospects of establishing a community of 'luminaries' on the shores of Lake Geneva beckoned as invitingly as the prospect of a milder climate. In May, Shelley and Mary, with Claire and baby William, left London, and a community did indeed come into being some three miles out of Geneva, with Byron and his retinue staying at the Villa Diodati, while the Shelleys took the less grand Montalègre nearby. It lasted from May until August 1816, and it was now that Mary began to write *Frankenstein*, working on it over the next two years before finally having it published in 1818.

When the time came for the Shelleys to leave, Byron refused to keep Claire with him, so she too returned to England. It was prudent to avoid London, so they found lodgings in Bath, from whence the attempt was made to urge Byron to accept responsibility for his child. A familiar pattern of events began to unfold: they had travelled towards a new life only for it to collapse around them, bedevilled by contending emotions and deceits; Mary now had to cope with the way Shelley and Claire had excluded her from the truth about Claire's child. On their return, their adventure turned swiftly to the stuff of nightmare. On 9 October Fanny committed suicide in Swansea. Of all Godwin's children, Fanny suffered most in the maelstrom of the Skinner Street household; she was evidently the butt of Claire's sharp wit. In her *Journal* for November 1814 she noted reading Henry Mackenzie's novel, *The Man of Feeling* (1771); its absurdly sensitive and tearful hero, she suggested, 'would have just suited Fanny for a husband'.[13] On 10 December Harriet Shelley was found, another suicide, drowned in the Serpentine. Just 20 days later Mary Godwin became Shelley's second wife at St Mildred's Church in London. In January 1817, Claire gave birth to a daughter; initially called Alba, she was subsequently to be known as Allegra.

Percy Shelley now began a vain attempt to get custody of his two children by Harriet, but legalising his relationship with Mary was scarcely going to cancel out the reputation he had in England as an irresponsible, immoral and seditious influence on all around him. Plans were laid for something more akin to a settled home, and in January when Mary wrote to inform Byron that he was a father, she added, 'We have taken a house in Marlow to which we intend to remove in about two months – And where we dare hope to have the pleasure of your society on your return to England.' (L I 26). With her own son thriving, and with a home in Marlow pending, Mary could begin to hope for better things. She continued through it all to work at becoming a publishable writer, reading with unabated determination, and drafting *Frankenstein, or The Modern Prometheus*, while Shelley worked on a large-scale poem, *Laon and Cythna*, eventually to be published as *The Revolt of Islam*.

In September Mary gave birth to a daughter, Clara, and in December she published her first book, *History of a Six Weeks' Tour*. In January 1818, *Frankenstein* was published anonymously, with a dedication to William Godwin. For John Croker, writing in the *Quarterly Review*, the dedication alone was sufficient to render the author 'as mad as his hero' (F 189). Walter Scott was more impressed, but he shrewdly observed that 'the execution is imperfect, and bearing the marks of an unpractised hand' (F 195).

We have an intriguing glimpse of Mary Shelley at this time in Peacock's satirical novel *Nightmare Abbey*, published in 1818, where there are thinly disguised descriptions of Percy, Mary and Claire. Claire is Stella, with whom Scythrop (Percy) 'could indulge freely in all his romantic and philosophical visions. He could build castles in the air, and she would pile towers and turrets on the imaginary edifices'; while Mary is the model for the far more down-to-earth Marionetta:

> She loved Scythrop, she hardly knew why ... she felt her fondness increase or diminish in an inverse ration to his ... Thus, when his love was flowing, hers was ebbing: when his was ebbing, hers was flowing. Now and then there were moments of level tide, when reciprocal affection seemed to promise imperturbable harmony.... He had no opportunity to take measure of her understanding by conversations on general subjects, and on his favourite designs; and, being left in this respect to the exercise of indefinite conjecture he took it for granted ... that she had great natural talents, which she wasted at present on trifles.[14]

The reference to Scythrop's notion that Marionetta was squandering her talents suggests tensions in a situation where Percy Shelley, frequently unwell, was being increasingly frustrated in his political ambitions while Mary, with her two children, was combining her intellectual and literary studies with home-making. It is hardly surprising, then, that when Shelley proposed taking to the road yet again, Mary's response was less than enthusiastic; but after a brief, and (for a change) pleasurable stay in London through February 1818, Percy, Mary and Claire, with the children William, Clara and Allegra, and two attendants, a Swiss nurse Elise and Milly Shields from Marlow, sailed from Dover to Calais in the teeth of a March gale.

Throughout this period Mary Shelley had been reading a series of more or less romantic accounts of the way an elect few might join together to form an enlightened society. Augustin Barruel's *History of Jacobinism* has already been mentioned in this respect, as has Godwin's *Fleetwood* and de Lisle's *Le Vieux de la Montagne*. Another contemporary author very much to the Shelleys' taste for the same reason was the American novelist Charles Brockden Brown.

Four of Brown's novels are recorded on the Shelleys' reading list for 1814, *Clara Howard, Philip Stanley, Edgar Huntley* and *Jane Talbot*; and for 1815 *Wieland; or, the transformation* and *Ormond* (J 638). *Wieland* in particular contains much that was clearly influential in the writing of *Frankenstein*. The female narrator tells us how her father was ostracised by his family because he married beneath him. We then hear how he becomes fascinated by the Camissards, an exclusive religious sect; his subsequent melancholia terminates in a spectacular death following spontaneous combustion in the summerhouse on his estate near Philadelphia. Peacock wryly noted that Shelley's enduring love of summerhouses dated from his reading of this novel.[15]

From one less-than-healthy religious secret society, Brown then moves on to consider an alternative, the seemingly happy and tranquil pastoral world in which the man's children and their friends live. The narrator's brother marries her best friend, whose brother then joins the coterie:

> Our tempers were remarkably congenial.... Every day added strength to the triple bonds that united us. We gradually withdrew ourselves from the society of others.... Our education had been modelled by no religious standard. We were left to the guidance of our own understanding.[16]

Wieland reminds us just how ubiquitous the communitarian idea was. Brown then describes the tragic disintegration of the idyll, and this must have struck a chord with Mary. The novel quite literally becomes darker as the relationships disintegrate, and Mary of course began her tale of Victor Frankenstein 'on a dreary night of November', perhaps even with Brown's description of Carwin, the man whose presence mysteriously threatens the coterie, on her mind:

> His cheeks were pallid and lank, his eyes sunken, his forehead overshadowed by coarse straggling hairs, his teeth large and

irregular, though sound and brilliantly white.... His skin was of coarse grain, and sallow hue....[17]

The appearance of Victor Frankenstein's creation would seem to owe something at least to Brown's Carwin: 'His yellow skin scarcely covered the work of muscles and arteries beneath; his hair was of a lustrous black, his teeth of a pearly whiteness...' (F 34).

Brown's interest in the psychology of his characters was equally influential; there was not a lot of difference between reading Brown and watching Percy wind himself and Claire up as the shadows lengthened, the candles guttered in their holders, and their copies of *Wieland* fell open at the appropriate page. Brown excelled at representing darkness as a palpable force of evil, where the individual becomes terrifyingly vulnerable. The coterie world of *Wieland* sinks into darkness and terror as supernatural powers of evil seem to violate its members. Mary had been an object of interest all her life on account of her parenthood; she will have been pointed out and stared at. Since 1814 she was the object of scandalised reports and bizarre gossip. She will certainly have felt for Brown's narrator, discovered by the neighbours in a darkened room with the mutilated body of her sister: 'They pried into the corners as if in search of some fugitive; next their gaze was fixed upon me...'.[18] It is Wieland himself whose derangement becomes responsible for the coterie's violent end. The trope was a familiar one to Mary; she was studying the way her father had explored it in *Caleb Williams*, in *St. Leon*, and to a lesser extent in *Fleetwood*, where hero, victim and villain combine in a series of overlapping personae all doomed to failure.

Frankenstein became in part a chronicle of Mary Godwin's search for light to relieve the darkness of the grimmer side of life within the Shelley circle. It is a novel that charts the disintegration of what its author perceives as her (rather than her husband's) ideal of the communitarian life. Mary's community comprises the extended family unit (the Frankensteins, the De Laceys); it is predicated on relationships which (whether or not confirmed by the existing marriage laws) remain fundamentally orthodox. Issues raised in the novel around science, education, gender and political justice combine to represent the potentially destructive power of a single-minded reforming zeal. In a novel which begins in distinctly Gothic mood by exploring transgression, the power exerted by Enlightenment wisdom was always going to be productive of tension rather than resolution. The extent to which Mary was nevertheless still holding to a belief that rational, radical reform was justified in *Frankenstein* will be further considered when her revised version of the novel, published in 1831, is considered.

The immediate circumstances in which the novel was begun are well documented. For days, talk at the Villa Diodati had turned on contemporary medical and scientific debates. Particular attention was given to galvanism, the theory that electricity was a prime agent in the principle of life. In the novel she describes how as a child Frankenstein witnesses the power of electricity in the form of lightning striking an oak tree: 'It was not splintered by the shock, but entirely reduced to thin ribbons of wood. I never beheld anything so utterly destroyed' (F 23). There are again echoes of *Wieland* here. The spectacle is described as though it were a case of spontaneous combustion; the lightning is not seen, rather 'I beheld a stream of fire issue from an old and beautiful oak' (F 23). In *Wieland* we read:

> At the same instant, a very bright spark was seen to light on his clothes. In a moment, the whole was reduced to ashes.... Meanwhile, the disease thus wonderfully generated betrayed more terrible symptoms. Fever and delirium terminated in lethargic slumber, which, in the course of two hours, gave place to death.[19]

The implications are clear: the Promethean gift of fire is essentially self-generated and ultimately destructive, the very opposite of the life-giving process that is being sought. This is not a light which can dispel the darkness of ignorance, fear and superstition. Talk of such things at the Villa Diodati was undertaken in the customary Shelleyan manner, which is to say interspersed with readings from gothic literature. Mary, normally able to withdraw herself from what was usually a psychic game for Percy and Claire, was unable on this occasion to remain as aloof as she would wish. She experienced her waking dream:

> I saw – with shut eyes, but acute mental vision – I saw the pale student of unhallowed arts kneeling beside the thing he had put together. (F 172)

The Diodati discussions were in fact predicated on two years of intensive debate and reading. In the summer of 1815 Shelley had sought medical help from Sir William Lawrence, an eminent London surgeon then engaged in fierce public controversy with John Abernethy over the origins of life. Lawrence's radical, atheistical thoughts found their way into Shelley's *Alastor*, and into the general tenor of intellectual life at Bishopsgate. The virtues of the old and the new science are debated in *Alastor* even as they were to be in the opening chapters of *Frankenstein*:

> O, that the dream
> Of dark magician in his visioned cave,
> Raking the cinders of a crucible
> For life and power, even when his feeble hand
> Shakes in its last decay, were the true law
> Of this so lovely world! But thou art fled
> Like some frail exhalation....[20]

The theme of 'life and power' moves from *Alastor* into *Frankenstein*, where the ambitious young doctor first dabbles in the magic arts of Agrippa and Paracelsus, and then turns to the study of modern science, 'natural philosophy, and particularly chemistry' (F 29); Frankenstein was, after all, a 'modern' Prometheus.

If the genesis of *Frankenstein* significantly predates the Villa Diodati meetings, then we should also remember that its composition stretched over the following two years. The novel became Mary's counterpoint to Shelley's *Laon and Cythna*, composed at Marlow after their return from Switzerland, and in the wake of the suicides of Fanny and Harriet. Even while Shelley looked over his wife's shoulder while she drafted and redrafted her novel, so she was also a party to the composition of *Laon and Cythna*, Shelley's elegy for the French Revolution. There she could see her husband telling the story of his own fight against tyranny and bigotry, and incorporating her into his dream of eventual liberation:

> Thou Friend, whose presence on my wintry heart
> Fell, like bright Spring upon some herbless plain;
> How beautiful and calm and free thou wert
> In thy young wisdom, when the mortal chain
> Of Custom didst thou burst and rend in twain ...

Their ultimate victory in this world deferred, Laon and Cythna head for a triumphant world of light:

> Motionless resting on the lake awhile,
> I saw its marge of snow-bright mountains rear
> Their peaks aloft, I saw each radiant isle,
> And in the midst, afar, even like a sphere
> Hung in one hollow sky, did there appear
> The Temple of the Spirit.[21]

Following her first attempt to get *Frankenstein* started with what became Chapter 4, 'It was a dreary night of November...', Mary subsequently enfolded Frankenstein's narrative in the story of Robert Walton, a polar explorer. She too, then, gives us 'snow-bright mountains', and the hope that from this region of light will come an enlightenment of the spirit:

> What may not be expected in a country of eternal light? I may there discover the wonderful power which attracts the needle; and may regulate a thousand celestial observations, that require only this voyage to render their seeming eccentricities consistent for ever. (F 7)

Unlike the protagonists of *Laon and Cythna*, however, Walton realises that his quest is doomed, and that he must turn for home.

When the writing of *Frankenstein* was joined to the task of preparing the 1814 *Journal* for publication, Mary no doubt found herself thinking hard about all the travelling they had done as well as the scenery they had witnessed. It all finds its way into *Frankenstein*; there is the brightness of the Alpine landscape, and the contrasting darkness of Frankenstein's laboratory; the high ideals, the endless process of travel, the heartbreak of rejection and failed relationships, and the trauma of untimely deaths. Both books are dominated by the need to be for ever moving on, and by the interplay of light and dark. In the letter of 1816 (probably to Fanny) which was added to the *Six Weeks' Tour* narrative, Mary wrote:

> We now inhabit a little cottage on the opposite shore of the lake, and have exchanged the view of Mont Blanc and her snowy *aiguilles* for the dark frowning Jura.... Unfortunately we do not now enjoy those brilliant skies that hailed us on our first arrival to this country.[22]

Writing the novel gave her the opportunity to explore the pain of her estrangement from her father, the emotional complexity of her life with Shelley, Claire, Hogg and their other friends, and above all, to address the major social and political issues associated with the love of 'life and power'. Here she observed the overwhelmingly destructive ego of the would-be reformer, Victor Frankenstein, describing his 'enthusiastic madness' from within the defining consciousness of Walton, a man equally driven by ambition to enlighten his fellow creatures, but one who is nevertheless prepared to turn his boat for home in the interests of the welfare of his crew (F 151). Would Shelley ever listen to his crew and turn his boat for home? Quite apart from his political convictions, it seemed that his health was unlikely to allow him to do so.

Though Percy Shelley wrote the Preface for the 1818 edition of *Frankenstein* in the first person, effectively appropriating the authorship, it was never his novel. It was a book in which Mary drew up a balance-sheet on what their pursuit of an enlightened community had cost to date. She had earned a place in the public eye, but only as one who belonged to a socially ostracised group of radical libertines. It had cost her the love of her father, it had effectively brought to an untimely end the lives of two women. She continued to be carried along with her husband on their great adventure, but she did so having to cope with nagging fears for Shelley's constancy and for his health, fears for her children, sorrow at the gulf that still lay between her and her father, guilt over Fanny and Harriet.

Frankenstein therefore suggests that there is everything for the young idealist to win, but the 'cheek grown pale with study' and the wasted body are also there to remind us that there is also everything to lose:

> No one can conceive the variety of feelings which bore me onwards, like a hurricane, in the first enthusiasm of success. Life and death appeared to me ideal bounds, which I should first break through, and pour a torrent of light into our dark world....
>
> These thoughts supported my spirits, while I pursued my undertaking with unremitting ardour. My cheek had grown pale with study, and my person had become emaciated with confinement. Sometimes, on the very brink of certainty, I failed; yet still I clung to the hope which the next day or the next hour might realize. (F 32)

The first paragraph catches something very close to the tone of the Dedication Shelley wrote for *Laon and Cythna*:

> Thoughts of great deeds were mine, dear Friend, when first
> The clouds which wrap this world from youth did pass.[23]

The second paragraph envisages the bright haven at the end of the long voyage promised in the same poem in a very different way.

Frankenstein describes himself as the epitome of Enlightenment man: 'I do not ever remember to have trembled at a tale of superstition, or to have feared the apparition of a spirit' (F 30). In 1814 Shelley will have reinforced Mary Godwin's rationalist upbringing in such matters in much the same way that he addressed the readers of his notes to *Queen Mab*:

> But even supposing that a man should raise a dead body to life before our eyes, and on this fact rest his claim to being considered the Son of God; – the Humane Society restores drowned persons, and because it makes no mystery of the method it employs, its members are not mistaken for the Sons of God.[24]

Mary will not have missed the bitter irony that might now be attached (after Harriet's death) to the restoration of 'drowned persons' as she read again her husband's denial of superstition, the husband who, with a few well-chosen lines from Gothic fiction, could scare himself and Claire half to death. Mary herself, now, was to use the story of Lazarus as a metaphor for the tale of one man's ambition to create a new society. What she now discussed was the nature of the difference between a new society and a reformed society. It is central to the reading of *Frankenstein* to appreciate that because of his impatience for success, reform is supplanted by the wish to make it new, thus 'I resolved, contrary to my first intention, to make a being of gigantic stature...', and this change of plan leads not to the creation of an oversize man but results in the creation of 'a new species' for which Frankenstein therefore becomes sole 'creator and source' (F 3). The creature is an embodiment of perfect rationality, and as such it constitutes an alien presence in the world. Its appearance is not mere difference, it is so totally 'other' as to be virtually impossible to look at, 'Oh! No mortal could support the horror of that countenance', the creature is 'almost too horrible for human eyes', and Walton writes, 'I dared not again raise my looks upon his face, there was something so scaring in his ugliness' (F 35, 65, 153). This difference in his appearance is matched by his superior physical strength, and the eloquence with which he is able to argue his case. We fear this intrinsically innocent creature because we cannot know it. It is not what we might become because it is not human, it does not answer to our God; its own God is (or was) a paragon of human Enlightenment, a modern Prometheus.

Hiding in the outhouse of a remote cottage, the creature is educated in human ways and values, but remains an outsider. Despite his progress with language there is much he fails to understand. He does come to perceive that the De Lacey family are in some way outsiders themselves:

> I saw few human beings beside them; and if any other happened to enter the cottage, their harsh manners and rude gait only enhanced to me the superior accomplishments of my friends. (F 75)

In due course he progresses to a more profound and disturbing knowledge of the history of government. Volney's *Ruins of Empire*, a rationalist critique of the political systems that have tyrannised mankind through to the present day was first published in 1791, and it occupied a central place in the Shelley library, where it helped to inspire the radical agenda of *Queen Mab*. The creature now listens as Felix De Lacey uses it as a primer to teach his sweetheart, a beautiful Arabian woman, his native language:

> Through this work I obtained a cursory knowledge of history .... Was man, indeed, at once so powerful, so virtuous, and magnificent, yet so vicious and base? He appeared at one time a mere scion of the evil principle, and at another as all that can be conceived of noble and godlike.... I learned that the possessions most esteemed by your fellow-creatures were, high and unsullied descent united with riches.... And what was I? Of my creation and creator I was absolutely ignorant; but I knew that I possessed no money, no friends, no kind of property. I was, besides, endowed with a figure hideously deformed and loathsome; I was not even of the same nature as man. (F 80)

The creature decides nevertheless to reveal himself to the De Laceys. Different as they may be from the 'harsh manners' of others, their difference is not his, and they drive him away.

It is this trauma of rejection that sets in train the creature's series of evil deeds of vengeance, that and Frankenstein's subsequent refusal to create a female of his creature's species. He murders Frankenstein's young brother, William; Justine, the maid, is found guilty and allowed to hang despite Frankenstein's knowledge of her innocence; he murders Frankenstein's closest friend, Clerval, and then his creator's bride, Elizabeth. The history of Mary's own haphazard education, her removal from home to Scotland, her continuing life as an outcast, the death of her own first child followed by those of Fanny and Harriet, all contributed to writing the history of a creature who explored the nature of its difference from humanity alongside an author who had reason to wonder if she might not have come to represent a new species. Like the creature in her novel, she desires to join with others to bring relief to the unenlightened masses; but like her mother, she is publicly branded as beyond the pale of humanity. Prometheus-like, Frankenstein's creature (rather than Frankenstein himself) would bring fire to aid stricken mortals; when he does bring fire, however, it is in anger, and is used to burn the De Laceys' cottage to the ground. The Gods of old triumph; a child is murdered and the innocent Justine eventually confesses so that she might gain absolution from the Church. Superstition mocks reason.

The creature's predicament was already a well-established part of Mary Shelley's literary life. Alongside Brockden Brown's Carwin, there is the central figure of Godwin's *St. Leon,* a man who becomes the keeper of the alchemical mystery of eternal youth in his efforts to aid humanity. Choosing this path as a means of bringing enlightenment to the world results in the death of his wife and the destruction of his family. Bethlem Gabor is the man St Leon attempts to reconstruct as an agent for human regeneration. The parallels between Gabor and Frankenstein's creature are striking. Here is Gabor rounding on his would-be benefactor:

> I hate mankind. I was not born to hate them. I have no native obliquity of character. I have no diabolical maliciousness of constitution. But they have forced me to hate them. And the debt of abhorrence shall be amply paid.[25]

Here is the creature rounding on Frankenstein:

> I was benevolent and good; misery made me a fiend.... Shall
> I not then hate them who abhor me? I will keep no terms
> with my enemies. I am miserable, and they shall share my
> wretchedness. (F 66)

Frankenstein has done with the new science what St Leon is shown to
have done with the old: stumbled into a new world which turns out
to be a curse, not a blessing.

Similarly, in Godwin's *Caleb Williams* (1794), Caleb, the 'new'
servant who challenges the principles of Falkland, the 'old' aristocrat,
are ultimately portrayed as one, pursuing each other towards a mutually destructive destination. In *Frankenstein* the pursuit and
exploration motifs bring us to the novel's climax on board Walton's
ship. Walton's retreat from his mission is Mary Shelley's means of
suggesting that an egotistically destructive drive towards revolution
might be honourably averted through recourse to pragmatic reform.

In the years immediately before *Frankenstein* began to be written,
Mary Shelley had been working on another literary project that
reveals an author far from clear on where she stood in relation to her
partner's political views. Her essay, 'History of the Jews' sets out to
attack the evils of priestcraft and superstition; Mary, however, slides
all too easily into the rhetoric of anti-Semitism. Her condemnation of
violence is similarly confused.[26] As Jane Blumberg has argued, we can
sense here an uncertainty that accords precisely with the debate over
reform and revolution that the activities of Frankenstein's creature
then went on to develop more thoroughly.

The subject for Shelley's next novel had been established before the
completion of *Frankenstein*. In the course of her studies at Marlow, she
had discovered the story of Castruccio, Prince of Lucca. As an enemy
of the republican Guelph party in fourteenth-century Tuscany,
Castruccio was the epitome of an aristocratic tyrant, and thus more
than earned himself a place on the Marlow syllabus. But there was
little opportunity, once *Frankenstein* had been delivered to the
publishers, to undertake serious research or composition for some
time. Once in Italy, Allegra was dispatched to Byron in the care of
Elise. At Livorno (May 1818) the Shelleys met Maria and John
Gisborne. Maria had previously been part of Godwin's circle, and he
had proposed to her after Mary Wollstonecraft's death. They finally

settled at Bagni di Lucca in early June. Anxious letters from Elise about Allegra's health sent Shelley and Claire hurrying to Venice. Shelley then decided that Mary must join them as a matter of urgency. She set off for Venice in the punishing August heat, fearful for Clara who was far from well. She joined the others at Este on 5 September 1818; on 24 September Clara died in Venice. At the end of October they moved on. Their travels took them to Naples, and eventually to Rome in March 1819.

Travelling had once more become a nightmare. Clara's death was followed by the appearance of a child, Elena, born in February 1819. Between them, Shelley, his servant Paolo Foggi, Elise and Claire, knew the answer to the origin of Elena, but it was treated as a mystery, and Mary was left to guess at what had gone on. The presence of Elena thus became one more cause of her increasing estrangement from her husband. In June William died from malaria, and this brought her to the point of almost complete breakdown. In April she had written to Maria Gisborne, giving her the news that she was pregnant, adding, 'We are delighted with Rome, and nothing but the Malaria would drive us from it...' (L I 93). From Leghorn at the end of June she wrote: 'I never know one moments ease from the wretchedness & despair that possess me' (L I 101). In her *Journal* she wrote, 'We have now lived five years together & if all the events of the five years were blotted out I might be happy' (J 293). Her condition was not improved by the intervention of her father, who thought he detected an opportunity to enlist his daughter's help in pressing Shelley to fulfil his promises to lend him money, while scolding a daughter of Enlightenment stock for wilting under such transient calamities. The Castruccio novel was laid aside, and instead Mary began to write a novel through which she might explore her own suicidal grief. This was *Mathilda*.

Prior to that, however, quite possibly during the period between the deaths of Clara and William, she had written a short story, 'Valerius: the Reanimated Roman'. Incorporating what must have been commonplace reflections in the Shelley circle on Italian history, and drawing on the mood conjured up in Byron's melancholy poem *Childe Harold*, Shelley imagines meeting a Roman returned from the dead to view his city in the early nineteenth century:

> When I awoke, Rome was no longer. That light, which I had hailed as the forerunner of perfection, became the torches that added splendour to her funeral....[27]

'Valerius' reminds us that Shelley was living a professional literary life that kept her busy on a number of marketable projects at any one time. Here, readers were invited to reflect on the shortcomings of the Enlightenment and its apostles in an attractively sentimental style.

If 'Valerius' signals the onset of a profound sadness in Mary's life, then *Mathilda* charts her dramatic decline into a state of chronic depression. Confronting rejection on all sides, she now fantasised on the fate of a child abandoned by her father because he has discovered that his love for her is tainted by an incestuous passion. Horrified by an urge he cannot control, he eventually commits suicide. Mathilda is discovered at the beginning of the novel alone in a bleak winter landscape that recalls the place where Frankenstein and his creation had met their deaths. This time there is no Walton prepared to make the return trip, there is only death:

> I see the desolate plain covered with white … a few birds are pecking at the hard ice that covers the pools … I do believe that I shall never again feel the vivifying warmth of another summer sun…. Others will toss these pages lightly over: to you, Woodville, kind, affectionate friend, they will be dear – the precious memorials of a heart-broken girl who, dying, is still warmed by gratitude towards you. (M 151)

Woodville is the Shelleyan presence in the novel. He is a tenderly perceived figure who attempts, unsuccessfully, to help Mathilda. He might once have been thought of as a saviour, but in the end is only an ineffectual 'affectionate friend' who looks on while the real tragedy of the broken relationship between father and daughter unfolds. Mary's treatment of Woodville suggests that a degree of reconciliation between Mary and Percy was achieved as the year wore on and the arrival of her next child became imminent:

> His genius was transcendent, and when it rose as a bright star in the east all eyes were turned towards it in admiration … To bestow on your fellow men is a Godlike attribute – So indeed it is and as such not one fit for mortality; – the giver like Adam and Prometheus, must pay the penalty of rising above his nature by being the martyr to his own excellence. Woodville was free from all these evils. (M 191)

The reference to Woodville as a 'bright star in the east' is undoubtedly a half-humorous comment on Percy Shelley's reputation as a heretic. He is neither Adam, Christ, nor yet Prometheus; he is in fact the Shelley she wanted, purified by the removal of political ambition, and crushed by the loss of the woman he loved before meeting Mathilda.

The literary sources of *Mathilda* emphasise the intimacy of its conception. Mathilda concludes her narrative on the point of death, as did the heroine in Wollstonecraft's *The Cave of Fancy*. Wollstonecraft had also written on the tragic story of George III's sister, Matilda, in her *Short Residence in Sweden*. Married to the brutal Christian VII of Denmark, Matilda campaigned for liberal reform, but died young. Matilda is also the name of Manfred's daughter in Horace Walpole's *The Castle of Otranto* (1765), and she is despised and harshly treated by her father. As Mary now regarded her father, so Mathilda describes hers:

> He was a sincere and sympathising friend – but he had met with none who superior or equal to himself could aid him in unfolding his mind, or make him seek for fresh stores of thought by exhausting the old ones. He felt himself superior in quickness of judgement to those around him ... he became at the same time dogmatic and yet fearful of not coinciding with the only sentiments he could consider orthodox ... at the same time that he strode with a triumphant stride over the rest of the world, he cowered, with self disguised lowliness, to his own party.... (M 153)

Godwin's intellectual brilliance is set alongside a streak of cowardice with clinical shrewdness.

Mathilda's life mirrors that of Mary's own, from the death of her mother, 'a few days after my birth', to her sojourn in Scotland, where she is looked after by an aunt (M 155). For Mathilda as for Mary, the great climax of her life comes at the age of 16, though in Mathilda's case this is because her father reappears. Before this she confesses she had often been tempted to run away (her aunt now doubling for her stepmother); here we glimpse the complex web of relationships and emotions that existed at Skinner Street: 'Sometimes when I had planned next morning for my escape a word of more than usual affection from her lips made me postpone my resolution' (M 159).

When Mathilda's father arrives in Scotland, Shelley is able to indulge in the fantasy of a reunion with her own father. In the novel what then transpires is the father's discovery of his incestuous love for his daughter; such a turn of events was relatively commonplace in the Gothic romances Shelley was reading, but the literary trope here almost certainly serves as a coded reference to the consequences of a Godwinian education. Mathilda's father admits to a 'strange narrowness of ideas' that in the novel lead to potentially scandalous consequences:

> I have betrayed your confidence; I have endeavoured to pollute your mind, and have made your innocent heart acquainted with the looks and language of unlawful and monstrous passion.... You are I doubt not prepared for what I am about to announce; we must separate and be divided for ever.
>
> I deprive you of your parent and only friend.... I, in the overflowing anguish of my heart, supplicate you to forgive me. (M 177)

While Mary Shelley had been analysing the anatomy of corrupt political systems, she had also been reflecting on attempts – specifically those in which her father had been a prime mover – to bring about the restoration of political justice. Godwin's relationship to Mary and the relationship of radical reform to a society as yet unable to bear its consequences are elided. The 'looks and language of unlawful and monstrous passion' that had 'polluted' Mary's mind were political rather than sensual. The personal catastrophes of her life were framed by failed political experiments; first Godwin's, then Shelley's. 'I am an outcast from human society', Shelley declared to Leigh Hunt in 1816.[28] It is the fate shared by both Frankenstein and his creature, and she had in mind now also the fate of Castruccio's lover, likewise betrayed by a man driven by political ambition. This theme is also paralleled in *The Cenci*, the verse drama that Percy Shelley was writing while Mary worked on *Mathilda*. In due course she was to claim it as his greatest work.

Life may have been over for Mathilda, but it continued for Mary Shelley. Determined to get the best medical assistance for her pregnancy, the couple moved to Florence. They arrived there on 2 October. With the birth of Percy Florence Shelley on 12 November 1819, Mary's spirits continued to improve. As winter came on, they moved yet again, this time to Pisa, where the medical care was good, and friends were not far away. They now settled down to live at the Cassa Frassi in Pisa for over two years. As the autumn of 1820 wore on,

Mary began to write in earnest, choosing *Valperga* as the title for her novel about Castruccio; Valperga was the name of the home of his ill-starred lover. It was her third novel, and the second she would see published.

5

The Wife of Shelley, 1820–22

In a short story that had probably been written by the time the couple moved to Pisa, 'The Heir of Mundolpho', Mary Shelley rehearsed the consequences of bad parenting; Fernando's dealings with his son, Ludovico, closely mirror Sir Timothy's treatment of Percy. Ludovico falls in love with a peasant girl and marries her. Fernando wants an heir of appropriate lineage to inherit Mundolpho, and therefore imprisons Ludovico's wife and child. All ends happily when the girl escapes with her child and is eventually reunited with Ludovico; but significantly the evil father remains unreconciled to the situation. Mary and Percy's relationship, however, was deteriorating rapidly; it had been under pressure from the first, given that Percy had never seriously envisaged entering a formal contract of marriage. Whatever her initial response to Shelley's communitarian idealism had been, Mary clearly came to look for a singleminded commitment from him, something he soon proved unable to provide even had he wished to. The partnership that survived through to their arrival in Pisa in 1820 had become little more than an agreement to share their literary lives, while both continued to take an active interest in the other's work.

Transcribing her husband's poetry, however, was a task that could now only feed Mary's sense of estrangement from him, a fact nowhere more apparent than in her tentative return to churchgoing. She wrote an embarrassed but frank account of this development to Maria Gisborne in January 1822: 'I have gone to the house of prayer ... and that from a truly Christian motive.... I went once, and then that I might not appear to despise his preaching, I went again and again' (L I 214). The 'Christian motive' might of course be construed as a wish not to offend the priest, George Frederick Nott, who ministered to a small English congregation in Pisa; but it is equally possible that her irony here is a defensive screen.

Her emotional withdrawal from Shelley did not make living with him any easier; she looked on while his affections were directed else-where, and by the time their Pisan interlude was drawing to a close, the *Journal* clearly signals Mary's recognition of the difference between her husband's recurring flights of romantic fancy and the nature of her own emotional needs. In an entry for February 1822 she attempts to sustain her spirits through the application of Godwinian rational analysis, but the final note reveals the Wollstonecraft in her, the bitterly disillusioned lover:

> let me in my fellow creatures love that which is & fix my affections on a fair form endued with imaginary attributes – where goodness, kindness & talent are, let me love & admire them at their just rate neither adding or diminishing & above all let me fearlessly descend into the remotest caverns of my own mind – carry the torch of self knowledge into its dimmest recesses – but too happy if I dislodge any evil spirit or enshrine a new deity in some hitherto uninhabited nook – Read Wrongs of Women.... (J 399–400)

Ever since the completion of *Mathilda*, Mary had been building a life for herself, alongside, rather than with her husband. It was a life that sought to distinguish clearly between the idealised 'fair forms' that entrapped her husband's thoughts, and her own commonsense commitment to love and admiration, bestowed at a 'just rate'. Her quest for self-knowledge might dislodge 'evil spirits', thereby estab-lishing a niche for a new deity (a reference perhaps to churchgoing). Mary was confronting the fact that Shelley was no longer central to her affections; there were other activities and indeed other people who might help her discover and adorn an 'uninhabited nook' in the 'remotest caverns' of her mind. The shade of her mother is summoned up to support her resolve.

Though she remained prepared to defend her marriage in public, privately Mary harboured a deep resentment over the failure of Shelley to modify his other relationships, not least the unabated strength of his feelings for Claire. Now rumours began to surface that Percy and Claire were the parents of Elena, the child born in Naples in 1818. Paolo Foggi, the Shelleys' servant at the time, sought to blackmail him with the claim, and – as had been the case with Claire's affair with Byron and her subsequent pregnancy – Percy and Claire sought to deal with the matter without informing Mary. When Elena died in June 1820, it was no longer possible to do this, and ready as she was to dismiss any idea of Elena as the child of Claire and her husband, Mary was forced to reflect on the uncomfortable likelihood (perhaps even her certain knowledge) that Elena was the child of Percy and Elise, the nurse who had travelled with them from England in 1818, and who was now Foggi's wife. There is also the possibility, explored by Richard Holmes, that Claire had indeed become pregnant around the time of Elena's birth, but had miscarried.[1]

It is hardly surprising that by June Mary's relationship with Claire had fallen to a very low ebb. Amid Mary's *Journal* entries noting her relentless reading, Scott's *Legend of Montrose* and *Ivanhoe*, Godwin's *Fleetwood* and *Caleb Williams*, Sterne's *Sentimental Journey*, Livy, Virgil, Lucretius, Mrs Macaulay's *History of England* (the list rolls on), we find the cryptic comment for Thursday, 8 June: 'A better day than most days & good reason for it though Shelley is not well. C[laire] away at Pugnano.' (J 320) The situation was bad enough for all to be persuaded that Claire should spend some time away from Pisa, though her vacation in Livorno was punctuated by regular visits from Shelley. In October she left for Florence.

The Shelleys' time in Pisa was notable for their integration into both an Italian and an English set of friends. There were the Gisbornes and their son Henry, Edward and Jane Williams, Thomas Medwin (a friend since Syon House school days), Count John Taafe, Edward John Trelawney, George Tighe and Mrs Mason. Trelawney, who did not arrive in Pisa until 1822, had served in the navy until 1812; he left it to pursue a life of travel that brought him eventually to Pisa in search of Byron and Shelley. Mrs Mason was the radicalised manifestation of Lady Margaret Mountcashell, who as a teenager had been tutored briefly in Ireland by Mary Wollstonecraft. The Elena affair now threatened to destroy this expanding circle. Problems arose after the Gisbornes returned from a visit to England. They had been on the receiving end of a furious tirade against Percy Shelley from Godwin, and Mary quickly became aware of their decision to snub her. It was soon after this that she learnt of the rumours around Elena's parentage. Shelley wrote to her about it from Venice where he was visiting Byron. Byron reported that the Hoppners were spreading Elise's version of Elena's parenthood to whoever they could get to listen. Richard Hoppner was the English consular-general in Venice, and he and his wife had helped the Shelleys and Claire in their dealings with Byron over Allegra, and had been on hand for Mary at the death of

Clara. Now they threatened, with the Gisbornes, to destroy the community of friends that Mary needed so badly.

Though she wrote in defiant terms to Maria Gisborne in October 1820, it is not difficult to perceive the panic and despair that lie just beneath the surface:

> A veil is now taken off from what was mysterious yesterday, and I now understand your refusal to visit us ... I see the ban of the Empire is gone out against us.... When you said that filthy woman said she would not visit Hunt how I gloried in our infamy. Now is the time! Join them, or us.... (L I 161)

James Henry Leigh Hunt was editor and co-owner of the *Examiner*, a weekly newspaper; he had long been an admirer of Shelley's poetry. The 'filthy woman' is Mary Jane Godwin. For the most part Mary avoided confronting the fact that her father, as much as Mary Jane, was working against her. In a later letter to Mrs Hoppner on the question of Elena's parents, she refuses to attach any blame to the two men (Shelley and Godwin) who, more than any, were in fact responsible for putting her in the state of an isolated outcast; indeed, she is more than loyal to both of them:

> Those who know me well believe my simple word – It is not long ago that my father said in a letter to me, that he had never known me utter a falsehood ... Shelley is as incapable of cruelty as the softest woman – To those who know him his humanity is almost as a proverb.... (L I 207, 10 August 1821)

This was the father she had so unmercifully unmasked in *Mathilda;* and this was the Shelley whose passion for Claire continued unabated, who may well have been the father of Elena, and who also, while at Pisa, had become obsessed with a young Italian countess.

Francesco Pacchiani, a retired academic, was largely responsible for introducing the Shelleys to an intellectual and artistic circle at Pisa, and in due course he took Claire to meet the Contessa Teresa Viviani. Teresa (known to the Shelleys as Emilia) was 19, and living in the Convent of St Anna while her parents negotiated for her marriage to a suitable husband. Eventually she was introduced to Mary and Percy. Mary wrote of her:

> It is grievous to see this beautiful girl wearing out the best

years of her life in an odious convent where both mind and body are sick from want of the appropriate exercise from each.... (L I 172, 29 December 1820)

Shelley wrote to her: 'Here we are then, bound by a few days' friendship, gathered together by some strange fortune from the ends of the earth to be perhaps a consolation to each other...'.[2]

With Mary unwilling or unable to give Shelley the emotional and physical companionship he craved (despite what was clearly his continued concern for her welfare), and with Claire increasingly out of bounds, Teresa Viviani became the occasion for a replay of Harriet in 1811 and Mary in 1814, 'a fair form endued with imaginary attributes', as Mary had wryly put it in her *Journal* entry for February 1822 (J 399). Percy's infatuation with 'Emilia' bore fruit in his poem *Epipsychidion*; 'It is an idealized history of my life and feelings', Shelley wrote to Gisborne,[3] and throughout the work he poured out his passion for Teresa:

> I never thought before my death to see
> Youth's vision thus made perfect. Emily
> I love thee.... [4]

He also expressed his continued abhorrence of marriage:

> I never was attached to that great sect,
> Whose doctrine is, that each one should select
> Out of the crowd a mistress or a friend,
> And all the rest, though fair and wise, commend
> To cold oblivion.... [5]

And he wrote of his regret for the way his passion for Claire, the 'Comet beautiful and fierce', had been thwarted:

> ... O Comet beautiful and fierce,
> Who drew the heart of this frail Universe
> Towards thine own; till, wreckt in that convulsion,
> Alternating attraction and repulsion,
> Thine went astray and that was rent in twain.[6]

Compared to Teresa, 'Poor captive bird ... Seraph of Heaven ... An antelope,/ In the suspended impulse of its lightness',[7] and Claire, the

'Comet', Mary appears in the guise of the moon:

> And I was laid asleep, spirit and limb,
> And all my being became bright or dim
> As the Moon's image in a summer sea,
> According as she smiled or frowned on me;
> And there I lay, within a chaste cold bed:
> Alas, I then was nor alive nor dead ... [8]

Epipsychidion presented Mary with an unambiguous statement of her husband's commitment to free love, as against the 'chaste cold bed' in which she herself chose to sleep. The poem suggests she might consider sharing her husband's love with Teresa as a 'bright regent':

> So ye, bright regents, with alternate sway
> Govern my sphere of being, night and day![9]

Just how bitter this pill was for her to swallow may be gauged by the brief, dismissive nature of her references to the poem subsequently ('There are other verses I should well like to obliterate for ever', J 561), and by the fact that in her 1839 edition of Shelley's poems, it is the one long poem she printed without comment.

She also – at some point during the course of these events – had recourse to fiction in order to ease the contempt she felt. 'The Bride of Modern Italy' tells the story of the young and impressionable Marcott Alleyn. He discovers Clorinda incarcerated in a convent, and becomes infatuated with her. What he fails to realise is that Clorinda does not really think of herself as being in any way victimised, and that the nuns are cynically exploiting his misplaced sense of chivalry. When Clorinda does get married, without a second thought for the besotted Alleyn, his friend Giacomo ironically recommends him to continue his visits: 'kiss the gentle nuns.... They miss your good cheer, and who knows what other nets they may weave to secure so valuable a prize.'[10] Teresa married in 1822; and though Mary's sardonic response remained unpublished then, it is interesting to note that despite the sense of guilt that prostrated her after Shelley's death – caused by the state of their relationship at that time – she agreed to the *London Magazine* publishing 'The Bride of Modern Italy' in 1824.

A further cause for anxiety at Pisa was the state of both her husband's and her father's finances. Mary knew that Godwin contin-ued to demand money from Percy; yet she remained loyal to him, explaining the situation to herself in terms of the baleful influence of her stepmother. It was this situation that made her all the more determined to succeed as a writer. Any money she might make from her second novel, *Valperga*, was intended to go to the assistance of Godwin. It thus became her research and writing, linked to a social life focused on contemporary political issues, that sustained her through these years.

In *Valperga* she wove together reflections on her own domestic tribulations with a meditation on the relationship between liberty and power in the state. In the latter instance she was influenced by the implications of Shelley's political convictions read alongside her observations of the faltering steps Italy was then taking to attain its liberty as an independent nation. In May 1820, Mary undertook to transcribe Percy's *A Philosophical Review of Reform*, which, though focusing on England, contained arguments on the function of literature in relation to social and political change that inevitably influenced her views on Italian and Greek current affairs. Her literary life was thus being defined not only by her reading for *Valperga* (which included a study of Scott's techniques as an historical novelist); it was profoundly influenced by her engagement with the progress of Italian unity after the defeat of Napoleon and the outcome of the Congress of Vienna. Equally significant was her continuing review of the place of Godwinian political principles in her life.

In *A Philosophical View of Reform*, Shelley continued to agonise (as he had in *The Mask of Anarchy* in 1819) over the justification of the use of physical violence in the cause of reform. Transcribing the essay (which Shelley never completed) will have taken up many hours of Mary's time; and she carried over into the pages of *Valperga* her reflections on the moral dilemmas that accompanied a belief in reform. Shelley wrote (and Mary copied):

> When the majority in any nation arrive at a conviction that it is their duty and their interest to divest the minority of a power employed to their disadvantage, and the minority are sufficiently mistaken as to believe that their superiority is tenable, a struggle must ensue.... [11]

The heroine of *Valperga,* Euthanasia, is forced to accept the need for just such a struggle. As she watches the armed conflict she has sanctioned, she appeals to the shade of her father for guidance, even as Mary had no doubt done herself many times:

'This is my work!' But she recovered herself – 'It must all be endured,' said she; 'I have undertaken a part, and will not faint on the threshold. Spirit of my father, aid me!' (V 293)

The eventual failure of Euthanasia's vision reflects Mary Shelley's realistic appraisal of the state of contemporary Italy. Metternich had famously declared that 'Italy' was no more than a geographical expression, and it was clearly the case that the partitioning of Italy at the Congress of Vienna of 1814–15 was made all the easier by the lack of any coherent nationalist movement. Italy's situation assisted Metternich's aim to ensure that nascent French nationalism received little or no encouragement from its neighbours. It was left to small, disparate groups to work for an end to foreign domination, and this was generally undertaken for immediate, local gain, rather than through any wider nationalist vision. Byron became involved in a group known as the Carbonari, a shadowy patriot movement with divided loyalties and ill-defined aims. In 1820 they were involved in an uprising in Naples as a result of which Ferdinand I was forced to grant a democratic constitution; but with Austrian aid he was restored as absolute monarch within a year. Mary Shelley's comments on the Neapolitan uprising (written in a letter to Maria Gisborne of 19 July 1820, while its success still seemed assured) show her reflecting on how the passage of time can influence the interpretation of history:

> Are you not ... delighted to hear of the Revolution at Naples.... Thirty years ago was the era for Republics, and they all fell – This is the era for *constitutions* ... in the end I hope the people here will raise their fallen souls and bodies, and become something better than they are. (L I 156)

The failed revolt in Naples was followed by a similarly ill-fated uprising in Piedmont. Pisa was a garrison town, and the Shelleys could not but be aware of intensified activity by the police and spies. Orders sent to the Venice police in 1820 graphically indicate how precarious the position of foreigners anywhere in Italy could become at this time. The police were urged to step up 'surveillance and control of foreign consuls, of diplomatic personnel and other agents of foreign powers, whether accredited or secret, of emissaries, adventurers, travellers, etc., especially of their machinations and contacts'.[12] The Shelleys' departure from Pisa was eventually to come about as a direct consequence of the volatile political situation.

Byron's arrival in Pisa in November 1821 made the likelihood of political mischief appear all the more probable to the authorities, not least because Byron's English set (surely to be included in the 'adventurers' and 'travellers' category) rode out regularly for shooting practice, and there was little love lost between the soldiers garrisoned at the city and the participants in the noble Lord's war-games. A minor incident on the road between Byron's shooting-range and Pisa involving the English (including Shelley) and a soldier galloping back to town, sparked off a series of ugly incidents. John Taafe was jostled as the soldier, Sergeant Major Masi, hurtled past him. An angry exchange followed and Masi was eventually wounded by an Italian member of Byron's household. The soldier did not die, and the matter was eventually dropped. But it marked the end of the Pisan circle, and in consequence precipitated the Shelleys' move to the Casa Magni in the Bay of Spezia.

The Masi affair belongs to the narrative of Shelley and Byron, where Mary is cast in the role of an anxious onlooker. Her engagement with the political issues of the day, however, were no less serious than those of the men. She came to know Prince Alexander Mavracordato, the exiled leader of the Greek patriots in Europe who was determined to bring the Turkish occupation of his homeland to an end. As Mavracordato set about instructing Mary in the labyrinthine details of Greek politics, he also undertook to tutor her in the language; it may well have seemed to her in consequence that the pretentiously militaristic activities of the English menfolk around her lacked the seriousness of her own commitment.

Shelley acquiesced in his wife's evident pleasure in the company of Mavracordato (he could scarcely do otherwise), and he dedicated *Hellas* (1821) to him; but his note to Claire at the time of Mavracordato's departure for Greece is revealing: 'He is a great loss to Mary, and *therefore* to me – but not otherwise.'[13] Mary, meanwhile, wrote excitedly to Leigh Hunt in December 1820 that Mavracordato had:

> related to us some very infamous conduct of the English powers in Greece of which I should exceedingly like to get the documents & to place them in Gray Bennet's or Sir F. B.'s [Francis Burdett] hands – they might serve to give another knock to this wretched system of things.

England was seldom far from her thoughts, and she continued,

'perhaps we exiles are ultra-political – but certainly I have some hopes
that something fortunate will soon happen for the state of things in
England' (L I 170–4). Mavracordato set sail from Livorno for Morea at
the end of June 1821. In the meantime Percy Shelley had bought a
canal boat. His doctor, Andrea Vaccà, had advised fresh air and exercise as the best way for him to regain his health. In April he therefore
went to Livorno with Edward Williams and Henry Reveley to buy a
horse. The boat he bought instead came close to terminating his life
almost at once. On the way home, around midnight, it capsized, and
but for Reveley's presence of mind Shelley would certainly have
drowned. Unfortunately the adventure did nothing to dampen his
enthusiasm for sailing.

Alongside *Valperga*, and the ever-present transcription work for
Shelley, Mary worked on various short stories; 'The Heir of
Mundolpho' and 'The Bride of Modern Italy' have already been
mentioned. From her historical researches she also worked up a story
to be called 'A Tale of the Passions'. Eventually in February 1822 she
could inform Maria Gisborne, 'I have sent my novel to Papa – I long
to hear some news of it – as with an author's vanity I want to see it in
print & hear the praises of my friends' (L I 218). Like *Frankenstein*
before it, *Valperga: or, the Life and Adventures of Castruccio, Prince of
Lucca*, had been a long time coming. The research had started in the
library at Marlow in 1817. After that came the satisfaction of seeing
her first books in print, only to be followed by the cumulative disasters of her life in Italy. The research had continued, but it had not
been until 1820 at Pisa that she had felt ready to begin writing in
earnest. She had to hand as primary sources biographies of Castruccio
by Machiavelli and Niccolo Tegrino, Sismondi's *Histoire de Républiques
Italiennes de l'Age Moyen*, Villani's *Florentine Annals*, and Morevi's
Grand Dictionnaire Historique. Once she began writing, *Valperga*
evolved as a novel crafted to allow its author to articulate both her
public enthusiasm for political liberty, and the difficulties that beset
her inner life as she struggled with the continuing frustrations and
disappointments of her marriage.

Writing to Peacock, Percy Shelley stressed the way in which Mary's
interest in the history of the period had burgeoned; the novel was
'illustrative of the manners of the Middle Ages in Italy' which she had
culled from 'fifty old books'.[14] Mary had prepared for *Valperga* by
doing considerably more than study 'old books', however. The
Shelleys had been reading Scott's historical novels since they first
began to appear in 1814. During the period when she was writing

Valperga Mary intensified her study of Scott's technique, reading (or in some cases rereading) *Ivanhoe, Kenilworth, The Abbot, Waverley, Rob Roy, The Bride of Lammermoor, A Legend of Montrose* and *The Pirate*. While Percy made no comment on this, what he wrote does indicate the extent to which she had become beguiled by the historical pageant that began to unravel before her. What was destined to be a long novel when it was published was certainly an even longer novel when it landed on Godwin's desk. His major editorial contribution was to take the pruning hook to passages of excessive historical detail in order to bring out more strongly the drama of the plot.

But if Mary discovered and indulged her historian's facility in *Valperga*, she manipulated plot and character to write with equal determination through her personal difficulties, and to explore her developing political ideas. Writing to convince the publisher, Charles Ollier, that the political drift of the novel was entirely safe, Percy described Castruccio as 'a little Napoleon' over against Euthanasia, 'whose love for him is only equalled by her enthusiasm for the liberty of the republic of Florence, which is in the same sort her country, and for that of Italy, to which Castruccio is a devoted enemy...'.[15] Subsequent critical readings of *Valperga* have all endorsed Percy Shelley's suggestion that Napoleon was a model for Castruccio, and this was certainly the case. It is also true, however, that Mary's novel explores the theme of liberty versus oppression in a way that is much closer to the bone. She uses the rivalry between Ghibelline and Guelph factions – between the forces of oppression and liberty – as a thinly veiled critique of reactionary political movements in her own time, and relates that story to the intimate affairs of her own life.

The novel begins with a portrait of the young Castruccio that makes it sound very much as though it is the young Shelley who has been exiled from Lucca by the Guelphs:

> Alone on the bare Apeninnes, over which the fierce wind swept, he felt free; there was no one near him to control his motions, to order him to stay or go.... He felt as if the air that quickly glided over him, was a part of his own nature, and bore the soul along with it; impulses of affection mingled with these inexplicable sensations.... (V 17)

Percy Shelley had been reflecting on the possibilities of a return from exile at this time, and the *Philosophical View of Reform* carried between its lines thoughts on how he might in due course achieve 'power and distinction' in his native land (V 17). Mary is as ever acutely conscious of the damaging effects of rejection and exile; like Shelley, Castruccio is 'a youth of high birth and nobly bred, an outcast and an exile' who comes to dream of compensating for his rejection by the acquisition of power (V 24). Shelley had planned to regenerate society through the influence of the enlightened community he was for ever striving to create; the atheist in him was dreaming, as Castruccio also did, of even conquering Heaven itself (V 29). Unlike Shelley, Castruccio has no time for dreams of introducing political justice for the masses, but Mary clearly explores from the outset how narrow the divide can become between the ambitions of two men otherwise so profoundly different.

Mary herself is undoubtedly a model for Castruccio's childhood sweetheart, Euthanasia. The daughter of an enlightened scholar, Antonio dei Admirari, Euthanasia is described by Anne K. Mellor very much as Mary would have thought of herself at Pisa, 'a highly educated woman with the capacity for both passionate love and political leadership'.[16] In *Valperga* we read that:

> she saw and marked the revolutions that had been, and the present seemed to her only a point of rest, from which time was to renew his flight ... and, if her voice or act could mingle aught of good in these changes, this it was to which her imagination most ardently aspired. She was deeply penetrated by the acts and thoughts of those men, who despised the spirit of party, and grasped the universe in their hopes of virtue and independence.... Her young thoughts darted into futurity, to the hope of freedom for Italy, of revived learning and the reign of peace for all the world.... (V 22)

While Percy Shelley might still just have fitted the bill for 'high song' (V 22), the reference to the active pursuit of 'virtue and independence' is more reminiscent of the enthusiasm Mary expresses in her correspondence for Mavracordato.

Castruccio's story is one of an impressionable Shelleyan youth lured into the belief that political liberty is a destabilising force in the world, to be resisted by every means possible. In 1309 he travels to England and becomes embroiled in the politics of the Court of Edward II. He is forced to return to Europe after killing a noble in a fight, and here he meets Alberto Scoto and Benedetto Pepi who teach him to match his soldier's craft to that of 'hypocrisy, and the wily arts of a hoary politician' (V 57). Through Pepi Shelley gives voice to the reactionary leaders of Europe in her own day. 'The world', he explains (helping us to interpret *Frankenstein* as he does so), '… will never go well, until the rich rule, and the vulgar sink to their right station as slaves of the soil.… If the rich would only know their own interests, we might chain the monster, and again bury Liberty.' The truth is simple, Republics have wars, the rule of Kings brings peace. 'While Liberty is a word, a breath, an air; it will dissipate, and Florence become as slavish as it is now rebellious; did not Rome fall?' (V 72–3)

In due course the opportunity arises for an alliance between Florence and Pisa (Guelph and Ghibelline), but the chance of peace evaporates and Castruccio exploits the situation for his own aggrandisement. Describing his 'ambition for power, conquest and renown', Mary now injects an unmistakably Byronic element into the portrait:

> somewhat of pride, and more of self-confidence, and much of sensibility, were seen in his upturned lip; his eyes, dark as a raven's wing, were full of fire and imagination; his open forehead was shaded by the hyacinth curls of his chestnut-coloured hair. (V 92)

Despite his overweening ambition there is still good in Castruccio, and he manages to save Lucca from being razed to the ground; but it is in order to play power politics that he comes to Valperga where his childhood sweetheart, Euthanasia rules.

Mary Shelley's debt to Scott is particularly evident in her description of Euthanasia's gothic castle and its surrounds:

> The road that led from Lucca to Valperga struck directly across the plain to the foot of the rock on which the castle was built. This rock overhung the road … forming a precipice on three sides; the northern side, at the foot of which the Secchio flowed, was disjoined from the mountain by a ravine, and a torrent struggled in the depth, among loose stones, and the gnarled and naked roots of trees that shaded the side of the cleft.… At the summit of the path was a drawbridge that connected it with the almost isolated platform of rock on which the castle stood … the castle itself was a large and

picturesque building, turreted, and gracefully shrouded by trees. (V 101)

Castruccio enters the castle, proceeds through various carefully described courtyards until eventually he discovers Euthanasia's room, which he duly enters. There is much here about the vulnerability of the heroine's individuality and integrity.

Behind the castle is a secret place where Euthanasia retires to meditate. In time, Castruccio will also violate this retreat. The scene that is conjured up – involving a bunch of myrtle that falls in her lap – is reminiscent of the scenes of intrusion that occur in Brockden Brown's novels, in particular those already referred to in *Wieland*:

> She had a favourite retreat near a spring that issued from a rock behind her castle.... Thither she now retired, and watched the coming night; when suddenly she thought she heard a rustling above her, and a small bunch of myrtle fell on her lap; she looked up; and, gazing earnestly, perceived Castruccio, with one hand grasping a myrtle shrub, leaning from the summit of the precipice. (V 128)

When Castruccio later besieges the castle, his knowledge of the secret paths around Valperga ensures Euthanasia's downfall. Again, this is the occasion for a poignant reference to Shelley's sense of the woman's violation:

> she glanced back once more at the castle, and looked up to the windows of her apartment; she had expected to find it deserted and blank; but it was filled with soldiers who stood looking from it at her departure.... (V 297)

It is difficult to resist a reading that reflects on Mary's capitulation to Shelley's initial overtures of love, and his subsequent behaviour. She was pregnant yet again when they left Pisa. It is equally true that there is little in her symbolic use of the castle that had not already been explored in the Gothic literature she read.[17]

The descriptions of the meeting and falling in love of Castruccio and Euthanasia undoubtedly do owe much to Mary's reflections on the history of her partnership with Shelley. She describes her heroine as having 'a wisdom exalted by enthusiasm, a wildness tempered by self-command.... She was frank, generous and fearless; therefore she instantly believed and trusted ...' (V 103, 105). Euthanasia is a woman whose essential qualities are soul, love and feeling; she is therefore no match for Castruccio's worldly wisdom, and their relationship is clearly doomed. But even as Mary continued to find Shelley (and Byron) attractive, so the doubts that Euthanasia has about Castruccio's motives when he is absent are all too easily dispelled when he reappears. Particularly disturbing is Castruccio's Byronic quality of 'Raillery and bitter irony, which, when he chose to exert it, seemed to enter into and wither the soul of its object' (V 18–19). Mary's awareness of the potential influence for the worse that Byron might have on her husband has its part to play in the way she develops Castruccio's character.

Euthanasia and Castruccio agree to marry, but the reappearance of Pepi Benedetto serves to draw Castruccio all the more deeply into the world of political scheming and duplicity. Before long, he has become inextricably committed to plotting against the Guelphs, against what Galeazzo calls 'the contagion of liberty' (V 167). He now also meets Beatrice, the woman who swiftly becomes a rival for Euthanasia's love. Readers of Shelley biographies might be forgiven for thinking that they have met Beatrice before: 'Her deep black eyes, half concealed by their heavy lids, her curved lips, and face formed in perfect oval, the rising colour that glowed in her cheeks...' (V 169). Over against Euthanasia's 'frank, generous and fearless' love, grounded in 'reason', we have in Beatrice a woman who is all passion: 'her eyes, black as the darkness which succeeds a midnight flash of lightning, full and soft as the shy antelope's, gleamed with prophetic fire' (V 105, 169).

Beatrice has been arrested in Ferrara on a charge of blasphemy when the Bishop of Ferrara introduces her to Castruccio. Shelley makes it clear that Beatrice is the victim of the political game being played out, but she is equally clear about what Beatrice's problem is – she had, after all, been brooding on it ever since Claire had been included in the escape party of 1814. Beatrice, raised by an eccentric and unpredictable mother (Wilhelmina of Bohemia in the novel) has 'a most ardent imagination' which 'she ought to have bound with fetters, and to have curbed and crushed by every effort of reason' (V 203). Falling in love with Castruccio destines her to the same fate that overtook the impulsive young lover of Shelley and Byron: 'she resigned herself entire to her visionary joys, until she finally awoke to truth, fallen, and for ever lost' (V 204). Beatrice is tried and found guilty. She survives an ordeal by fire only because the event has been rigged; she is progressively forced to come to terms with the fact that her life has been based on a deceit. Castruccio eventually leaves her to pursue his military and political ambitions.

In Chapter 7 of Book II Euthanasia finally learns of Castruccio's implacable determination to crush the Florentine Republic; she now faces a choice between her love for him and her political commitment. Once again, Shelley drew heavily on personal experiences to write what is probably the most powerful chapter of the book. Euthanasia must refuse the man she has come to love so deeply:

> Yet when, in the silence of night and solitude, she consulted her own heart, she found that love had quenched there every other feeling, and not to love was to her to die.... 'Must I then fight to love?... I loved! God and my own heart know how truly, how tenderly! How I dwelt on his idea, his image, his virtues, with unblamed affection.... Is this a dream? Oh! Then all is a dream ...' (V 242–3)

At this point Beatrice arrives at Valperga and Euthanasia hears her tale. Both women are victims, and no doubt with Shelley's charge of 'coldness' in *Epipsychidion* still preying on Mary's mind, we learn that Euthanasia's 'imagination furled its wings, and the owlet, reason, was the only dweller that found sustenance and a being in her benighted soul' (V 258).

Valperga is besieged by Castruccio, and whether consciously or not, Mary Shelley writes a thinly veiled account of her situation in Pisa. Her dead children lay between her and the man she had so willingly loved; Euthanasia's friend is put to death by Castruccio for plotting against him; 'I can never forgive the death of Leodino', she says; and Castruccio, using his knowledge of the secret paths around Valperga, attacks the castle. It is nothing less than rape; she is forced to submit to him: 'it was she, whose castle he was about to take and raze' (V 276). Volume II ends with the fall of Valperga and Euthanasia taken captive to Florence.

In Volume III Euthanasia and Beatrice are brought together, both victims of a man who treads the mistaken path of Victor Frankenstein: 'Desire of dominion and lordship was the only passion that now had much power in his soul ...' (V 314). Beatrice is now prone to ungovernable bouts of hysteria, she attacks Euthanasia's liberal optimism with a belief in the omnipresence of evil. She is a caricature of Shelleyan atheism embodied in his favourite pupil (V 328–32). The novel allows Mary to assume and carry through the role she must so often have longed to have been empowered to adopt in reality:

> 'I will endeavour to teach you the lessons of true religion;
> and, in reducing the wandering thoughts of one so lovely and
> so good, I shall in part be fulfilling my task on the earth.' (V
> 333)

The autobiographical route through the novel serves to emphasise the
extent of Mary and Percy's estrangement, and the way in which their
relationship – before and after Percy's death – dominated Mary's literary life. Percy was Mary's Castruccio for whom she liked to think 'She
felt neither hatred, nor revenge, nor contempt colder than either; she
felt grief alone, and that sentiment was deeply engraven on her soul'
(V 339). But this was a Godwinianly idealised assessment based on
rational analysis, there were emotional consequences not so easily set
aside. The novel suffers from Shelley's inability to resist exhaustively
analysing the differences between Beatrice and Euthanasia. Against
Euthanasia's enlightened intellect Beatrice displays an unchecked
imagination which continues to draw her towards superstition and
necromancy. Her continued longing for Castruccio puts her in the
power of the witch Fior di Mandragola who fools her into thinking
that she can summon up Castruccio through magic. The whole
scheme is a fabrication, and when Castruccio finally appears, it is
without the help of necromancy. He is not alone, however, and
Beatrice is terrified to recognise his companion as the man who
imprisoned and violated her as a girl. The shock sends her into a
decline from which she is destined not to recover.

Euthanasia has now to recognise that Castruccio is irredeemable,
and she takes what positive action she can to foil his plans: 'Ambition,
and the fixed desire to rule, smothered in his mind the voice of his
better reason' (V 233–4). Yet even here, condemnation cannot be
absolute; Tripaldi, the de Sadian villain who destroyed Beatrice's life,
is shown as the evil genius who directs Castruccio's pride and ambition into evil channels, even as Scoto and Pepi had done earlier.
Euthanasia is drawn into a plot intended to overthrow Castruccio
while sparing his life; she still dreams of reforming him. The plot fails
and the conspirators are arrested. Their fate, decreed by Castruccio, is
torture and death.

When he is with Euthanasia in her cell, Castruccio is still able to
agonise over the role he has chosen to play; away from her, however,
he reverts swiftly to the cynical tyrant. When Euthanasia agrees to

allow him to save her by smuggling her off to Sicily, she does so not through any wish she has to live, but as a gesture of sympathy to a man tortured by guilt and self-doubt. Her ship, however, is overtaken by a storm, and she is drowned. Castruccio himself dies soon after; aged just 47, he is burnt out by the rigours and pressures of his life.

Shelley clearly used *Valperga* to work through her personal situation, and though in some respects the author of *A Philosophical View of Reform* may seem a bizarre model for Castruccio, there can be no doubting its appropriateness from Mary's point of view in many respects. Castruccio is a man whose best interests lay in being prepared to submit to the counsels of the woman who loved him. His sense of honour and commitment was to be tragically misapplied when her place as the voice of his conscience was usurped by the demonic (Byronic) libertine, Tripaldi, and her place as his lover was taken by Beatrice. Mary had clearly come to believe that, like Castruccio, her wayward lover would most probably be the death of her. The writing of *Valperga* enabled its author to enact a victory over the disruptive influence of Claire, and it explored the steadily widening division of opinion between Percy and Mary over central tenets of Percy's radical programme of thought and action, reinstating through Euthanasia a commitment to religion grounded in rationalism, as against a Shelleyan rationalist atheism that perversely seemed to encourage recourse to emotional excess and occultism. The novel affirms an ideal of domestic felicity (represented in glowing terms by Euthanasia's hospitable court at Valperga); it was a domesticity fated to be brutally destroyed by Castruccio.

In the end, though, Euthanasia – like Mary – cannot, or will not, be rid of the man. Mary pursued the same theme in 'A Tale of the Passions', written at this time and using the same historical material. Despina, one-time lover of the cruel Guelph Lostendardo, smuggles herself into his presence disguised as a man, and there, by attempting to appeal to his better nature, begs him to join the young Ghibelline Corradino. Despina clings to the belief that love will win the day, both for political justice and for personal fulfilment. She is wrong, and Lostendardo's response is terrible indeed:

> The tempest of passion that arose in his heart seemed too mighty to admit of swift manifestation; it came slowly up from the profoundest depths of his soul, and emotion was piled upon emotion before the lightning of his anger sped to its destination.[18]

When 'A Tale of the Passions' was published in *The Liberal* in 1823 it was criticised for the summary way it dealt with the fate of the main players, Corradino and Lostendardo. But of course Mary Shelley's main interest was in the fate of the beleaguered Despina who, like the deserted Euthanasia, finds that she pays for her grand passion with her life. With hindsight, the tragic conclusion of *Valperga* appears an uncannily misheard prophecy of tragic events that were soon to come.

Mary Shelley's belief that *Valperga* was a novel destined for greater popularity than *Frankenstein* was soon called into question; Lackington, who had published *Frankenstein*, turned it down, while Percy Shelley's publisher, Ollier, hesitated despite Percy's eloquent recommendation. In January 1822 she sent the manuscript to Godwin with instructions to do the best he could with it. It was finally published in February 1823. By that time, however, Mary's situation had altered dramatically, and the story of the publication and subsequent fate of *Valperga* belongs to the time when she was looking to create a literary life for herself in the shadow of her husband's death, and in the teeth of Sir Timothy Shelley's determination to remove all record of his son's name from the public eye, including as he did so the name of the woman he married.

At the end of April 1822 Shelley and Mary, with their child Percy Florence (now in his third year), Claire, Edward and Jane Williams and their two children, moved together into the Casa Magni on the Gulf of Spezia. Shelley's first task was to find a way of breaking the news to Claire that her daughter Allegra had died of typhus fever. It seems she had already guessed. It was an inauspicious start to life in their new home. Mary was now three months pregnant and very ill, wearily aware of an increasingly close relationship developing between Percy and Jane Williams.

On 12 May a new boat Shelley had ordered arrived (Byron had christened it the *Don Juan*) and for Williams and Shelley at least, an enjoyable summer seemed assured. Claire appeared to be recovering well from her loss, and she left to spend some time in Florence in mid-May. Mary continued ill and depressed. Early in June she suffered a miscarriage, and only survived because of Percy's prompt but extreme action of immersing her in a bath of freezing water to staunch the bleeding. Claire returned and did her best to help her, but she remained withdrawn and morbidly depressed. On 1 July Shelley and

Williams sailed to Livorno, and from there travelled on to Pisa. It was a spirited reunion of the set; Byron, Trelawney and their Italian friends were joined by Leigh Hunt, who had arrived from England to discuss launching a new magazine to be called *The Liberal*. On 8 July, with ominous clouds gathering on the western horizon, Shelley, Williams, and their boat-boy Charles Vivian set sail once more for La Spezia. In the ensuing storm the *Don Juan* went down. There were no survivors.

For Mary, the consequence of the tragedy was to be a crushing burden of guilt which she determined to alleviate by publishing Shelley's collected poems, and writing his life. She wrote what was, in effect, a draft of the final chapter for the biography in mid-August 1822, when she sent Maria Gisborne 'some account of the last miserable months of my disastrous life' (L I 244–51). It is the first of many statements that were to retell Shelley's drowning as a defining moment in the history of English Romanticism. Mary's letter is not the work of a woman whose spirit is broken. It is a strong, dramatic narrative where the author sets about dealing with the trauma through the use of literary form.

The first part of the letter describes her own state – 'My nerves were wound up to the utmost irritation' – over against Shelley's good health. She then relates a series of premonitions, dreams and quasi-supernatural events, all of which serve to build expectation, in the best Gothic tradition, towards the moment of disaster. Jane Williams, 'a woman of sensibility', who 'has not much imagination & is not in the slightest degree nervous – neither in dreams or otherwise', thought she saw Shelley walk by the window on the terrace twice, going in the same direction, impossible at the best of times, 'and it proved indeed that Shelley had never been on the terrace & was far off at the time she saw him'. Then, with the menfolk gone, there is the waiting. Letters finally arrive, among them a letter from Hunt to Shelley:

> it said – 'pray write to tell us how you got home, for they say that you had bad weather after you sailed Monday & we are anxious' – the paper fell from me – I trembled all over – Jane read it – 'Then it is all over!' she said. 'No, my dear Jane,' I cried, 'it is not all over, but this suspense is dreadful – come with me, we will go to Leghorn, we will post to be swift & learn our fate.' We crossed to Lerici, despair in our hearts.... I knew that Hunt was at Pisa at Lord Byron's house but I thought that L. B. was at Leghorn. I settled that we should

drive to Casa Lanfranchi that I should get out and ask the fearful question of Hunt, 'do you know any thing of Shelley?' On entering Pisa the idea of seeing Hunt for the first time for four years under such circumstances, & asking him such a question was so terrific to me that it was with difficulty that I prevented myself from going into convulsions – my struggles were dreadful – they knocked at the door & someone called out 'Chi è?'.... I staggered upstairs.... They knew nothing – he had left Pisa on Sunday – on Monday he had sailed – there had been bad weather Monday afternoon – more they knew not.... I had risen almost from a bed of sickness for this journey – I had travelled all day – it was now 12 at night – & we, refusing to rest, proceeded to Leghorn – not in despair – no, for then we must have died....

Just as the device of fiction in *Mathilda* and *Valperga* had carried Mary through and out of her depression before and during her time at Pisa, so here it enabled her to cope with the next, even more demanding crisis. The letter casts the terrible reality into fictional form, and in that way it can be confronted, written and read through to its devastating conclusion. The middle section is taken up with the interminable waiting, the situation not helped by the fact that a carnival was being celebrated, though for the dramatic effect it lends the narrative, it could not have been better timed:

San Arenzo was illuminated for a festa – what a scene – the roaring sea – the scirocco wind – the lights of the town towards which we rowed – & our own desolate hearts – that coloured all with a shroud – we landed; nothing had been heard of them.... reports were brought us – we hoped – & yet to tell you all the agony we endured during those 12 days would be to make you conceive a universe of pain – each moment intolerable & giving place to one still worse. The people of the country too added to one's discomfort – they are like wild savages – on festa's the men & women & children in different bands – the sexes always separate – pass the whole night in dancing on the sands close to our door running into the sea then back again & screaming all the time one perpetual air – the most detestable in the world – the scirocco perpetually blew & the sea for ever moaned their dirge. On Thursday 25th Trelawney left us to go to Leghorn to see what was doing or what could be done. On Friday I was very ill but as evening came on I said to Jane – 'If anything had been found on the coast Trelawney would have returned to let us know. He has not returned so I hope.' About 7 o'clock P. M. he did return – all was over – all was quiet now, they had been found washed on shore – Well all this was to be endured.

We hear of the 'last offices' to be performed on the shore, of some other tales of foreboding, and a postscript adds further details of a possible eye-witness account.

This devastating moment in Mary Shelley's life was also a key moment for the development of her literary life. From this point on she was driven to write and rewrite in fictional form different versions of the narrative of her life with Percy. The formal biography remained a book she could never write, despite several abortive attempts. Even had Shelley's father been prepared to sanction it, she could not bring herself to complete it – it was simply too painful a task, given the terms on which they had parted company in 1822. Though Percy's death was a brutal reality for Mary, it became also a Romantic fiction in which Mary Shelley – in so many ways the least appropriate candidate – was destined to play out the role of the tragic Romantic heroine. In due course, Edward Trelawney's account of the drowning helped to fix Mary's persona as the widow of Shelley in the public mind, and it was the literary life of the widow of Shelley that the public now began to observe:

> And now by the blow of an idle puff of wind the scene was changed. Such is human happiness.
>
> My reverie was broken by a shriek from the nurse Caterina, as, crossing the hall, she saw me in the doorway. After asking her a few questions, I went up the stairs, and, unannounced, entered the room. I neither spoke, nor did they question me. Mrs Shelley's large grey eyes were fixed on my face. I turned away. Unable to bear this horrid silence, with a convulsive effort she exclaimed –
>
> 'Is there no hope?'
>
> I did not answer, but left the room.... [19]

6
The Widow of Shelley, 1822–26

On 2 October 1822, Mary Shelley began to write what she called her 'Journal of Sorrow'. 'But for my Child', she declared, 'it could not End too soon' (J 428). Two things above all else appear to have made it possible for her to go on: one was her son, now 3 years old; the other was her writing. Her despair spilled across the pages of her *Journal* and flooded into her letters to become a therapeutic enactment of the devastation she felt; and she soon resolved to dedicate her life to the project of memorialising her husband through the publication of his work, and the writing of his life:

> If I were alone I had already begun what I have determined to do – but I must have patience – & for those events my memory is brass.... France – Poverty – a few days of solitude & some uneasiness – A tranquil residence in a beautiful spot – Switzerland – Bath – Marlow – Milan – The Baths of Lucca – Este – Venice – Rome – Naples – Rome & misery – Leghorn – Florence Pisa. – Solitude The Williams – The Baths – Pisa These are the heads of chapters – each containing a tale, romantic beyond romance. (J 447)

After the tragedy she had returned to Pisa. Before moving on from there to Genoa, she wrote to Maria Gisborne that not even Percy Florence could always be considered a consolation, 'when I think how He loved him, the plans we had for his education, his sweet & child-ish voice strikes me to the heart' (L I 252). It was in the *Journal* in particular, however, that Shelley undertook to approach the most distressing issue of all, the terms on which she and Percy had parted. She constructed a highly literary, melodramatic context from which she might contemplate her feelings of guilt; she reconstructed a time that was 'romantic beyond romance', that was 'happy though chequered', and while she wonders if her writing is up to the task, she also wonders just how honest she can bear to be with herself:

> For eight years I communicated with unlimited freedom with one whose genius, far transcending mine, awakened & guided my thoughts... Now I am alone! Oh, how alone!... White paper – wilt thou be my confidant? I will trust thee fully, for none shall see what I write. But can I express all I feel? Have I the talent to give words to thoughts & feelings that as a tempest hurry me along?... What a change! Oh my beloved Shelley – It is not true that this heart was cold to thee ... How often during those happy days, happy though chequered, I thought how superiorly gifted I had been in being united to one to whom I could unveil myself, & who could understand me. (J 429–30)

'It is not true that this heart was cold to thee.' Though this statement might well be read as evidence that Mary was still smarting from the rebuke levelled at her in *Epipsychidion*, it was in fact a reference to Hunt's subsequent treatment of her. Jane Williams had told Hunt of Mary's coldness to Percy in the years before his death, and how unhappy that had made him. Though at this point she was unaware of Hunt's source, Mary soon became only too aware of his attitude:

> No one seems to understand or to sympathise with me. They all seem to look on me as one without affections.... I feel dejected and cowed before them ... the presence of those who do not love me, makes me feel as if I were of marble. (J 441)

Though the insensitivity of it is hard to credit, Hunt went so far as to lodge a counter-claim against Mary's for the custody of Shelley's heart (if that is what it was), preserved from the funeral pyre on the beach at Viareggio, and given to Hunt by Trelawney.

The autobiographical strands in *Valperga* make clear the extent to which Percy Shelley's death had put his wife on an emotional rack. In the novel she had been prepared to focus the action of the story around a relationship between two incompatible individuals, neither of whom, however, can bear to lose the other; the relationship is doomed because of the man's actions, and Mary imaginatively projects herself into the disaster of emotional loss only to escape almost at once by having her *alter ego*, Euthanasia, perish at sea. The blame falls on Castruccio, and once written, the verdict could not be negated with Percy's death. Paradoxically, however, it was her husband's death that now offered Mary the chance of rescuing that situation, replacing the once living Shelley she now believed she had wronged with his presence on the written page. Here, no matter how barren and distressing the exercise, she might at least reconstitute a lasting relationship.

The task of rewriting her life with Shelley came to dominate her literary life, and the composition of her next novel, *The Last Man*, was driven by this need. Mary's life with Percy after his death reveals two distinct aspects of their previous, living partnership: the intellectual and the physical. There was Mary's relationship to Shelley's ideas, to his radical atheism and communitarianism, and there was her relationship to him as her husband and the father of her children. *Frankenstein*, *Mathilda*, *Valperga* and *The Last Man* delineate a widening rift between Mary and her husband's ideas, in death as surely as in life. She was driven, however, to pursue an act of atonement when it came to memorialising their life together. When she turned to her task as a biographer, therefore, she sought to write a life where she might be understood as an harmonious accompaniment to the inspired poet she had married, rather than the radical thinker. The life and the work were to appear as complementary texts, and she began work at once on a collection of poetry left unpublished at his death.

Besides writing fiction, Mary had committed much of her time to the study and practice of biography. Percy had encouraged her in this respect back in 1814, when her first attempt at novel-writing was petering out, and the couple's pecuniary circumstances and personal relationships – combined with a debilitating pregnancy – were making it difficult for Mary to settle to anything. The proposed subject then had been the radical French journalist, Jean Baptiste Louvet, and a start at least was made (J 44). In *Valperga*, she overlaid biographical fiction with strands of autobiography (to the point of self-indulgence) while *Mathilda* and *The Last Man* (1826) were autobiography projected into fiction, as was *Lodor*, the novel she published in 1835, and her final novel, *Falkner* (1837). Before *Lodor*, however, she had returned to the historical-novel format with *Perkin Warbeck* (1830), having all the while been proposing and frequently publishing biographical essays. Her essay on Madame D'Houtetot came out in Hunt's *The Liberal* in the early 1820s, and in the 1830s she contributed a series of biographical essays to a prestigious collection edited by Dionysius Lardner. She was destined never, however, to write the one life that in normal circumstances should have given her the least difficulty, that of Percy Shelley.

In June 1824 Mary achieved what should have been a major step forward in her campaign to rehabilitate Shelley in the public eye, a public largely hostile where not indifferent to his work and reputation. John and Henry Leigh Hunt published the *Posthumous Poems of Percy Bysshe Shelley*. The editorial effort had been immense; Mary had worked tirelessly to decipher illegible manuscripts, in the process repeatedly reliving the trauma of her bereavement. But it was at this point that the full significance of her relationship with Shelley's father for the future direction of her literary life becomes clear. Sir Timothy Shelley responded swiftly and uncompromisingly; his preparedness to provide financial help for his grandson and daughter-in-law since his son's death had always been grudging and uncertain, but at least to some degree it had been there. He now announced that if any kind of contact was to be maintained, the book must be suppressed at once, and Mary was asked to relinquish custody of all manuscript material (this included the prose writings being prepared for a future volume) along with all papers relating to her proposed biography. Percy Shelley's name was in no way to be brought before the public during Sir Timothy's lifetime. Of the 500 copies of *Posthumous Poems* printed, some 200 remained unsold when the ultimatum was issued, and these Mary agreed to withdraw, lodging all the allegedly offending material with Peacock. She knew well enough that there was nothing to be gained from contesting the demand, having read Sir Timothy's version of her relationship with Percy in a letter he sent to Byron in 1823:

> Mrs Shelley was, I have been told, the intimate friend of my son in the lifetime of his first wife, and to the time of her death, and in no small degree, as I suspect, estranged my son's mind from his family, and all his first duties in life.... (in J 453)

The Preface to *Posthumous Poems* provided a brief character-sketch and began to make a case for the calibre of Shelley's work; it came nowhere near a formal biography. 'It had been my wish', she wrote, 'on presenting the public with the Posthumous Poems of Mr. Shelley, to have accompanied them by a biographical notice.' She goes on to explain that she feels the narrative 'would come more gracefully from other hands than mine', and nominates Leigh Hunt for the task.[1] This statement must be set against her avowed determination expressed in the *Journal* to undertake the task herself: 'Well I shall commence my task, commemorate the virtues of the only creature on earth worth loving or living for ... I shall write his life – & thus occupy myself in the only manner from which I can derive consolation' (J 434, 444-5). The *Journal* reveals Mary's true mind; only she is to be trusted with the task; what she writes in *Posthumous Poems* is more by way of an excuse offered to the public for limiting herself to a eulogy where more biographical detail might have been hoped for:

> The comparative solitude in which Mr. Shelley lived, was the occasion that he was personally known to few; and his fearless enthusiasm in the cause, which he considered the most sacred upon earth, the improvement of the moral and physical state of mankind, was the chief reason why he ... was pursued by hatred and calumny. No man was ever more devoted than he, to the endeavour of making those around him happy; no man ever possessed friends more unfeignedly attached to him.[2]

She goes on to dwell on the ignorance of his enemies:

> Before the critics contradict me, let them appeal to any one who had ever known him: to see him was to love him; and his presence, like Ithuriel's spear, was alone sufficient to disclose the falsehood of the tale, which his enemies whispered in the ear of the ignorant world.[3]

She then begins to describe him as quintessentially a poet of nature: 'he could interpret without a fault each appearance in the sky, and the varied phoenomena of heaven and earth filled him with deep emotion. He made his study and reading-room of the shadowed copse, the stream, the lake and the waterfall.'[4] Reading Shelley as a poet of nature provided Mary with a route she could take in the direction of something approaching the biographical mode. Her husband's work memorialises the beautiful places in which they stayed; no mention here of the poet of contentious, radical atheism, of the man who refused to treat his marriage-bond with the seriousness required of him by the state (and, in due course, by his wife):

> 'Prometheus Unbound' was written among the deserted and
> flower-grown ruins of Rome, and when he made his home
> under the Pisan hills, their roofless recesses harboured him as
> he composed 'The Witch of Atlas,' 'Adonais' and 'Hellas.' In
> the wild but beautiful bay of Spezia, the winds and waves
> which he loved became his playmates.[5]

The critical tradition of calling Shelley back from his political radicalism to be a poet of nature begins here. It was on this basis that
subsequent critics sought to retrieve Shelley as a poetic genius
throughout the nineteenth century. Mary goes on to write of the time
she and Percy spent at the Casa Magni in a way that enables us also to
hear the voices of those who would write a very different version of
events being firmly overruled:

> I am convinced that the two months we passed there were the
> happiest he had ever known: his health even rapidly
> improved, and he was never better than when I last saw him,
> full of spirits and joy, embark for Leghorn....[6]

In the midst of all the worry and uncertainty that followed his death,
Mary Shelley was taking possession of her dead husband with the
intention of establishing him in the public mind as a great poet and a
saintly person. It was the only way she now had of working a reconciliation with him. Sir Timothy might forbid it, but Sir Timothy could
not live for ever, and so – despite the demise of *Posthumous Poems* –
she continued with the task of collecting and editing his work. Since
it was impractical to contemplate a biography, she began to use the
composition of notes accompanying the poems as a means of writing
his life; this provided a far more easily handled medium than the
direct biographical approach. *The Poetical Works of Percy Bysshe Shelley*
eventually appeared in 1839, the notes providing a biographical gloss
and a critical commentary of a kind that she could write, and that Sir
Timothy (still alive) would find it hard to object to, since notes could
not constitute a biography. How Sir Timothy came to agree to the
publication of his son's poems at all will be considered in a later
chapter.

Preparing the *Poetical Works* inevitably forced Mary into revealing a
more intellectually challenging poet than the one found sailing 'alone
in his little shallop to the rocky caves' that bordered the bay of Spezia,
the retired poet of nature who enjoyed 'the refined pleasure which he

felt in the companionship of a few selected friends';[7] but still it revealed essentially the poet, an ethereal lover of nature who might also have had less than orthodox views on society (as Mary herself still did to a degree). Had she ventured any further it would have been very hard to avoid writing of her estrangement from her family, of Harriet's suicide, of Fanny's suicide, of Claire's presence, of her dead children, of precisely the kind of detail she so neatly sidestepped when denouncing Mrs Hoppner for her role in peddling rumours about the origins of Elena.

The only way she could approach the Shelley she remembered (as opposed to the poet she eulogised) was through fiction. *Valperga* had been published in February 1823, and through the winter of 1823–4 she was writing her next novel, *The Last Man*. Here Shelley, Byron, Claire Clairmont and Mary herself could be allowed to move freely, to share the stage with tyrannical aristocratic peers, cowardly political demagogues and frail, innocent children. In her Preface to *Posthumous Poems* Mary wrote of Shelley's death that 'The real anguish of these moments transcended all the fictions that the most glowing imagination ever pourtrayed…'; in *The Last Man*, as in *Valperga* and *Mathilda*, she opted for 'fiction' and a 'glowing imagination'.[8] She had to, because a part of her remembered the man as he had been, and like Euthanasia, while she could not let go, she would not easily give way. A part of Mary was therefore willing to go ahead in April 1824 with the publication of her satirical story (told tacitly at Shelley's expense), 'The Bride of Modern Italy', while another part of her resurrected Shelley in the persona of the sensitive, saccharine poet of nature Edmund Malville in 'Recollections of Italy', an article published in the *London Magazine* in January 1824.

By the time *Posthumous Poems* was published, Mary's social life had undergone significant changes. The Shelley community – such as it had been – dissolved swiftly. On 20 September 1822, Claire left to join her brother Charles in Vienna, noting bitterly in her *Journal* as she did so:

> I remembered how hopelessly I had lingered on Italian soil for five years, waiting ever for a favourable change…. I was now leaving it, (after) having (lost every object of) buried there everything that I loved.[9]

In the same month Mary and Jane Williams travelled together as far as Genoa, which Jane left almost at once for London. Mary remained, eventually moving in with the Hunts, since her reputation as the wife of Shelley meant that no respectable English person there would have anything to do with her. Trelawney was on hand to oversee these various events, while Byron, clearly feeling an obligation to assist, tended to keep himself relatively aloof. At Byron's request, Mary found him a house in Genoa, and as the year wore on, her main employment became writing for the new Journal, *The Liberal*. She transcribed Shelley's 'May-day Night; a Poetical Translation from Goethe's Faust' for the first number (published 15 October); for the second number she prepared Shelley's 'Song, written for an Indian Air', and her own 'A Tale of the Passions, or, the Death of Despina'. The third number (April 1823) included her biographical essay on Madame D'Houtetot and Percy's 'Lines to a Critic'. Her essay on Giovani Villani, written some time before, was resurrected for the fourth number (July 1830).

Money was not an immediate problem. Lodging with the Hunts and their six children kept the cost of living down, while writing for *The Liberal* took care of her immediate needs. She was able, therefore, to find time to begin collecting and transcribing Shelley's prose and poetry for what was to become the ill-fated *Posthumous Poems*. She wrote to Peacock (Shelley's executor) and his publisher Charles Ollier asking them to search out manuscripts. She contacted the Gisbornes, and consulted Hogg, who set about attempting to retrieve any poetry and letters that Harriet might have had. Godwin was also brought in on this latter, delicate project. A desk, used by Mary in Marlow and full of letters and other items, was recovered and shipped out to Genoa. Imagine her settling herself before it once more, opening it, and beginning to unfold and read the letters it contained:

> What a scene to recur to! My William, Clara, Allegra are all talked of – They lived then – They breathed this air & their voices struck on my sense, their feet trod the earth beside me & their hands were warm with blood & life when clasped in mine. Where are they all? This is too great an agony to be written about. (J 435)

But write about it was exactly what she did. Her editing, her letters, her *Journal*, and the determination with which she set about promoting herself as an essayist for other literary magazines testify to an objectivity that enabled her to translate her feelings into words, frequently at considerable length. She was encouraged to pursue her career as a writer by Godwin, who was, as ever, living on the brink of insolvency (he would eventually become bankrupt in the spring of 1825). It was very much in his own interest to encourage the career of a daughter who had already – as he told her – made a promising start:

> Frankenstein is universally known, and though it can never be a book for vulgar reading is everywhere respected. It is the most wonderful book to be written at twenty years of age that I ever heard of ... most fortunately you have pursued a course of reading, and cultivated your mind in the manner most admirably adapted to make you a great and successful author. (J 456–7)

Byron initially urged Mary to remain in Italy rather than return to England with Jane Williams. It must soon have become apparent, however, that this was not a practical proposition. Living with the Hunts and their unruly children proved taxing to say the least, while the commitment of both Byron and Trelawney to her welfare had its limits. Tensions soon arose; in particular, Mary became angry with Byron over his unwillingness to give Claire financial support. He further outraged her by advising her to accept Sir Timothy Shelley's offer of a settlement which required her to relinquish her child. One further encouragement for her to return home was the knowledge that it was in England that her literary career was destined to develop. In February G. and W. B. Whittaker published *Valperga*. Mary – having no illusions about the attitude of reviewers to the Shelley circle – expected the worst, only to find that many critics were surprisingly positive. A 'clever and amusing romance' was how the reviewer in *Blackwoods* summed up his impressions; Mary was probably too relieved to feel patronised.[10]

She set out for England on 25 July 1823. By 12 August she was in Paris where she probably met John Howard Payne and Washington Irving. Both men were to become an important part of her social circle in London. Payne was an American actor and dramatist; Irving, born in New York as was Payne, was a satirical essayist who spent much of this period in England working for the American government in various capacities. He was becoming increasingly well-known and respected as a writer.

Mary and Percy Florence arrived in London on 25 August. Initially she moved in with her father who now lived in the Strand; in the following month she took lodgings of her own off Brunswick Square. Just four days after her arrival she was taken to see an adaptation of *Frankenstein* at the English Opera House; she was reunited with Jane Williams and the Gisbornes, was introduced to Charles Lamb, and met Isabella Baxter once more. She renewed an acquaintance with the musician Vincent Novello. Through Novello her contacts widened to include – among others – Charles Cowden Clarke, the lecturer and essayist, and the writer Edward Holmes. As an author of some repute, with stimulating intellectual circles opening to her, the prospects for her future might have appeared promising; but to her the situation seemed very different. In her *Journal* for January 1824 she looked back to her life in Italy: 'I was worth something then in the catalogue of beings; I could have written something – been something.... Now I am exiled from those beloved scenes ... I am imprisoned in a dreary town ...' (J 471). Though she doesn't mention it, her sense of 'imprisonment' was due in no small measure to the success of *Frankenstein*; and whatever else might now serve to convince her that she had been robbed of an opportunity to attain intellectual and literary eminence among her peers, the fact was that her reputation as 'the author of *Frankenstein*' was to act as a continuing obstacle to her literary career. The critics may have been less than enthusiastic, but all the evidence points to a steadily growing enthusiasm on the part of the public for the book. We have seen that the story's theatrical potential had already been recognised and naturally, an intrigued readership was waiting eagerly for more of the same.

The consequences can easily be imagined, and they were duly voiced by an anonymous reviewer of *Valperga* writing in *Knight's Quarterly* in 1824. 'I do not think I ever was so much disappointed in any book as in Valperga', he wrote. 'I had the very highest expectations of the maturing of the genius which could produce such a work as Frankenstein.' What was wanted was another thriller, only better. The review moves swiftly on into a lively and very personal discussion of *Frankenstein*, only briefly returning to *Valperga* in the final paragraph. Throughout the rest of her career it was the story, and beyond that it was the idea of *Frankenstein* that continued to contribute significantly to the way in which Shelley's literary life was defined for her. After *Frankenstein*, declared the *Knight's Quarterly* reviewer, almost anything – and certainly *Valperga* – is going to appear 'cold and common-place' (F 197–200).

Quite apart from the consequences of her authorship of

Frankenstein, Shelley's life was now fated to be lived under a constant cloud of uncertainties. She could never be sure what Sir Timothy Shelley's next move might be and this meant that the fate of her son hung in the balance; this concerned her more than anything. Her relationship with her stepmother was as difficult as ever, and she knew that before long her father's finances were destined to collapse, and that neither *Frankenstein* nor *Valperga* would earn enough to pay the bills. It should also not be forgotten that though she had established a presence in the literary life of the capital, there was no shortage of evidence around to remind her that the name of Shelley remained anathema to many.

A further cause for her increasing discomfiture was the development of an intimacy between Jane Williams and Thomas Jefferson Hogg. After her reunion with her father, it was Jane's companionship she craved the most; she was now having to cope with seeing the man once recommended by Percy as her own paramour becoming firmly attached to the woman she had assumed would be her resident confidante. Her effusions of feeling for Novello and his music are perhaps best understood as to some degree an act of displacement. Such was their intensity that Novello felt bound eventually to distance himself from her. She also indulged in a brief flirtation with Bryan Waller Proctor. Proctor (whose pen-name was Barry Cornwall) was instrumental in guaranteeing publication of the *Posthumous Poems*. He was an enthusiastic Shelleyan, content to have Mary's admiration while he courted and in due course married Anne Skepper. Mary also came to admire, and perhaps even felt herself to be in love with Washington Irving; but this too proved to be an unrequited passion.

Characteristically, though, a positive resolve counterbalanced her anxieties and the sense of degradation she felt as she continued to write pieces for the magazines. Early in 1824 she wrote to Hunt that she intended to 'plunge into a novel' (L I 412). This referred to *The Last Man*, and in May 1824 she wrote, 'The last man! Yes I may well describe that solitary being's feelings, feeling myself as the last record of a beloved race, my companions, extinct before me –' (J 476–7). On 14 May news of Byron's death at Missolonghi in the previous month reached England. Byron had died in his attempt to aid the Greeks in their struggle for independence, reminding Mary all the more vividly of her Italian days, her lessons in the politics and language of the Greeks from Mavracordato, against which she now set her fixed circle of friends, her playgoing, and the grind of magazine work:

> Why am I doomed to live on seeing all expire before me? God
> grant I may die young.... At the age of twenty-six I am in the
> condition of an aged person – all my old friends are gone....
> (J 478)

In June Mary moved to Kentish Town to be near Jane Williams. It was
now that the publication of *Posthumous Poems* incurred the wrath of
Sir Timothy, and in the relative isolation of her new home, the *Journal*
records a mounting unhappiness and an increased longing to return
to Italy. It was an impossible dream, against which she suffered a
severe crisis of confidence in her ability to write. In *The Last Man* she
set out to celebrate her experience of having been part of a uniquely
gifted intellectual élite. Looking around her now, at the likes of Lamb,
Peacock, Beddoes, Proctor and Payne, she knew there was no comparison, and even more painfully she knew she herself dare not aspire to
the greatness of Shelley and Byron: 'What folly is it in me to write
trash nobody will read ...' (J 489). She clung to Jane's companionship
as the English winter gave way to the spring of 1825, and for all the
doubts, she stuck to her task. In February she wrote to John Cam
Hobhouse, a friend of Byron, requesting permission to view the House
of Commons in session: 'I am engaged in a tale which will certainly
be more defective than it would otherwise be, if I am not permitted to
be present at a debate.' (L I 466) She was also faced with the problem
of how to respond to a proposal of marriage from John Howard Payne.
Her feelings for him, she explained, were not of a romantic nature,
and there the matter rested (L I 493–4). That summer, Mary and Jane
visited Windsor for ten days, and then it was back to work on *The Last
Man*, which was duly published by Colburne on 23 January 1826.

   Though Shelley wrote her *Journal* entry beginning 'The last man!' on
the same day that news of Byron's death reached London, his loss was
almost certainly no more than the occasion for reflection on themes
and images she had encountered over the years in a steady stream of
'last man' narratives available to her. As far back as 1816, when the
Shelley circle were all alive and trying to frighten themselves to death
with ghost stories in the Villa Diodati, Byron had written 'Darkness':

> The bright sun was extinguish'd, and the stars
> Did wander darkling in the eternal space,
> Rayless, and pathless, and the icy earth
> Swung blind and blackening in the moonless air.... [11]

It is the kind of thing you would expect to find haunting literature and visual art in a millennial context, and certainly the immediate origins of this theme may be traced back to the 1780s and 1790s. As with many of their generation, the Shelleys were readers of the German dramatist and poet Johann Schiller; in 1795 Schiller diagnosed the fragmentation of society in apocalyptic terms, and his description of a lifeless future calls Frankenstein's creature to mind:

> The simple organisation of the first republics ... now gave place to an ingenious piece of machinery, in which out of the patching together of a vast number of lifeless parts a collective mechanical life results.[12]

Thomas Malthus's *Essay on the Principles of Population*, which had warned of the catastrophic consequences of overpopulation in 1798, was in its fifth edition in 1817, and concern for the social effects of the growth of cities were the cause of increasing anxiety. Fiona J. Stafford has written of the impact that men like Edward Irving, the evangelical preacher, were having on their audiences in the 1820s. In 1825 Hazlitt included him as part of *The Spirit of the Age*:

> He literally sends a challenge to all London in the name of the KING of HEAVEN, to evacuate its streets, to disperse its population, to lay aside its employments, to burn its wealth, to renounce its vanities and pomp.... The grape-shot of rhetoric, and the cross-fire of his double vision reduce the British metropolis to a Scottish heath....'[13]

By the time Irving and others were preaching Armageddon, the findings of the French geologist Georges Cuvier had become well-known. Byron had produced a series of works since 'Darkness' that echoed Cuvier's conviction that 'Life ... has been often disturbed by terrible events.... Numberless living beings have been the victims of these catastrophes...'.[14] Following the archaeological findings of William Butler in Yorkshire, Cuvier was led to conclude that there had been a series of apocalyptic exterminations, with God creating new species in the wake of each disaster.

Byron found in Cuvier the suggestion of a steadily degenerating succession of races, the complete opposite of the Christian model of progression towards perfection. Prior to leaving Italy, Mary Shelley spent a good deal of time transcribing Byron's poetry and so will have confronted these ideas at an intimate level. They appear with increasing frequency in the shorter poems, and then dominate *Cain* and *Heaven and Earth* (1821). *Heaven and Earth* is Byron's version of the story of the flood, where Japhet is made to envy those who die:

> ... happier in that doom
> Than to behold the universal tomb,
> > Which I
> Am thus condemn'd to weep above in vain.
> Why, when all perish, why must I remain?[15]

In the same year Shelley was no doubt prompted to look again at Malthus following the publication of a refutation of his thesis by her father. Malthus had argued that the population was growing at a rate that would soon render it unsustainable, and that poverty, disease and starvation were nature's God-given way of imposing the controls needed for the survival of civilised society. The topic remained as controversial as ever two decades on, and *The Quarterly Review* of October 1821 began its attack on Godwin's *Of Population* by reminding its readers that they were confronted by the author of *Political Justice*, 'The work bore the stamp of a mind ... of such overweening confidence in its own powers, as rashly to pull down, in its imaginations, whatever had been held most venerable and valuable in society...'[16]

Shelley's acquaintance with Byron's work alone would have been sufficient to set her on to her 'last man' theme. Stanzas 27 and 28 of *Don Juan*, Book IX come close to a prediction of how she was to stage the opening of her novel. The poet is about to offer some 'good advice' to authors, but then forgets what it is:

> But let it go:– it will one day be found
> With other relics of 'a former world,'
> When this world shall be *former*, underground.... [17]

The narrator of the 'Introduction' to *The Last Man* describes his (or her) discovery of the cave of the Cumaean Sybil, and then the discovery of numerous 'Sibylline leaves', upon some of which the story to be told is written. It is a story, in Byron's words, of a world 'Like all the worlds before us ... ':

> ... which have been hurl'd

> First out of, and then back again to chaos,
> The superstratum which will overlay us.[18]

To which he adds in the opening words of the next stanza, 'So Cuvier says'.

But there were other literary models besides Byron that Shelley will have known about, including one – perhaps the most interesting – that she never mentions. Although it failed to find a popular readership in England, it is unlikely that Shelley remained unaware of Jean-Baptiste Cousin de Granville's *Le Dernier Homme*. The English translation appeared in 1806 under the title of *The Last Man: a Romance in Futurity*. Even if Mary Shelley did not include it in her programme of reading, de Granville's title was there to prompt the notion that she might consider setting her own 'Last Man' narrative in the future. Shelley certainly did know Thomas Campbell's sanctimonious little poem, 'The Last Man'. When it was criticised in 1823 as a pale shadow of Byron's 'Darkness', Campbell responded that it was he, all those years before, who had given Byron the idea. The other Last Man project Shelley will have been aware of was Thomas Lovell Beddoes' attempt at the subject; he was never to complete it. It was composed during the period when, with others, he volunteered to cover the expenses of Percy Shelley's *Posthumous Poems*.

A further source of inspiration was to be found in the visual art of the time, particularly in the apocalyptic strain of subject-matter to be found in the paintings of J. M. W. Turner, John Martin and Francis Danby. Godwin's links with the art-world dated back to the 1790s, and although after Percy Shelley's death Mary's *Journal* ceases to include details of her cultural life in the way it previously had, her reading, theatregoing and enjoyment of music continued to be accompanied by a keen interest in visual art. On her return to London in 1823 Mary came to know Sir Thomas Lawrence well enough to be deeply affected by his death in 1830; her comment was, 'I see all those I love die round me while I lament' (J 512).

There was, therefore, a well-established literary and intellectual context for Mary Shelley's third published novel. It becomes important for the study of her development as a novelist to consider how she related to it in a very personal manner. *The Last Man* is a *roman à clef*, openly inviting its readers to find the major players in the Shelley circle represented through its fictional characters. The novel therefore clearly implies that with their passing the world has lost its hope for an enlightened, civilised future. *The Last Man* is thus intimately informed by Shelley's perception of the people she had lived with up to the point of her departure from Italy in 1823. Her engagement with issues of a broader social and political nature emerge from this context, and it is this aspect of the novel that will be considered first.

In *Frankenstein* the story addresses the radical political ideas of her father and Percy Shelley by way of engaging with 'science' as the potential ennabler of enlightened progress. In *Valperga*, science gives way to history as a means of analysing, with perhaps even more scepticism, the likely progress of political justice. In *The Last Man* she announces with the title her disenchantment with contemporary manifestations of cultural and political progress. In *Frankenstein* one of her narrators at least, Walton, is saved in order that he might presumably teach the world a greater wisdom. In *Valperga* she has both protagonists die; in *The Last Man* we confront the death of everything human, and her narrator, Lionel Verney, survives only to roam a world whose population has been completely exterminated by plague. The plague, however, does not make its appearance until Volume II. Prior to this, we observe the world nearing the end of the twenty-first century, and coming within reach, it would seem, of establishing a perfect society.

An important part of the narrative in Volume I concerns the way in which England has evolved as a republic, the last king having abdicated relatively recently in 2073. All the central male characters in the novel are major players on the political stage. Shelley was clearly fascinated by the task of envisioning the evolution of a political system in England which realised the changes that radicals of her father's and her own generation were still striving for. The situation is not a settled one, however. Though the King of England has abdicated, the future remains uncertain, with growing friction between three power-groups: aristocrats, democrats, and royalists (LM 49). At the point when civil war begins to look likely, the country is saved by the intervention of Lord Raymond. He returns from a victorious campaign in the world's one remaining theatre of war, Greece, where Turkish ambition continues to threaten Grecian liberty. Raymond becomes leader of the Royalist party, and brings the political crisis to a head when he confronts his opponent, Ryland, in what is now an amalgamated House of Representatives. 'Ryland was the leader of the popular party, a hard headed man, and in his way eloquent; he had obtained leave to bring in a bill making it treason to endeavour to change the present state of English government and the standing laws of the republic' (LM 55).

As Raymond travels to London with Verney, he speaks openly of his political ambitions, but only in the most reserved way of the conflicting private passions that beset him. Verney is moved to exclaim:

> '... whither will thy actions tend, in all this maze of purpose in which thou seemest lost?'
>
> 'Whither indeed? To a crown, a golden, begemmed crown, I hope ... and though I dream of a crown and wake for one, ever and anon a busy devil whispers to me, that it is but a fool's cap that I seek, and that were I wise, I should trample on it, and take in its stead, that which is worth all the crowns of the east and presidentships of the west. (LM 57)

The tension here between political ambition and human relationships restates the central theme of *Valperga*, and will be returned to later. The chapter continues with an account of the debate in which Ryland defends the republic. Shelley has sown the seeds of doubt as to Ryland's credibility before this, 'a man of obscure birth and of immense wealth, inherited from his father, who had been a manufacturer' (LM 58), but she reports his defence of republicanism in glowing terms, and draws our attention – as Ryland does to the assembled representatives – to Raymond's evident discomfiture at the exposure of his ambition. But Raymond, 'his voice softly melodious, his manner soothing' (LM 60), wins the debate. Shelley based Ryland on the radical politician William Cobbett, Raymond opposes him in a manifestly reactionary, Burkeian fashion: 'Nor did Raymond make an end without drawing in vivid and glowing colours the splendour of a kingdom, in opposition to the commercial spirit of republicanism' (LM 61).

A considerable amount of time passes before Raymond, no longer seeking the crown, is elected Lord Protector. The warrior thus deserts his ambitions and commits himself to ushering in a perfect society, a moment Shelley uses to refute the enemies of her father's recent book on Malthus:

> Raymond was occupied in a thousand beneficial schemes ... The arts of life, and the discoveries of science had augmented in a ratio which left all calculation behind; food sprung up, so

to say, spontaneously – machines existed to supply with facility every want of the population. (LM 106)

Throughout this political narrative, a good deal of space has been devoted to describing the development of a set of complex personal relationships between her main characters. Verney's sister Perdita marries Raymond. Raymond falls in love with Evadne, the daughter of the Greek Ambassador. Evadne had had another lover, Adrian. He is the son of the deposed King, whose mother continues ceaselessly to plot for a return of the old order. As part of these schemes she intends her daughter Idris to marry Raymond. In due course, however, it is Verney who marries Idris, while Adrian's loss of Evadne threatens to unsettle his mind. Verney is the son of a one-time favourite of the old king, who was eventually (Falstaff-like) cast aside. Verney's first task is to overcome the bitterness he feels towards the deposed royal family. The first chapters of the novel describe how he is won over by Adrian's unaffected concern for his welfare. Raymond's reflections that despite his ambition to be king, there exist longings that might render political ambition 'a fool's cap' point up Shelley's primary interest in all this. Raymond was hinting here to Ryland of his love for Perdita, and it is their marriage and commitment to domestic life and care for their daughter, Clara, that effectively postpone Raymond's political elevation after his triumph over Ryland.

Evadne leaves England only to reappear once Raymond (now Perdita's husband) is busily engaged realising his Utopian dreams as Protector of England. There is a sentimental account of their reunion, 'her head sunk unconsciously on the shoulder of Raymond; he held her hand: he kissed her tear-stained cheek...' (LM 110). But having thus performed the sentimental novelist's duty, Shelley turns in far more detail to the theme that concerns her most, addressing the harmful consequences of Raymond's 'visions of power and fame' on his domestic life as essentially a Byronic fault:

> Thus, while Raymond had been wrapt in visions of power and fame ... the territory of his own heart escaped his notice; and from that unthought of source arose the mighty torrent that overwhelmed his will, and carried to the oblivious sea, fame, hope, and happiness. (LM 117)

Raymond's family life is shattered by his revived passion for Evadne, and in consequence the government of the country falls into disrepair. The circle is irrevocably broken in the last two chapters of Volume I when Raymond decides to resume his role as a freedom-fighter in Greece (there is always Greece), and he finds a willing companion in Adrian. 'A moral tempest had wrecked our richly freighted vessel,' concludes Verney, 'and we, remnants of the diminished crew, were aghast at the losses and changes which we had undergone' (LM 155). The charmed circle of friends is broken (if not entirely dispersed) well before the plague begins to destroy the rest of humanity. The implication is that with the dissolution of this group, there is nothing left for anyone to live for. The plague becomes, arguably, little more than a framework within which may be set an extended coda to Shelley's negative verdict on the culture of the Romantic Movement as personified in the lives of Percy Shelley, Byron, Godwin, Wordsworth and William Cobbett.

Most accounts of *The Last Man* tend to begin by exploring the portraits of Byron and Shelley as they appear in Raymond and Adrian respectively. Both men are viewed compassionately, both are at times effusively idealised; but both are portrayed as irretrievably flawed. As Adrian overcomes Verney's prejudices against him in the early part of the novel, we encounter Shelley as Mary chose to remember him in the days of their courtship:

> his sensibility and courtesy fascinated everyone. His vivacity, intelligence, and active spirit of benevolence, completed the conquest.... In person, he hardly appeared of this world; his slight frame was overinformed by the soul that dwelt within. (LM 26–7)

In that last sentence lies the identification of weakness. Adrian's character is unbalanced. His love for Evadne is misplaced; she does not love him, and his loss of her brings him close to madness. This is about Claire and the Percy Shelley who failed to respond to Mary's love for him, though Evadne also at times has clear affinities with Byron's mistress, Teresa Guiccioli. Adrian's mother, dictatorial, powerful, and for ever scheming, ensures the separation of Adrian and Evadne; here surely we catch a glimpse of Percy Shelley's vexed relationship with his father grafted on to some vivid recollections of the behaviour of her own stepmother.

Characteristically, Mary found herself returning to lick the wounds of her conduct towards Shelley at the time of his death, and she does so through the estrangement of Raymond and his wife Perdita.

Raymond, though manifestly the Byronic hero, is made use of to give voice to Shelley from beyond the grave when it comes to reconciliation with Perdita. All the accusations of Mary's coldness come to mind:

> 'One word more concerning unkind, unjust Perdita. For a time, I thought that, by watching a complying moment, fostering the still warm ashes, I might relume the flame of love. It is more cold within her, than a fire left by gypsies in winter-time.... Present her with a mirror, in which she may know herself ... she will wonder at her present mistake, and hasten to restore to me, what is by right mine, her kind thoughts, her love.' (LM 154)

This was a passage of autobiography Mary needed to write, but it was too painful to deliver in anything other than a context several times removed from her own experience. As with Evadne, Perdita has a dual function within the *roman à clef* format; she can be Mary, but when playing opposite Raymond's Byron, she can also be Claire.

The fatal disease in this novel is not so much the plague as misplaced pride, the sickness that destroys Frankenstein and Castruccio. In *Posthumous Poems* Mary had already begun the work of delivering Shelley from this failing by reconstructing him as the greatest nature-poet of his generation. In the opening paragraph of the novel she reflects on the way that Shelley's generation were in danger of responding to nature as an adjunct to power in its most unhealthy manifestation; she attacks the tendency of English Romantics to consider themselves peculiarly blessed in both their nationality, and in their intimacy with the powerful forces of nature. Verney tells us that 'England, seated far north in the turbid sea, now visits my dreams in the semblance of a vast, well manned ship, which mastered the winds and rode proudly over the waves.' (LM 9) The past tense alerts us to the intended irony; the notion of a 'well manned ship' is to be exposed as only ever a dream, and this becomes dramatically apparent when the lives and the loves of its principal citizens come under close scrutiny in Volume I.

Verney's father retires in ignomiy to the birthplace of English Romanticism, the Lake District. His subsequent history reads like a parody of many of Wordsworth's poems, not least 'The Female Vagrant' from *Lyrical Ballads* (1798): first comes his death, then his wife's penury as she struggles to raise her two children in their

Lakeland cottage; she dies and the children are given over 'to the close-handed charity of the land'; Lionel Verney works as a shepherd, but it is no Wordsworthian idyll: 'its pains far exceeded its pleasures' (LM 13). Verney's first encounter with Adrian takes place, and events, it would seem, take a decidedly brighter turn. But as Mary Shelley was to discover, an alliance with Percy was no guarantee for future happiness. Human nature is fatally flawed, and subject in the end to the indifferent forces of nature. The plague exposes Verney's misplaced confidence in England as a place of especial virtue, the 'well manned ship':

> The plague was in London! Fools that we were not long ago to have forseen this.... we fancied that the little channel between our island and the rest of the earth was to preserve us alive among the dead.... truly we were wise in our generation, to imagine these things! (LM 248)

It remains important to keep in mind the way Shelley had set about remodelling her husband in the Introduction to *Posthumous Poems*. He was a poet who 'made his study and reading-room of the shadowed copse, the stream, the lake and the waterfall'.[19] In *The Last Man*, under cover of fiction, she is prepared to reveal the personality of Shelley with far greater candour. The appeal to nature might be a means of rescuing his memory for public approbation, but in truth nature was also likely to prove a false God, and Verney (still within the first paragraph of the novel) questions the basis of Romantic nature worship: 'So true it is, that man's mind alone was the creator of all that was good or great to man...' (LM 9). Even Godwin's utopianism is challenged through the portrayal of the misplaced optimism of Merrival, an astronomer whose ideas read like a parody of *Political Justice* and *Queen Mab* combined. When, much later, Verney confronts man's savagery on the battlefield as he accompanies Raymond on his last campaign, he uncompromisingly dismisses the sentimental notion of nature as a benevolent healing power. Nature, though beautiful, has nothing to do with the 'corse-strewn earth' Verney surveys:

> Now, I looked on the evening star, as softly and calmly it hung pendulous in the orange hues of sunset. I turned to the corse-strewn earth; and felt ashamed of my species. (LM 180)

Among the dead and dying is Evadne; her dying speech is an indictment of Raymond's fickle temperament. Before long he too dies, crushed to death in the ruins of Constantinople. Verney then has to convince Perdita that she should return to England; her wish to remain near the spot where her husband has died introduces a peculiarly Shelleyan poignancy to the situation: '"... it is not a matter of choice; I can live here only. I am a part of this scene; each and all its properties are a part of me."' (LM 211) Eventually she does agree to return, but commits suicide on the homeward voyage. Mary thus weaves into the book her own sense of spiritual death since the loss of her husband, leaving a part of herself still living through the narrative voice of Verney. The central character now becomes Adrian; the Shelleyan hero replaces the Byronic, showing courage and compassion as the country (and the world) slides into anarchy. Yet what Mary writes is in the end an uncompromising denial of the Shelleyan dream.

Adrian assumes the leadership of a doomed remnant of humanity. Where Percy Shelley's dream had been of an expanding community of enlightened individuals, eliminating injustice, famine and disease, all Adrian can do is urge his diminishing followers onward to oblivion. At the end of Volume II they leave England, and by the time they reach Venice there are only Verney, Adrian and Clara, the daughter of Raymond and Perdita, left. Adrian decides to cross the Adriatic to Albania and head for Greece. Verney reluctantly agrees. A storm follows, and both Adrian and Clara are lost in the shipwreck, leaving Lionel Verney as the last man.

How the story comes to be told at all takes us back to Shelley's Introduction. Verney's narrative is found written on Sibylline leaves at Baiae. It is, of course, a 'prophecy'; but with Cuvier's theory to hand (and Byron's embellishment of it in *Don Juan*) we should remember that the 'future' in question might conceivably already belong in the distant past. If this were so, Shelley's sense of being forced to live in a world wholly different from the one inhabited by her circle is reinforced all the more. The consequences of this sense of alienation are inscribed across her fiction; Shelley's creative drive emanated from the composition of autobiographical testimony that claimed also to have relevance to broader political and social issues; but the overwhelming need clearly lay in rehearsing the devastating events of her own past and the breaking of the Shelley circle. When it came to peopling her fiction, therefore, she returned repeatedly to the powerful personalities of Percy Shelley, Byron, Claire, Godwin, her stepmother and Sir Timothy Shelley, and to the tragic ghosts of her children and of Fanny and Harriet. Her novels thus retained that sense of a closet view of things, revolving around the heightened sensibilities of her central characters who were made to relive in various ways the peculiar and particular experiences of her set. The larger world of political and social change tended only to be glimpsed beyond the walls of her own private estate.

While the English novel was gradually extending its terms of reference in relation to a diversifying readership (even as cockney Sam Weller moved in to steal the limelight from the respectable, rotund Pickwick in 1836), Mary Shelley (along with others) continued in her vein of coterie *roman à clef* novels, drifting to one side of the mainstream to produce well-crafted tales of sentimentality whose ultimate focus was the rarefied personal issues and concerns of the author. Her three remaining novels, *Perkin Warbeck*, *Lodore* and *Falkner*, all tackle contemporary social issues, but with very particular reference to Shelley's own relationships and experiences, most of which belonged in the past. None of these novels engage in any profound sense with the way the world was changing around her, and nor did the revised version of *Frankenstein* published in 1831. For Shelley, confronting the present was essentially to confront the issue of her personal survival, a harrowing and heroic struggle accompanied always by the fear that close friends might let her down, that the malign intentions of her father-in-law would rob her of her son, and that she would fail in the duty she had of establishing her husband as a poet of genius and a good man.

7
Writing to Live, 1826–34

Despite what seem to have been some relatively low-key flirtations with the opposite sex, Mary Shelley had become increasingly dependent on women for companionship since her husband's death, and this applied in particular to Jane Williams. In July 1827, shortly after Jane and Thomas Jefferson Hogg married, Mary wrote to Jane, coquettishly implying a subversive union of their own:

> Loveliest Janey – to thee tranquillity & health … I am not sure that male eyes will not trace these lines, so I will endeavour to be as demure as an old maid – I wonder if you will understand the fitting supplement to that unfinished sentence. (L I 556)

Jane Williams and Hogg had long found Mary's attentions something of an embarrassment; and while Jane continued to act as Mary's confidante, she found the latter's championship of Percy Shelley hard to bear in the light of her own memories of how things had been during their final months in Italy. More than a little in love with Shelley herself, she had gossiped then to Hunt about Mary's frigidity and she continued to do so now. Eventually Mary was bound to find out; indeed it is hard to believe that she did not have some inkling of who was involved in talking behind her back well before the summer of 1827, when Isabel Robinson finally told her of it:

> My friend has proved false & treacherous! Miserable discovery – for four years I was devoted to her – & I earned only ingratitude…. (J 502–3)

In addition to this crisis Sir Timothy's unpredictability continued to cast the shadow of constant financial worry over everything. In 1823 an edition of *Frankenstein* edited by Godwin named Mary Shelley as the author. This gave Sir Timothy reason to claim that when *The Last Man* was published, its attribution to 'the author of Frankenstein' meant that the name of Shelley had been publicised against his expressed wishes. The £50 he sent Mary in July 1826 was therefore pronounced to be the final payment he would make. The *Journal* for 1826 indicates clearly enough what Jane (and Hogg) were having to put up with as the crisis deepened:

> I need companionship & sympathy only – & the only one I love can afford me so little ... I cannot live without loving & being loved – without sympathy – if this is denied to me I must die.... (J 498)

It is Jane who 'can afford so little'; she was clearly being asked to give a lot.

In September Harriet's son, Charles Shelley, died of tuberculosis, leaving Percy Florence heir to the baronetcy. A settlement of £250 a year was reached in February 1827, but payments were not to begin until September. With herself and Godwin to think of, Mary ended up borrowing money from Hogg and being helped by Claire. Some relief from brooding upon her troubles came with the reappearance of Thomas Moore, a longstanding friend of her father's. Mary's reminiscences of life in Italy provided Moore with valuable material for his projected biography of Byron. 'He seems to understand & to like me', Mary noted in her *Journal*, and Moore was genuinely impressed by her (J 501).

But then came the bombshell from Isabel Robinson. Losing her trust in Jane Williams amounted to a late development in her grieving over the loss of Shelley, and the second half of 1827 may be considered as something of a watershed in her life. In her letters to Jane she attempted to pretend that nothing had changed; they are full of a laboured jocularity that she sustained until February 1828. There followed a confrontation after which Mary wrote to Jane, 'Though I was conscious that having spoken of me as you did, you could not love me, I could not easily detach myself from the atmosphere of light & beauty that for ever surrounds you – I tried to keep you, feeling the while that I had lost you ...' (L II 25-6)

The summer of 1827 also marks Shelley's increasingly close relationship with the Robinson family as she masterminded a bizarre scheme, where yet again fiction seemed to have invaded the real world. In July, Mary and Percy Florence, Isabel Robinson and her illegitimate baby, and Mary Leigh Hunt (a daughter of James and Marianne Leigh Hunt) travelled to Sompting on the Sussex coast. Mary was the prime mover in a plan to deliver Isabel and her child to France with a 'husband' so that Isabel's shame might be avoided. The husband was David Lyndsay, a successful writer whom Mary already knew; David Lyndsay was in fact the pen-name of Mary Diana Dods who now rechristened herself 'Sholto Douglas' and sailed to France with Isabel as her husband in September. Shelley had persuaded John Howard Payne to obtain false passports for them in London, and had got letters of introduction for Isabel and her husband to the Garnett family in Paris from a recent acquaintance, Frances Wright. It was the Garnett circle that Mary joined when she travelled to Paris herself in the spring of the following year. Its major figures included Lafayette, Prosper Mérimée, Stendhal, Benjamin Constant and the critic and historian Claude Fauriel.

Frances Wright had been an important addition to Shelley's circle. Born in 1795, she travelled to the United States in 1818, where she established the Nashoba settlement in Tennessee, a communitarian venture guaranteed to strike a chord in Shelley's heart. The settlement did not survive, but Wright continued her reformist work, and in August 1827 she wrote to Shelley from Paris where she was recuperating from illness. Wright was a friend of Robert Dale Owen, who had been introduced to William Godwin by his father, the socialist reformer Robert Owen. Here was a contact for Shelley who reaffirmed the ideals she felt she had once lived for herself. Her reply to Wright's letter reveals a considerable degree of embarrassment. Wright's admiration for Mary's parents carried with it the assumption that the daughter continued in the same path. Mary was forced to apologise for her own lack of activity in the public domain (L II 5). She was obviously dying to say more of the recent goings-on on the Sussex coast, but how petty it must have seemed in comparison with Wright's labours.

By the summer of 1827 Shelley was working on *The Fortunes of Perkin Warbeck: A Romance,* an historical novel set in the aftermath of the defeat of Richard III at Bosworth in 1485. In mid-October she travelled with Percy Florence to Dieppe to visit the Douglases. On her return to England she moved to Portman Square, ending an eventful year in bleaker mood than ever: 'I look back with wonder to the last year – the stream flowed struggling & dark – suddenly it dashed down a precipice of horrific depth – Whither now do the waters tend?' (J 504) Shelley was far from friendless, however. Moore was in London once again, and helping her out financially. Though it proved impossible to interest the publisher John Murray in *Perkin Warbeck*, a loan of £100 was negotiated. Besides her continuing closeness to the Robinson family, she made an important friend in Georgiana Beauclerk, the daughter of Charles George Beauclerk, a neighbour of Sir Timothy Shelley at Horsham. Georgiana married John Dean Paul in 1826, and their son Aubrey became a friend of Percy Florence. The opportunity eventually presented itself for Georgiana to speak of Mary and her son to Sir Timothy, and thus establish grounds for hope that eventually his intractability might ease.

In March 1828 Shelley travelled to Paris to see the Douglases once more, and once more the possibility of a romantic attachment arose, this time with the writer Prosper Mérimée; but as in previous cases, nothing came of it. Both Mérimée and Trelawney (who was now back in England) were keen to impress on her that she was worthy of better friends than the Robinsons. Certainly the prospect of meeting Trelawney had the effect of stirring vague hopes of a revitalised future:

> Trelawney in England! – where? – how ardently I desire to see him – Dear dear darling ... it is useless to talk of my plans – Trelawney's arrival may change them.... (to Jane Williams-Hogg, 5 June 1828, L II 42)

They finally met in November; Claire had meanwhile arrived in London from Dresden where she had been working as a governess. Such reunions only served to underline the fact that the Shelleyan dream was dead. Claire and Mary found it hard as ever to get on while Trelawney continued to grouse about the mediocrity of Mary's friends and the fading of Claire's beauty. He returned to Italy early in 1829; Claire stayed until September, when she returned to Dresden.

In January 1829, Shelley moved to 33 Somerset Street, off Portman Square, where she was to remain for the next four years. Though she continued to fill her *Journal* with complaints about the loneliness she suffered, she began to entertain on a regular basis, and the opportunity arose to publish a clandestine edition of Percy Shelley's poetry. In the absence of any international copyright laws, the Galignani brothers were reprinting pirated editions of English books in France. Through Cyrus Redding, Mary was happy to assist in the production of *The Poetical Works of Coleridge, Shelley and Keats*. She supplied Redding with material for a Memoir of Shelley, and the book appeared in mid-December.

Work went steadily ahead on *Perkin Warbeck* while she continued writing short stories for publication in the increasingly popular annuals. 'The Sisters of Albano', published in 1828 in *The Keepsake*, tells the story of two sisters, Anina and Maria. Anina falls in love with a robber, Domenico, who is arrested despite his determination to reform. When Anina attempts to take him food she is also arrested and condemned to death. Maria contrives to change places with her sister, who realises too late what has happened. Shelley's point is both the general one: 'was not Anina innocent also? Her sole crime had been disobeying an arbitrary command', and a specific one about loyalty and commitment in relationships.[1] Between the lines there is a message for the disloyal Jane Williams, and perhaps even for Trelawney. In her *Journal* Shelley hints at a lost hope for happiness with 'Isabel' (which could mean either Robinson or Baxter), '... that dream is over' (J 510).

'Ferdinando Eboli: A Tale' was published in 1829 in *The Keepsake*, and explores the already well-worn theme of the *doppelgänger*. Ferdinando is imprisoned and impersonated by his double, a situation that allows Shelley the opportunity to explore the hero's rage at his sense of powerlessness. Looking between the lines once more, we glimpse the humiliation she felt as a result of her dependence upon Sir Timothy Shelley's charity, a situation that incarcerated her financially, and balked her ambition to publish her husband's work, to which should be added (now that she had to reply to letters from Frances Wright) her sense of failure to pursue a Shelleyan campaign for political justice. The anxiety of it all resulted in physical illness that persisted through most of the summer of 1829.

Entertaining in Somerset Street got under way in earnest in 1830 as work on *Perkin Warbeck* drew to a close; but it did little for her self-esteem:

> People like me & flatter & follow me, & then I am left alone again. Poverty being a barrier I cannot pass – still I am often amused and sometimes interested.... (J 512–3)

In fact Shelley was beginning to move into elevated company, partly as a result of her friendship with Georgiana Beauclerk. Georgiana's sister-in-law, Anne-Frances Paul married Francis Hare. The Hares presided over an impressively fashionable set that included the Manners-Suttons. Sir Charles Manners-Sutton was Speaker of the House of Commons, and his wife Ellen clearly took to Mary. In August she reports regular meetings with Mrs Hare, and in September she notes, 'nothing can be more friendly than these dear good people ... an intimacy between me & Georgiana is beginning' (J 515). Another important member of this group was Edward Bulwer-Lytton (1803–73), a successful writer with ten novels to his credit by 1830. He had sought out Godwin and read and admired his novels; he was now on the verge of a career in politics. Not surprisingly, therefore, Shelley read his work with an approval that soon developed into admiration.

Behind the public persona of an active writer and intellectual, Mary Shelley remained the profoundly insecure widow of the man still anathematised by significant sections of society. Sir Timothy had increased his daughter-in-law's allowance to £300 in June 1829, but this hardly covered Percy Florence's school fees, and was certainly not enough to keep Godwin and his aged amanuensis Marshall out of serious debt. *Perkin Warbeck* was sold to the publisher for only £150; it came out in May 1830, and Shelley began at once to search for new commissions. In addition to her long-term financial commitments, she was now also lending money to Claire. Maria Jewsbury reported that in company, Mary Shelley's 'hilarity... contrasted with the almost sadly profound nature of some of her remarks', adding that this contrast 'somewhat puzzled me' (J 513). Had she known more about Shelley's financial situation, she would no doubt have been less puzzled. In 'The Mourner', published in *The Keepsake* of 1830, a Shelleyan narrator (Horace Neville), tells the story of an orphaned girl, Ellen, whose love for her father engulfs her, and who finally perishes at sea. It was a potboiling exercise in sentimentality; but it was also an outlet for the feelings of an author who, as Maria Jewsbury commented, 'could never be described as a happy woman' (J 513). At the end of 'The Mourner' Neville is made to say, 'Still she was to be viewed as the wreck of beauty. What must she not have been in happier days, with her angel expression of face, her nymph-like figure, her voice, whose tones were music?'[2]

Shelley had written to Frances Wright about the way her life had been channelled away from participation in the larger political issues of the day into a concentration on personal and domestic affairs. The main reason this had happened was lack of money. She had to write to live, and the control Sir Timothy had over her fate will have inevitably made her as cautious of establishing a radical political presence (worthy of Percy Shelley) as she had to be of displaying the Shelley name. However, the company she now kept was at least fashionably liberal, if not radical in conviction. The debate over the need for political reform was beginning to gather momentum, and when news of the French Revolution of July 1830 broke, Mary wrote to Lafayette, 'I rejoice that the cause to which Shelley's life was devoted, is crowned with triumph.' She went on to sound a more cautious note with respect to England:

> May England imitate your France in its moderation and heroism. There is great hope that any change operated among us, will originate with the Government.... But our position is critical and dreadful – for what course of measures can annihilate the debt? And so reduce taxation, which corrodes the very vitals of the suffering population of this country. (L II 43)

Behind these and similar comments lay her awareness of rising disaffection across the country. The winter of 1829 was exceptionally harsh, and the spring and summer weather was poor. Desperate labourers hardly needed rumours of revolution in France, or the defiant articles of William Cobbett in the *Political Register*, to encourage them into taking direct action. In the course of 1830 the Government's determination to stamp out insurrection led to the trial of 1976 prisoners; 19 men were hanged, 481 were transported, many others were given prison sentences.[3] Should there be any danger of assuming that the 481 who were transported had been in some sense let off by escaping the death sentence, we should remember the words of Mr Glumford in Bulwer's *The Disowned*, published in 1829. Hoping for the worst possible sentence on a political radical, he says, 'I wish to heaven you may be transported instead of hanged.'[4] E. P. Thompson concludes that 'indirectly' the riots of 1830 'gave a final push to Old Corruption. Many farmers, and a few of the gentry, had been ashamed of the business, had negotiated with the mobs, or given them passive support. The revolt both sapped the confidence of the gentry, and helped to arouse the Reform agitation of 1831–2.' And he goes on to quote Cobbett's claim that the hearts and minds of the middle classes were now increasingly with the working class instead of against them: '"Among the tradesmen, even of the metropolis, *ninety-nine out of a hundred are on the side of the labourers."'[5]

Like Mary Shelley, Bulwer was concerned to explore contemporary political issues through his fiction. It is instructive to compare the way Shelley set about this task in *Perkin Warbeck* with Bulwer's similar attempt in *The Disowned*; the central concern for both novelists is the fate of victimised outcasts.[6] There is no record of Shelley having read *The Disowned*, but her enthusiasm for Bulwer's work should leave us in little doubt that she did. Bulwer's reference to Castruccio in Chapter 4 affirms his knowledge of Mary's work, while Percy Shelley is alluded to in Chapter 14 as 'a great, but visionary mind'.[7] Bulwer's depiction of the hero-figure in *The Disowned* illustrates the extent to which idealised images of both Shelley and Byron were combining to provide early-nineteenth-century novelists with a stereotype for their leading men. Mary will have enjoyed such passages as this:

> He had only just passed the stage of boyhood ... and the attitude which he had chosen fully developed the noble and intellectual turn of his head and throat. His hair, as yet preserved from the disfiguring fashions of the day, was of a deep auburn, which was rapidly becoming of a more chestnut hue, and curled with short close curls from the nape of the neck to the commencement of a forehead singularly white and high....[8]

Bulwer not only employed the integrated Byron/Shelley look (frequently combined in this novel with specific references to the originals); the circumstances of such heroes would also tend to coincide with the Shelleyan model.

Clarence Linden (our hero) has been wrongfully dispossessed by a tyrannical father, while Algernon Mordaunt (friend of Linden, but not quite dashing enough to be entirely heroic) conforms even more closely to type by taking his beloved with him into penury when he is disinherited: 'It is past, Isabel: henceforth we have no wealth but in each other. The cause has been decided – and – and – we are beggars!'[9] In addition to this, the pride and bigotry of Linden's father, and the miserliness of Vavasour, Mordaunt's enemy, seems to bear more than a passing likeness to the antagonism between Percy Shelley and his father:

> 'Why do you not kneel?' cried the old man, vehemently.
> 'It is the attitude of the injurer, not of the injured!' said Clarence, firmly.

'Injured – insolent reprobate – is it not I who am injured?. . .
Boy, boy, what are your wrongs to mine?'[10]

Bulwer sets cultural points of reference such as these in a far more firmly delineated political context than Mary Shelley was ever to achieve. Arguably, with a real-life tyrannical father-in-law (cheque-book in hand, breathing down her neck) she dare not do it.

The Disowned is set in the early 1770s. The closest we get to establishing a precise date is from a reference to England's approaching crisis with the American colonies. Clarence Linden has been disowned by his family; Algernon Mordaunt is disowned as much by the law (manipulated by an unscrupulous relative) as by another individual. At the beginning of the novel Clarence joins a band of gypsies, portrayed by Bulwer as people disowned because they themselves have chosen not to adopt a modern way of life. They live free from all boundaries and restrictions, both in the literal sense of late-eighteenth-century enclosed land, and in the sense of legal boundaries. There are those in the novel whom society disowns because of their radical, commonwealthman politics; and there are those (in this case a young artist) who are disowned because of their temperamental make-up. Bulwer expresses both an enthusiasm for and a criticism of Romanticism throughout the text. We have already met a somewhat cautious reference to Shelley as 'a great, *but* visionary mind'. Thus Warner is shown to be an ambitious young artist destined for a tragic end because, despite his undoubted talent, he suffers from the 'inexperience of unregulated taste, and an imperfect professional education'.[11] Bulwer, in common with another of his Romantic heroes, Wordsworth, no doubt felt that the fate of the gifted but unbalanced Thomas Chatterton (who had taken his own life in 1770) constituted a lesson to be learned by all who aspired to greatness in the arts.

As the political issues present in *The Disowned* progressively invade the private lives of the central characters, Bulwer's representation of these lonely, frequently desperate and haunted men register his debt to Godwin's characterisation of Caleb Williams, and to his later versions of that character in subsequent novels. Through Mordaunt, he also develops a specifically Godwinian investigation of crime: to what extent is it a social phenomenon for which society is answerable, and to what extent is it the sole responsibility of the individual who commits it? Shelley will also have recognised Bulwer's interest in magic, and in particular with the secret world of Masonic ritual, as an area of common ground with both her father's and her late husband's work. Bulwer's novels frequently include a magician character of some sort; while *The Disowned* does not obviously do so, Mordaunt indulges in a series of Shelleyan reflections on the metaphysical mysteries of good and evil, and life and death, in the latter chapters.

The political strands of Bulwer's plot converge when plans are laid to hold a demonstration in a provincial town in support of the American colonists. Wolfe, a fanatical Quaker radical, is an heroic libertarian, but ready to use violence if need be. Mordaunt wisely counsels against sending in the troops, and the event passes off peacefully. Here, then, is a lesson about the need for tolerance, compassion and pragmatism appropriate to the troubled 1820s, and expressed in such a way as to justify the zeal of an earlier generation of radicals; it was, after all, written by a man who knew and admired *The Mask of Anarchy*, Percy Shelley's attack on the violent way the army had dealt with the peaceful 'Peterloo' demonstration in Manchester in 1819. Bulwer wished his readers to appreciate that believing in liberty was no straightforward matter, and to this end he has the erstwhile gypsy 'King' (latterly settled in a comfortable house and garden), and the radical Wolfe argue through their libertarian beliefs. Neither really listens to the other:

> Had we time ... it would have been a rare and fine contrast to have noted more at large the difference of thought and opinion between the companions; each in his several way so ardent for liberty.... The one guided only by his poetical and erratic tastes, the other solely by dreams, seeming to the world no less baseless, yet, to his own mind, bearing the name of stern judgement and inflexible truth.[12]

In *Perkin Warbeck*, Mary Shelley addresses the issue of how to introduce reforms into a society where many remain alienated by ruling-class cynicism and corruption, in a more tangential manner than Bulwer, but she does so with no less determination to engage with matters of current social and political concern. The story is based on the premise that Perkin Warbeck, pretender to the throne of England in 1485 when Henry Tudor defeated Richard III at Bosworth to become Henry VII, was in fact the rightful heir. In *Mary Shelley Revisited*, Johanna M. Smith shows how in doing this Shelley's work perpetuates the tradition of the Jacobin novels of the 1790s, 'this romance calls into question the chivalric ideals which underpin ... official history'. The official history here is specifically David Hume's *History of Great Britain* (1754–62).[13] Warbeck's true identity, Shelley argues, was Richard, son of Edward IV and nephew of the defeated Richard III. In following his career she therefore, like Bulwer, focuses our attention on a set of individuals all of whom qualify as 'disowned' by society, an alienation that increases as Henry VII inexorably tightens his grip on government. Unlike Bulwer, however, Shelley's disowned are for the most part aristocratic in origin, and her main interest lies in the standards of behaviour and morality exhibited by the ruling classes. There are exceptions; like Bulwer in *The Disowned*, she finds a use for gypsies, who figure towards the end of the novel.

In a way that reflects her reading of Scott's exploration of the passing of an age of romance, Henry VII is portrayed as the harbinger of modernity; cold, calculating and efficient, he personifies the end of a more attractive world of chivalry which the young would-be Richard IV represents. In this respect, Shelley implies (rather than overtly states) that, compared to the new King, Richard represents the interests of ordinary people. Her account of Audley's Cornish rebellion, with its emphasis on the sufferings of the labourers and the horrors of war for the underprivileged majority, is handled very effectively. At other times, warfare is described as little more than a sport for the aristocracy, and one that Shelley the historical researcher clearly relished writing up. Richard's attempt to gain the crown takes him to Scotland, Ireland, France and Spain; in each case Shelley is careful to show that the most powerful people in society remain wilfully ignorant of the conditions in which the lower classes live.

Jane Shore is a key figure for Shelley in this respect. She is introduced in Volume II. Shore was for a while the mistress of Edward IV, and during the radical years of the 1790s she had been rediscovered as a potent symbol for the hypocrisy of the aristocracy. Nicholas Rowe had written two plays early in the century on the theme of women whose suffering at the hands of royalty raised questions about privilege, authority and moral accountability. One was *Jane Shore* (1714), the other was *Lady Jane Grey* (1715). At the end of the century, Sarah Siddons made the role of Shore very much her own. In *Perkin Warbeck* we are introduced to Shore as an old woman. She has joined a band of gypsies, and lives in a world that has renounced the increasing restrictions of modernity. She advises Richard's lover, Monina, to abandon any thought of a union with him. In due course, Richard, seeking to cement an alliance with James IV of Scotland, becomes convinced that a marriage predicated as much on political opportunism as personal affection is advisable. His wife, Katherine Gordon, is sympathetically portrayed – as is Richard – but the reasons why Richard's political and domestic worlds fall apart are made very clear. As we read the sentimentalised account of Shore's gypsy life, and of the unaffected simplicity of the life of Richard's true love, Monina, we learn that rank, privilege and position continue to be as life-denying in the 1830s as they were in the fifteenth century:

> The Lady Katherine saw a vain mask in all the common-place pomp of palaces; she perceived that power failed most, when its end was good; she saw that in accomplishing its purposes in the cottage, or in halls of state, felicity resulted from the affections only. (P III 60)

The end is a tragic one. Richard is eventually caught and executed; Katherine is left to grieve. Richard is portrayed as an innocent young man, unspoilt by the cynicism and hypocrisy that normally characterise his class; in many ways he is a mirror-image of Bulwer's Clarence Lindon, and like Lindon he is every inch a Percy Bysshe Shelley. The extent to which Richard loses his innocence is the extent to which he is drawn unwittingly into the cynical world of political double dealing. In telling her tale, therefore, Shelley continued to draw heavily on the players in her own life. Richard's Shelleyan pedigree is established within the first thirty pages. He is 'the fair-haired, blue-eyed boy… the gentle, noble-looking being' doomed to live a life of exile because of the unjust tyranny of his elders:

> 'Farewell England,' said the royal exile; 'I have no country, save these decks trodden by my friends – where they are, there is my kingdom and my home.' (P II 172)

There can be little doubt that when Mary came to write up the character of Henry VII she had her father-in-law in mind. Henry treats his family with disdain, unashamedly using his wealth to crush others while he extends his own power throughout England. Meanwhile Richard, like Castruccio before him, finds himself in love with two women: the faithful Katherine Gordon, and the more exotic (but no less sympathetically portrayed) Spaniard, Monina. If here we find a mellower version of Claire (compared to Beatrice in *Valperga*), it is because Monina recognises Katherine's right, and sails off with her swashbuckling, seafaring father, Hernan de Faro. De Faro is written in part as a tribute to Trelawney. The Byronic role is s⠇ Edmund Plantagenant, an idealist and a warrior ᴸ Richard, ultimately fickle. We are told that 'a l⌐ the best points of his character', but that he i as such prone to be drawn into the labyrinthi⠤ day (P I 145).

In Volume III where Richard, several times⟍ 10/14/2009 recaptured, contemplates his death, Mary her⠤ of the forsaken wife Katherine with undiluted self-indulgence: ⠤⠤ ʏes, they are all gone ... all who linked me to the past ... they are gone from before me ...' (P III 343). Particularly interesting from the point of view of an autobiographical reading is the speech she gives to Elizabeth, the widow of Edward IV. Here too is Mary Shelley reflecting on her own state, allowing herself a degree of candour that not even the *Journal* could be trusted with:

> When our days of prosperity are fled we cling fondly to all that reminds us of their brightness, and turn with augmented distaste from everything that marred their splendour. Elizabeth loved to remember herself as the chosen bride of Edward, and any circumstance that spoke of his inconstancy, or detracted from the entireness of her influence over him, then inspired her with indignation, now with abhorrence. (P I 75)

The disowned of Shelley's novel bear a striking resemblance to the disowned of the Shelley circle in the enforced nomadic life they are destined to lead. The restlessness which becomes such an important ingredient of *Frankenstein*, and which constituted such a formative experience for her in her late teens and early twenties, is a central motif in *Perkin Warbeck,* and it is used to critique a political system that undermines stable social order and offers freedom only in return for an impoverished gypsy life.

Though she was no longer a wanderer, impoverishment certainly remained the dominating experience in Shelley's life, and to read the *Journals* is to be constantly reminded just how frightening she found it; but the despairing tone of the *Journals* should not blind us to a more positive, entrepreneurial side to her character. Ever since Hunt, Shelley and Byron had begun to plan *The Liberal*, Mary Shelley had been employed creating a niche for herself as a contributor to the increasingly popular magazines and annuals of the day. She was particularly favoured by *The Keepsake*, which ran from 1828 to 1861. As with her later successful bid to write for Lardner's *Cabinet Cyclopoedia*, this was work not necessarily considered in any sense demeaning (though Mary herself resented the implications). Lardner employed only those he understood to be in the first rank, and when the *Athenaeum* reviewed *The Keepsake* for 1829, it noted with approval the presence among its contributors of Coleridge, Scott, Southey and Wordsworth, alongside Mackintosh, Moore and Mrs Shelley.[14]

Mary was never slow to follow up the possibility of new work. Just such an opportunity occurred when Henry Colburne and Richard Bentley launched a series of 'Standard Novels'. These were new editions of established works priced to ensure a popular readership; the second novel in the series was to be Godwin's *Caleb Williams, St. Leon* followed soon after, and number nine, published in 1831, was *Frankenstein*.

Given what was said in the previous chapter about the popularity of *Frankenstein*, it comes as no surprise that it was on the publisher's list; and given also that it remained, despite the publication of *Valperga*, *The Last Man*, *Perkin Warbeck* and a string of popular short stories, the work for which Mary Shelley continued to be best known, it is not surprising that she was happy to return to it and revise it for a reader-ship that was potentially much larger than any she had previously enjoyed. Her revisions provide us with a valuable insight into the way her ideas had developed and changed over the previous 13 years alongside the changing social and political complexion of England. The text had never been far away; there had been reprints, and we have seen that the story had already begun to spawn derivative texts. In H. M. Milner's 'Peculiar Romantic, Melo-Dramatic Pantomime Spectacle' (dated 1826 but probably first performed in 1823), Frankenstein exclaims, 'Oh, horror! horror! – let me fly this dreadful monster of my own creation.'[15] In 1831 Shelley expressed no such repugnance: 'And now, once again, I bid my hideous progeny go forth and prosper. I have affection for it, for it was the offspring of happy days ...' (F 173). Here we have a clue to the way the novel read for her in the 1830s. We know that those 'happy days' contained some very unhappy moments, but she was comprehensively rewriting the past around a reconstituted Percy Shelley. It is hardly surprising, therefore, that the events at the villa Diodati as recounted in the 1831 Introduction are not recalled entirely accurately; but then, the Introduction itself becomes a fictional device (loosely based on fact) telling the tale of a group of 'disowned' Romantic philanthropists and their adventures.

The 1818 text of *Frankenstein* has been read here as in part at least a record of Mary's questioning of Percy Shelley's ideas. The novel criticised an unjust society; but equally it questioned through Frankenstein himself the means by which political justice might be attained. The dangers attendant on Frankenstein's singleminded ambition to become the liberator of modern society, its Prometheus, register the problem Mary had with her egocentric, idealistic husband throughout their life together. It is hardly surprising, therefore, given the way she had rewritten Shelley in the Introduction to *Posthumous Poems*, to find that the chief beneficiary of the revised *Frankenstein* is Frankenstein himself.

Reprehensible as the reader of 1831 may still have found Frankenstein's ambition and vanity, he was certainly easier to understand and thus forgive. The following information, for example, was new to the 1831 text:

> while I followed the routine of education in the schools of Geneva, I was, to a great degree, self taught with regard to my favourite studies, my father was not scientific, and I was left to struggle with a child's blindness, added to a student's thirst for knowledge.[16]

But it is not now just a matter of Frankenstein lacking the guidance needed to avoid disaster; in due course Shelley implicitly absolves him of all responsibility: 'Destiny was too potent, and her immutable laws had decreed my utter and terrible destruction.'[17] The fact that Shelley intends the reader to sympathise much more with Frankenstein than was originally the case is also indicated in revisions made to the way Walton responds to him. In 1831 Walton sees the reconstituted Shelley, and makes sure that we do too:

> Will you laugh at the enthusiasm I express concerning this divine wanderer? ... Sometimes I have endeavoured to discover what quality it is which he possesses, that elevates him so immeasurably above any other person I ever knew. I

believe it to be an intuitive discernment; a quick but never-failing power of judgment; a penetration into the causes of things, unequalled for clearness and precision; add to this a faculty of expression, and a voice whose varied intonations are soul-subduing music.[18]

Nothing is lost of Mary's attack on the materialism and inhumanity of a society grounded in imperialistic ambition; the circumstances of the creature's education remain the same. But the textual additions emphasise the desirability of domesticity; in this respect our sense of a political solution applied to a political problem is blunted. In 1831 Frankenstein turns his 'reluctant steps from my father's door'; and as his climactic confrontation with the creature on the glacier approaches, there are a series of additions that locate the solution to the problem in the maintenance of social, family life, rather than in retirement from the world. In 1818 Elizabeth says: '"We surely shall be happy: quiet in our native country, and not mingling in the world, what can disturb our tranquillity?"' (F16) In 1831 there is an added emphasis on 'the friends around you':

> Remember the friends around you, who centre all their hopes in you. Have we lost the power of rendering you happy? Ah! While we love – while we are true to each other, here in this land of peace and beauty, your native country, we may reap every tranquil blessing, – what can disturb our peace?[19]

Since publishing *Frankenstein* in 1818, Mary had explored the *doppelgänger* phenomenon on several occasions. A particularly interesting example occurs in 1831 with her story for *The Keepsake*, 'The Deformed Transformed'. It is 'a tale of impious tempting of Providence and soul-subduing humiliation', reflecting sadly on why '*Power*, in all its shapes, is venerable to man.'[20] It reads as an endorsement to the revised *Frankenstein*, strengthening the suggestion that Frankenstein and his creature may be thought of as one. The close identification of Frankenstein with his creature is one important reason for the emasculation of the original novel's political meaning. The creature of 1818 seeks reconciliation with society every bit as much as he seeks a private domestic acceptance. For both creature and creator in 1831 (as essentially one being) it all comes back to family life. Victor is wooed by Elizabeth only to reflect fearfully on 'the fiend ... in my heart' who stands between them. The mirror-image is confirmed when (in an a passage also added in 1831) the creature gazes on the sleeping Justine knowing she can never be his, knowing that if she wakes she will curse him, not love him; 'it stirred the fiend within me',[21] he says. Shelley is here working to absolve her husband from blame for the consequences of his misguided attempts to force the pace of much-needed reform.

Shelley was of course by no means alone in encouraging an interest in the personality of her dead husband and the Romantic generation he – along with Byron – had come to symbolise. We have seen Bulwer using the Shelleyan archetype for his heroes, and the popularity of biography and memoir as a genre also reflected continuing public interest in the Shelley circle. During the period that *Frankenstein* was being revised, Thomas Moore's *Life of Byron* was published, and in the late twenties Trelawney began to ask for material to enable him to write a biography of Shelley. Mary was clearly alarmed at the prospect:

> Shelley's life so far as the public had to do with it consisted of very few events and these are publicly known – The private events were sad and tragical – How could you relate them? (15 December 1829, L II 94)

She had been comparatively relaxed about another hand executing a Memoir for the Galgnani edition, 'since it is favourable in its way & I ought to be content …' (To Cyrus Redding ?September/November 1829, L II 87), but in Trelawney's case she was worrying about the content of a full-scale biography, not its tone.

Since Percy Shelley's death, Mary had established an identity for herself which came increasingly to revolve around her career as a respected writer. The novel she now began to plan and write as a successor to *Perkin Warbeck*, however, reflects the way that the legacy of Shelley and his generation retained a firm hold on her mind. In *Lodore* she recreated yet again the men and women who had dominated her youth and early womanhood, thus failing once more to escape from an approach to fiction that was earning her no more than a limited success as a novelist. While *Valperga* and *Perkin Warbeck* had proved serviceable historical romances, both had contained passages of undigested research that kept the narrative marking time, both had tended to dwell too long on character-dissection at the expense of dramatic action. Shelley was unable to blend history and fiction as artfully as Scott, and she was unable to resist the business of analysing the lives and loves of the Shelley circle within her novels. Comparing her achievement in this field with highly successful novels like Bulwer's *The Disowned* and *Paul Clifford* illustrates what the reading public of the day were looking for, and why Shelley failed to become as popular an author as her competitors.

Of *Paul Clifford*, published in 1830, Shelley declared, 'It is a wonderful book, a sublime book – What will Bulwer become? The first author of the age? I do not doubt it – He is a magnificent writer.' (J 517) It was an enthusiasm that did not last, and she was later to describe him as a man 'spoilt by vanity and disappointed ambition.... I admired his novels so much I wanted him to be a great man but he is envious as well as vain.' (J 605) In 1830, however, Bulwer was still an admirer of Percy Shelley, and *Paul Clifford* manifestly paid homage to a Godwinian view of society.

Clifford is the son of an ambitious lawyer who deserts his wife, taking the child with him. The wife steals the boy back, but dies soon after in penury. Paul is brought up as an East End urchin, falls into bad company and is wrongly convicted of thieving. It is his own father – by now a rising legal and political star – who unwittingly sends him to gaol. Society is thus deemed responsible for fashioning him into a criminal, and he becomes a highwayman. Having fallen in love with his father's niece along the way, he is eventually caught and tried by his father. The true identity of the prisoner is revealed to the judge at the very moment he is condemning him to death.

Shelley will have relished Bulwer's lively Godwinian irony when comparing the progress of a politician's career to that of a young criminal:

> We enter our career, Mr. Nabbem, as your embryo ministers enter parliament – by bribery and corruption. There is this difference ... *we* are enticed to enter by the bribery and corruption of *others* – *they* enter spontaneously, by dint of their *own*.... What is this but a picture of your member of parliament ripening into a minister – your patriot mellowing into your placeman?[22]

At his trial, Clifford eloquently accuses the judge (on the verge of becoming Lord Chancellor) of being guilty of making him what he is (he is unwittingly correct in every respect, of course). The denouement is profoundly reminiscent of *Caleb Williams*; the crowd in the Courtroom suddenly begin to notice the physical likeness that exists between accuser and accused. They have already heard in Clifford's final statement how distinctions may become blurred:

> The Government of a state profess to provide all for those who 'obey'. Mark! A man hungers! – do you feed him? He is naked! – do you clothe him? If not, you break your covenant, you drive him back to the first law of Nature, and you hang him, not because he is guilty, but because you have left him starving.[23]

After this we read that, 'as the eyes of the spectators wandered on each, a thrilling and electric impression of a powerful likeness between the doomed and the doomer, for the first time in the trial, struck upon the audience.'[24] Shelley – and no doubt many other readers – will have recalled at this point the relationship that develops between Caleb Williams and Falkland in the course of Godwin's novel.

Paul Clifford is a lively, witty exploration of criminality; it shamelessly sentimentalises the trade of the highwayman, but it rarely loses sight of its more serious business in exposing the double standards operating in an unreformed British political system. Two years later, using material based on an actual case, Bulwer produced a much darker novel, *Eugene Aram*, which concentrated more specifically on the individual case of a murderer's conscience. Here he also indulged his fascination with the influence of occult powers on human nature, but his concern with a society controlled by problematic codes of etiquette and manners remained central to the narrative.

In most respects, the model for the evolving nineteenth-century novel is here, and both culturally (with the lost generation of Romantic poets providing the role-models for the heroes) and politically, it was the model Mary Shelley followed. Yet she never equalled Bulwer's pace, wit and variety. It might be argued that she simply lacked his talent; but we should never underestimate the consequences of the peculiar circumstances in which Shelley found herself when it came to responding to the cultural icons of Romanticism. Bulwer was in receipt of the Shelleyan and Byronic model for his heroes, and he had Godwin's writings as a primer when it came to formulating progressive political ideas. Beyond that, he was committed only to furthering his own literary and political career. In the

1840s he was to have no qualms about criticising Shelley's verse, much to Mary's anger.

Shelley's situation was very different. She wrote as the guardian of Percy Shelley's flame; his story was her story, and she lived under the continuing and very real threat of the man who would dearly love to snuff it out for good. The widow of Shelley was always, in the end, destined to divert Mary Shelley the novelist back into the process of rewriting her own and her husband's lives in a way designed to ease the pang of his loss. *Perkin Warbeck* rehearsed the larger issues of freedom and power, but it did not herald any significant movement in Shelley's fiction away from the *roman à clef* genre of *The Last Man*. Her new novel, *Lodore*, concerned itself with broader potentially controversial political themes, while in many ways Shelley's use of irony denotes an important stylistic development; but the plot and characters, not here set within the framework of a researched historical novel, provided her with the means whereby she could become all the more involved in writing a covert form of autobiography and hagiography.

The short stories that Shelley published in the early 1830s are all primarily concerned to explore the power of love. In 'The Swiss Peasant' of 1831, love effectively manages to annul the political differences between the aristocracy and the lower orders. The heroine is an orphaned Swiss peasant girl brought up by an aristocratic family. When her lover returns from revolutionary France determined to obliterate the aristocracy, she saves her foster-family by claiming to be the wife of her adopted parents' son. She saves the family, but loses her revolutionary lover. At the end of the story he reappears. Fighting with the French army has left him physically wounded and politically disillusioned. The two are reconciled and at last reunited. Familial reconciliation and reunion are similarly at the centre of 'The Brother and the Sister', 'The Invisible Girl', and 'The Smuggler and his Family', all of 1833. We should never forget that when Shelley laid down her pen and looked up from her work, she saw not only the threat of economic disaster, but the likelihood of her son being taken from her by Sir Timothy. Her *Journal* entries, therefore, take up the narrative where her fiction leaves off, and when she turns from the *Journal* back to the fiction, she continues to weave the realities of her literary life into her latest plot. At the end of 1834 she noted in the *Journal*: 'My heart and soul are bound up in Percy [Florence].... But life is over for me – while I regret that the cruelty of Percy's relations will obscure his existence as it has mine by their wickedness ... their malice is so excessive, so awake, so mischievous ...' (J 541–2).

In the years between *Perkin Warbeck* and *Lodore* (published in 1835) Shelley retained her position in the circle of friends established since her move to Somerset Street in 1829. There had been difficulties, including a scandal involving Georgiana Beauclerk. Mary stood by her, but her ever-vigilant father-in-law was there once more to make it known that he disapproved. Percy Florence had gone to Harrow in 1832, and Shelley moved to Harrow the following year partly to have it seen that she was putting distance between herself and those of whom Sir Timothy disapproved. He had agreed to help his grandson financially and it was help his mother could not afford to lose. In April 1833 Godwin was made a Yeoman Usher of the Exchequer. Almost at the very point when he ceased to be a financial burden on Mary, her aunt, Everina Wollstonecraft, began to ask for help: 'There is something quite savage in this new misfortune', was Claire's comment (J 537). There had been tragedy too; Mary's half-brother William had died in the cholera outbreak of 1832. Through it all she continued to live her busy literary life, but increasingly now her mind turned to her major task as Percy Shelley's widow, the publication of his poetry. Sir Timothy seemed indestructible, but the editing and planning went ahead while she continued work on *Lodore*. If the fate of the *Poetical Works* remained uncertain, the novel at least offered the prospect of keeping the spirit of Percy Shelley alive in the hearts of some discerning readers.

8
Fiction and the Marketplace: *Lodore* and *Falkner*, 1834–38

In 1804 James Barry completed a large-scale neo-classical canvas, *The Birth of Pandora*.[1] The prophetic implications of the painting were clear. Barry, a defender of the liberties of the American colonists against British tyranny in the 1770s, sought to herald a new era in Britain's political and cultural life; but in doing so he also implied that the future would be a perilous place in which to live. Pandora had been created by Zeus as a means of avenging himself on Prometheus for delivering the fire of the Gods to mortals. She was sent as a gift to Prometheus's brother, Epimetheus, where her mischievous character was intended to wreak havoc on humanity. It was after Epimetheus (wary of any gift from the Gods), refused to accept Pandora – despite her great beauty – that Zeus chained Prometheus to a rock and initiated the savage punishment where vultures tore at his liver all day, while at night, in the frost and cold, his wounds healed, only to be attacked once more by the vultures when day returned. On hearing of this, Epimetheus agreed to marry Pandora. In due course she displayed her untrustworthiness by opening a jar (the mythical equivalent to the tree of knowledge in the Christian tradition), and letting loose into the world all the ills that from then on became the condition of life. These included old age, sickness, vanity and despair. Hope, however, was also released, and this (a no less cruel device on the part of Zeus) had the effect of reconciling humanity to a life of suffering.

It was precisely this kind of meek acceptance of suffering against which radical minds like those of Godwin and Shelley had raged:

> Men of England, wherefore plough
> For the lords who lay ye low?

> Wherefore weave with toil and care
> The rich robes your tyrants wear?
>
> Wherefore feed, and clothe, and save,
> From the cradle to the grave,
> Those ungrateful drones who would
> Drain your sweat – nay, drink your blood?[2]

The story of Pandora symbolises the eternal untrustworthiness of the gods. Barry's painting was executed in severely neo-classical style, and therefore had the outward appearance of conformity with established taste, but at the same time it was proposing a profoundly subversive agenda. The gathering on Mount Olympus appears magisterially impressive. A closer view, however, reveals a corrupt, decadent gathering, where the fate of humanity is cynically written off, and where the perpetuation of wealth, power and sensual pleasure among those on Olympus (or its equivalent within the British political establishment) governs every act.

Barry's combination of apparently acceptable taste in execution with a subversive meaning epitomises the course of much cultural evolution in England in the late eighteenth century. His classicism was, of course, by no means in line with the drift towards sensibility to be found in much prose, poetry and painting at this time. But other artists who continued to work in the classical style like Benjamin West and Gavin Hamilton, were as conservative in their politics as they were in their aesthetics. Barry's painting illustrates the way cultural forms of representation were increasingly open to scrutiny, and, since the American War, subject to a degree of politicisation previously unknown. What was true for visual art was true also for the production of novels and poetry. Authors consciously experimented with form, adopting styles in order to challenge the assumptions they carried with them, producing in most cases composite forms through which they might establish an independent voice.

The period during which Mary Shelley wrote her novels, from 1816 to 1837, is frequently written up in literary-historical terms as 'transitional', lying between an 'Augustan' eighteenth and a 'Victorian' nineteenth century. Eighteenth-century novelists were all in various ways in receipt of the lessons of Enlightenment rationalism, and tended to reflect a degree of scepticism when it came to the credibility of tradition and established authority. The humble Pamela's outburst against the ignoble advances of the well-born Mr. B. in

Samuel Richardson's *Pamela* (1740) illustrates what Gary Kelly has called eighteenth-century 'Enlightenment sociology':

> One may see how the poor people are despised by the proud and the rich! Yet we were all on a footing originally: and many of those gentry, who brag of their ancient blood, would be glad to have it as wholesome and as really untainted as ours![3]

Richardson appealed to middle-class aspirations of grandeur, to a generation of industrialists and entrepreneurs who aimed to replace the gentry 'who brag of their ancient blood' in their positions of power; there is no hint yet of the kind of subversion that informs Barry's *Pandora*, the kind of subversion to be found in Godwin's *Political Justice* or Percy Shelley's *Song to the Men of England* or his Preface to *Prometheus Unbound*.

It was writers of Godwin's generation who first seriously subjected the formal process of cultural representation to rational analysis while working from a genuinely radical political agenda. Considerably before this, the young Edmund Burke's conservative response to the impact of 'Enlightenment sociology' on the arts had been published in 1759. In *A Philosophical Enquiry into the Origin of Our Ideas of the Sublime and Beautiful*, Burke sought to impede the potentially egalitarian progress of rationalism with an argument claiming that the emotional side of man's nature was a driving force in the production of the greatest art. He enumerated the major sources of creative inspiration that, within a few years, and with the help of an equally reactionary, dilettante writer, Horace Walpole, would become collectively known as 'Gothic': 'Terror ... Obscurity ... Power ... Vastness ... Suddenness ... Pain ... Darkness ... Blackness...'.[4]

Godwin and the radical Jacobin novelists he inspired, all combined the Gothic format with the vogue for sensibility to reaffirm that the way forward for society was through the application of reason and common sense. Readers were drawn in by the use of popular, congenial fictional devices; no such novel was complete without a Gothicised tyrannical father-figure, or a pair of sentimentalised, star-crossed lovers. Comfortable, conformist resolutions to such plots, however (reunions and reconciliations) were denied or postponed, and increasingly radical proposals emerged in relation to every aspect of social and political life. The child catechised in Mrs Inchbald's *Nature and Art* (1796) confounds his reverend questioner because of his innocent application of rational thinking. He is told that 'the poor are born to serve the rich', and that if this seems hard, they have a life in Heaven to look forward to:

> '... But cannot this world try to be as good as that?'
> 'In respect to placing all persons on a level, it is utterly impossible – God has ordained it otherwise.'
> 'How! Has God ordained a distinction to be made, and will not make any himself?'[5]

The threat is two-fold: to the way a sentimental novel might resolve its narrative, and to comfortable assumptions about how society is ordered to maintain the *status quo*.

The latter years of the eighteenth century see an increasing tendency to deconstruct established cultural forms, and to pose fundamental questions about the relationship of those cultural forms to the societies that produce them. Wordsworth raises the issue in his Preface of 1800 to *Lyrical Ballads*, while Percy Shelley, like Blake before him, reflected on the origins and implications of Milton's portrayal of good and evil in *Paradise Lost* in his Preface to *Prometheus Unbound*. Blake and Shelley produced a subversive reading of Milton that matches Barry's subversive reading of neo-classical taste in *Pandora*. *Frankenstein* is in this sense typical of much Romantic fiction in its formal restlessness. It has a series of narrators; it is not entirely 'Gothic': it possesses all the ingredients of a novel of sensibility, and frequently employs the style of one. The De Lacey episode is an excellent example of this: the aged, blind father, penury made bearable by love, the arrival of the mysterious, beautiful Saphie. But for them the creature lurks without, and eventually destroys their way of life.

Fiction was being written for a readership increasingly aware that power and authority were moving from the aristocracy to the middle classes. Jane Austen points up the need for a responsible, professional, Christian middle-class leadership by referring her readers to the nation's reading habits: in *Northanger Abbey* (1798–99) Gothic fiction is censored and its readers ridiculed, while in *Mansfield Park* (1814) the proposed performance of Kotzebue's play *Lovers' Vows* occupies a defining role in the novel's critique of middle- and upper-class irresponsibility. In *Sense and Sensibility* (1811) Elinor's ironic account of her sister's frame of mind instructs us that a superficial literary taste is symptomatic of a superficial, untrustworthy character:

> 'Well Marianne … you have done pretty well. You have
> already ascertained Mr Willoughby's opinion in almost every
> matter of importance. You know what he thinks of Cowper
> and Scott; you are certain of his estimating their beauties as
> he ought, and you have received every assurance of his admir-
> ing Pope no more than is proper. But how is your
> acquaintance to be long supported, under such extraordinary
> dispatch of every subject for discourse?'[6]

In the early 1800s, Austen was responding to a proliferation of litera-
tures encouraged by a burgeoning readership. Mary Shelley had seen
the Gothic novel challenged for popularity by the novel of passion,
she had seen the success of novels written expressly to counteract such
harmful popular taste, and she had witnessed the rise to popularity of
the so-called 'Newgate' novel, romanticised stories of robbers and
highwaymen of the past (of which Bulwer's *Paul Clifford* was an
example). All these novels readily appropriated what had become
known as 'silver-fork' fiction. Stories of scandalous goings-on in high
places have always made for lucrative copy, and in the 1820s novels
began to appear that were almost exclusively concerned with the lives,
loves and fashions of the rich and powerful. Catherine Gore, Disraeli
and Bulwer owed much of their literary success to the inclusion of
significant helpings of 'silver-fork' material in their work.

Inevitably – given the subject matter – the *roman à clef* ingredient
was an important part of this genre. Celebrity-spotters reading
Shelley's *The Last Man* had cut their teeth long before on sensationalist texts like Lady Caroline Lamb's *Glenarvon* (1816). Set in Ireland
against the backdrop of the Irish revolt of 1798, this novel provided
its readers with a breathlessly melodramatic account of aristocratic
life, and the impact upon it of the satanic and distinctly vampiristic
presence of the subversive Lord Byron. Lamb's text is a bizarre blend
of sentimentalism and personal confessional, and it was a seminal
influence upon the way in which the Romantic artist came to be
perceived in the public mind:

> Even the storms of nature could not move Glenarvon. In
> the dark night, when the tempest raged around and the
> stormy ocean beat against the high impending cliffs, he
> would venture forth, would listen to the roaring thunder
> without fear, and watch the forked lightning as it flashed
> along the sky.

> The rushing winds but seemed to smooth his perturbed
> spirit; and the calm of his brow remained unaltered in every
> changing scene. Yet it was the calm of hopeless despair....[7]

Lamb fails to control her subject-matter in the way that Lady Morgan,
Mary Robinson, Mary Hays or Amelia Opie do, though she does have
a controlling authorial presence as she steers us from dramatic Gothic
setting to picturesque landscape, and from passages of passionate
introspection to more measured reflections on the political circumstances that contextualise the personal histories involved. But above
all she established Byron – and by implication Shelley – in the public
mind as figures existing more in fiction than reality.

Fifteen years later, in 1831, Mary Shelley was to assist in the publication of a book that played a very similar game with the Byron and
Shelley set. Trelawney's *Adventures of a Younger Son* was a *roman à clef*
that claimed autobiographical status, and that perpetuated the
Byronic myth through the tale of the author's own life. Trelawney's
request that Mary help came after the acrimony that followed her
refusal to assist him in writing a life of Shelley. In her letter to
Trelawney of 14 June 1831, she avoided expressing her own judgement of the book by quoting Horace Smith's comments: 'it is a most
powerful, but rather perilous work, which will be much praised and
much abused by the liberal & bigoted – I have read it with great pleasure, & I think it admirable ...' (L II 138–9). Mary's letter reveals that,
in addition to insisting on a number of cuts in the name of decency
('any gross piece of ill taste will make your bookseller draw back'), she
took the initiative in replacing Trelawney's title, *History of a Man*, with
the altogether more marketable *Adventures of a Younger Son* (L II
119–20). Trelawney, one of the greatest poseurs of his literary generation, took on the mantle of the fictional Byron in the *Adventures*, and
made himself famous with what William St Clair summarises as 'a
celebration of rape and plunder'.[8] His fantasy (read at the time as a
true record of his life) indicates also the continuing popularity of tales
of the Orient, where much of it is set, and of the influence of pornography on novelists aware of the lucrative market in clandestine
literature.

By the 1830s, the public appetite for embellished retellings of the
myth of a Romantic generation of writers showed little sign of
abating. The opening section of Disraeli's *Henrietta Temple* (1837), for
example, bids to outdo even Trelawney in its account of the remarkable career of Sir Ferdinand Armine. It should be added that Disraeli

scrupulously avoids Trelawney's penchant for 'ill taste', while indulging in the genre's love of sensationalism:

> Beautiful, brilliant and ambitious, the young and restless Armine quitted, in his eighteenth year, the house of his fathers, and his stepdame of a country, and entered the Imperial service.... The world rang with the stories of his romantic bravery, his gallantries, his eccentric manners, and his political intrigues, for he nearly contrived to be elected King of Poland.[9]

Mary Shelley found herself with an abundance of options to choose from when casting around for a suitable vehicle for her fiction. After the Godwinian influences on *Frankenstein*, the historical model of Scott for *Valperga* and *Perkin Warbeck*, the *roman à clef* for *The Last Man*, and then the experience gained from revising *Frankenstein*, she had arrived at a point in the early 1830s where she might reasonably be thought of as feeling the need to extend her range as a novelist both for her own satisfaction, and given her need to succeed in the marketplace. In her letters to the publishers Charles Ollier and John Murray she carefully displayed her reading and appreciation of successful writers (notably Bulwer and Disraeli), while she plied them with lucrative projects for her own pen.

Lodore was probably started early in 1832. William Walling has written it off as a gloomy diatribe against the Byronic stereotype in which 'Mary failed to control fully the theme she had originally planned'.[10] The novel is, in fact, one of her most ambitious, complex and interesting achievements; Fiona Stafford reads *Lodore* as 'a serious attempt to explore the deepest human emotions ... it ... retains a belief in the power of the suffering individual, and in transcendent human values, that harks back to the literature of the Romantic period.'[11] Shelley's intentions can be gauged from a letter to Murray written on the eve of beginning the novel. She proposed a project that might sound potentially controversial: 'a history of the manners and ... Literature of England from Queen Anne to the French Revolution – from Pope to Horace Walpole'. This, she went on to assure him, would afford 'scope for novelty and amusement'. Shelley no doubt intended to produce a fundamentally serious work in a style that would offset its deeper import. At a time when the press was still being carefully vetted, and when she herself continued to be under the close scrutiny of her father-in-law, she was attempting not to lose sight of her commitment to the truth; the publisher, however, was to appreciate that she understood the market: 'my book while it would be conscientiously accurate would not at all fail on the score of *amusement*, which is one of the necessary adjuncts' (L II 114). The 'History' was never written; in its place came *Lodore*.

Revising *Frankenstein* was instrumental in the planning of a new novel that would review the 'history of the manners' of eighteenth-century England. It would contain many of the subversive themes rooted in her work since writing her first novel, and it would proclaim her intellectual strength and integrity; it would also need to make money for her. She set herself to write a very clever book indeed.

The opening could hardly have been more promising for a reader of popular fiction. We are introduced to an aristocratic family, the Fitzhenrys (duly ennobled to Lodore) whose fortunes are in eclipse; nothing intrigued a middle-class readership more than to see how the high-born coped with hard times. The young Lord Lodore leaves his sister behind at the great house in Essex where she dreams of his eventual return. She knows something of his story: his marriage, the birth of a child, a mysterious tragedy that follows the christening, but in the first chapter the reader is placed alongside the ignorant villagers:

> Some mystery there was – Lodore was gone – his place was vacant: he lived; yet his name, like those of the dead, haunted only the memories of men, and was allied to no act or circumstance of present existence. (L 52–3)

The second chapter strikes an equally fashionable note, moving the action to Illinois, where 'an English gentleman, advanced to middle age, accompanied by an infant daughter' arrives and proceeds to establish a small estate (L 54). He is wealthy, and before long builds a beautiful house and creates an idyllic setting for it. Throughout the eighteenth century, travellers' tales from North America had been popular. Besides Brockden Brown's novels, there was information to be had from Morris Birckbeck, William Cobbett, James Fenimore Cooper and Frances Wright (L 483–500); she would also have known Thomas Hamilton's *Men and Manners in America* (1833). In the 1840s Dickens sought to exploit continuing English interest in the progress of the new American nation in his novel, *Martin Chuzzlewit*.

The 'English gentleman' in Illinois is of course Lodore, showing clear signs of a Byronic temperament as he carries a secret sorrow with him in his search for solitude. His is the temperament of the high-born, yet: 'Even while he shrunk from familiar communication with the rude and unlettered, he took an interest in their welfare.' (L 57) In Chapter 3 attention is turned to the child, Ethel. Under Lodore's guidance, Ethel is destined for perfect womanhood; her father 'kept her far aloof from the very knowledge of what might, by its baseness or folly, contaminate the celestial beauty of her nature' (L 65). It is a charming experiment, but as Ethel grows up we sense the increasing fragility of her situation: 'Ethel's visionary ideas were all full of peace, seclusion, and her father' (L 67).

When a young suitor appears, Lodore recognises that his American home has not brought him the peace he sought, and he resolves to return to Europe with Ethel. The 'silver-fork' reader will be well aware of what lies ahead: Volume II will begin to unravel Lodore's secrets, but before we get to that Shelley fills in the narrative details that preceded Lodore's emigration. It is here that the *roman à clef* comes into its own. In 1835 a reader might have discovered either Percy Shelley or Byron in the story of Lodore's unhappy time at Eton, though Byron is the most likely candidate, since his meek and sensitive friend, Derham, has Shelleyan qualities over against the decidedly masculine spirit of rebellion that leads Lodore to quit both Eton and his home. A lack of purpose confirms the Byronic note:

> Lodore was one of those men ... whose early youth is replete with mighty promise; who, as they advance in life, continue to excite the expectation, the curiosity, and even the enthusiasm of all around them ... and yet to the end, as it were, they only gild the edges of the clouds in which they hide themselves, and arrive at the term of life, the promise of its dawn unfulfilled. (L 88)

Lodore falls in love with Cornelia Santerre; her background and the nature of their meeting is tailor-made for the reader of romance. Unfortunately Cornelia's mother turns out to be the worst kind of mother-in-law, retaining a powerful hold over her daughter, rendering her indifferent to him, and also – in due course – to their daughter. We are then given another high-society mystery to guess at. The Lodores become acquainted with a Polish Countess and her son, Count Casimir. It is not long before Cornelia and Casimir begin to flirt, while

Lodore becomes increasingly anxious and angry. The truth is that Casimir is Lodore's illegitimate child brought to London by his mother out of spite. Eventually driven to strike the Count (who of course demands satisfaction) Lodore tells Cornelia all. He cannot duel with his own son; honour demands nothing less than voluntary exile: 'The simple question is,' he says, 'whether you are prepared on a sudden to accompany me?' (L 115) The answer is no, and mother and daughter retreat to a villa at Twickenham. So it is that Lodore travels to America, taking with him his daughter, the child he has cherished as the one beautiful thing to come from a disastrous marriage. Avid Shelley and Byron watchers, recalling the scandalous gossip that surrounded their set in the recent postwar years, readers of *Glenarvon*, of the Reviews and the gossip columns in the papers, of Mary Shelley's *Last Man*, will have had a wonderful time imagining the proud yet sensitive Lodore as a type of Byron, which in turn will have suggested Cornelia as a sketch of Byron's wife Annabella Millbanke. Such readers will have been on the lookout also for a Shelley, a Claire, a Mary Jane Clairmont and no doubt a Godwin.

What, then, would they have made of the opening lines of Volume I, Chapter 11, which brings us back to the arrival of Lodore in Illinois?

> Accustomed to obey the more obvious laws of necessity, those whose situation in life obliges them to earn their daily bread, are already broken in to the yoke of fate. But the rich and great are vanquished more slowly. Their time is their own ... and cloyed by the too easy attainment of the necessaries, and even the pleasures of life, they fly to the tortures of passion, and to the labour of overcoming the obstacles that stand in the way of their forbidden desires, as resources against *ennui* and satiety.... In the midst of this, their thoughtless career, the eternal law which links ill to ill, is at hand to rebuke and tame the rebel spirit.... The young are scarcely aware of this; they delight to contend with Fate, and laugh as she clanks their chains. But there is a period ... when the link envelops them, the bolts are shot, the rivets fixed, the iron enters the flesh, the soul is subdued, and they fly to religion or proud philosophy, to seek for an alleviation, which the crushed spirit can no longer draw from its own resources.... This dark moment had arrived for Lodore. (L 118–9)

This reads as an ironic dismissal of Lodore's entire history to the point of his arrival in America. People who have to earn their living 'obey the more obvious laws of necessity'. The likes of Lodore have the opportunity to indulge themselves in arcane codes of honour and etiquette in an unreal, decadent world. If it was not apparent before, we must now take into account the evident scorn with which Shelley views the aristocracy: 'such a tissue of pain and evil is woven from their holiday passtime, as checks them midcourse, and makes them feel that they are slaves'. Only 'feel'; these people have no idea what true slavery is. The rest of the chapter reflects ironically upon the acts of Lodore, in particular his decision to take Ethel to America with him. By the end of the chapter we may pity him, but it has been made clear that his problems are the fruits of aristocratic self-indulgence.

This is the second time that the reader has arrived in America with Lodore, and our revised view of the circumstances of his exile must take us back to the first ten chapters of the book. They were read originally to illustrate Shelley's intention of writing in the popular taste. As with her scheme for a history of English manners and literature, the history of Lodore provides boundless 'scope for novelty and amusement'; but as with James Barry's employment of a tastefully neo-classical form, from page 1 the silver-fork genre is manipulated to incorporate a subversive strand in the narrative. Only slightly concealed behind her description of the Lodore family seat lies the sorry tale of ordinary people who live outside the park-gates:

> Longfield is distant eight miles from any market town, but the simple inhabitants, limiting their desires to their means of satisfying them, are scarcely aware of the kind of desert in which they are placed. (L 49)

Longfield and its inhabitants, set – as the opening sentence of the book explains – in 'the flattest and least agreeable part of the county of Essex', is Shelley's metaphor for a society bled dry by an effete, self-indulgent aristocracy. The name of Longfield is surely a glance in the direction of Field Place.

Returning to America, the superficial attractions of Lodore's idyllic estate are undercut by ironic references to the financial advantages he has over his fellow settlers. This inequality goes largely unnoticed because 'the people were too busy securing for themselves the necessaries of life' (L 54). Lodore swiftly establishes a prosperous estate and builds a beautiful house, 'while the dark forest, or untilled plain, seemed yet to set at defiance the efforts of his fellow settlers.' Lodore's wealth has rendered him blind to what is actually going on around him in the name of equality. He swiftly acquires 'comforts of so civilized a description, that the Americans termed them luxuries ... although to his eye everything was regulated by the strictest regard to republican plainness and simplicity' (L.54). If another settler disturbs Lodore when the Byronic fit is upon him, 'he was irritated to fury. His resentment was expressed in terms ill-adapted to republican equality ... he involuntarily looked upon himself as a distinct and superior race to the human beings that each day crossed his path' (L 57). Similarly, Shelley's ironic tone is never far away when describing Ethel's Rousseauistic education:

> [Lodore] drew his chief ideas from Milton's Eve, and adding to this the romance of chivalry, he satisfied himself that his daughter would be the embodied ideal of all that is adorable and estimable in her sex. (L 65)

It is a beautifully judged passage, laden with implicit references to her husband's subversive reading of the myth of the fall, to Burke's reactionary politics, and to her mother's arguments on behalf of the rights of women. Yet for all that, it might be read without offence.

Lodore insists that the nobility are for ever nobility, bound by outmoded custom and deadened to the true needs of others by the unjustified excess of their wealth and misguided notions of honour. Lodore leaves his American retreat 'as if it had never been a place of shelter to him, unthankful for the many happy hours which had blessed him there' (L 77). Shelley had used a circular narrative strategy before, but never with this degree of sophistication; it becomes the key to the way in which she challenges orthodox expectations of style and plot with an impressive input of irony. Her boldest stroke comes at the end of Volume I, when Lodore is killed in a duel, thereby focusing our attention on the major political theme of the novel; it is what Thomas Paine had inveighed against in 1792:

> There never did, there never will, and there never can exist a parliament, or any description of men, or any generation of men, in any country, possessed of the right or power of binding or controlling posterity to the '*end of time*'.... Man has no property in man, neither has any generation a property in the generations which are to follow.... I am contending for the rights of the *living*, and against their being willed away, and controlled and contracted for, by the manuscript assumed authority of the dead....[12]

Shelley could apply Paine's sentiments directly to Sir Timothy Shelley; he was rich enough to ensure that his oppression of her would continue long after his death. In the remaining two volumes of *Lodore* Shelley explores the consequences of Lodore's actions upon those he leaves behind; she contends for the rights of the living against the 'manuscript assumed authority of the dead', where 'the dead' constitute an aristocratic ruling class who still extend an unhealthy influence over the ordering of early-nineteenth-century English society.

Before the climax of Volume I, we read how Lodore and Ethel travel to New York, where Lodore discovers Fanny Derham, the daughter of his friend at Eton. She is to travel home with them to be reunited with her father. Letters arrive, telling of the death of Lodore's mother-in-law; the letters also indicate that the reconciliation he has been hoping for with his wife is impossible; his sister writes that Cornelia is 'given up to pleasure' and 'naturally shrunk from being reminded of her exiled husband and her forgotten child' (L 153).

The uncontrollable pride and anger of the aristocrat in Lodore is aroused by an abusive American who knows of his refusal to fight Casimir. He is unable to withstand the dictates of the barbaric conduct he and his class consider 'honourable', and a duel is arranged. A young Englishman named Villiers, who seems acquainted with the family, steps forward to act as Lodore's second. Lodore is killed, and in his dying breath asks Villiers to make sure that Cornelia knows he bears her no malice, and that, despite her wish to the contrary, he longs for her to be reunited with Ethel. In the event it is Lodore's will, made long before, that dictates how things shall be (or, in Paine's words, 'governs beyond the grave'). Here Lodore had forbidden Cornelia any access to their daughter. Ethel is thus twice orphaned: once as a consequence of the barbaric rights of aristocratic combat, and again as a result of the law at its most inhumane. Shelley could identify closely with both sets of circumstances. Villiers returns to England with Ethel and Fanny Derham, and this handsome, chivalrous young man of mysterious origins shadowing a frail orphan child provides us with a promising start for Volume II.

'The abstracted, wounded, yet lofty spirit of Lodore was totally dissimilar to the airy brightness of Villiers' disposition' (L 181). For the *roman à clef* addict, Chapter 1 of Volume II moves us on from Byron to Percy Shelley. While she wrote up the Shelleyan Villiers, Mary continued to work her way through her husband's poems and letters: 'I am copying one of Shelley's letters', she noted in 1833. 'Great God! What a thing is life! In one of them he says "The curse of this life is that what we have once known, we cannot cease to know"' (J 532–3). There were of course things about Percy that Mary would have preferred to forget:

> Villiers was imprudent from his belief in the goodness of his fellow-creatures, and imparted happiness from the store that his warm heart insured to himself. The one [Lodore] had never been a boy – the other [Villiers] had not yet learnt to be a man. (L 182)

Both Villiers and his cousin, Henry Saville, are given a Shelleyan persona, and Volume II concerns itself initially with the love-affair between Saville and Cornelia. This is why Villiers knows about Lodore; though in conversation with Ethel's aunt Elizabeth, he realises that there is much he has yet to learn about Lodore's widow.

Shelley weaves this new strand of her narrative back into the action of Volume I. The idealist Saville takes it upon himself to travel to America to plead with Lodore for the return of Ethel to her mother. Villiers accompanies him, and we learn that the two Englishmen arrive in Illinois as Lodore and Ethel leave for New York. Saville discovers what has happened, and assuming this to be the prelude to Ethel's return to Cornelia, he decides to travel in America before leaving. Villiers heads straight for home, and it is at this point that the reader first meets him in New York. This latest loop back into Lodore's narrative confirms how easily – in an unenlightened society – we become prisoners of the past, in this case specifically Lodore's aristocratic past. Saville and Cornelia ought to be free to acknowledge their true feelings and move forward in their relationship. But both are impeded by the stale transactions of the past. Saville returns to England to find her in mourning, as custom demands: 'His delicate nature caused him to respect the weeds she wore, even though they might be termed a mockery...'. She is even more a victim of society and its customs than is he: 'all this was but a painted veil' (L 202–3). Shelley delivers a comprehensive critique of aristocratic power and privilege at a time when hopes for the future of a reformed political nation ran high. The foundering love-affair between Cornelia and Saville also rehearsed memories of the final bitter years of her time with Percy:

> Neither of them could afterwards comprehend what divided them; or why, when each would have died for the other's sake, cobweb barriers should have proved inextricable ... (L 202)

The solution to the problem is, predictably, education. Volume I dwells on the major impediment: the 'Lord' in 'Lord Lodore'. Volume II illustrates the misery and unhappiness of an unenlightened, unreformed society governed by outmoded laws and traditions. Saville, having lost Cornelia, travels abroad, believes himself once more in love, and marries an Italian. Volume III, with the reappearance of Fanny Derham, offers to explore the way forward through an enlightened commitment to learning.

The misery of Cornelia and Saville is now matched by the difficulties of Villiers and Ethel. Were it not, of course, for the unnatural separation of Ethel from her mother, the poverty of the young couple would easily be avoided. The sentimental tale of the young lovers, however, is repeatedly challenged by ironic asides: the moment the wedding is over, we are told, Villiers's father 'hastened down to his castle to kill pheasants' (L 251). Shelley now used her own miserable experience of dodging the bailiffs with Percy in London in 1814–15, and many of her readership would have been able to recognise this. She even wonders whether they will approve:

> a risk is run, on the one hand, of being censured for bringing the reader into contact with degrading and sordid miseries; and on the other, of laying too much stress on circumstances which will appear to those in a lower sphere of life, as scarcely deserving the name of misfortune.... But all beautiful and fairy-like as was Ethel Villiers, in tracing her fortunes, it is necessary ... to employ terms of vulgar use, and to describe scenes of common-place and debasing interest.... (L 302)

This passage illustrates one reason why Shelley failed to achieve the popularity she aimed for. Readers had no objection in seeing their own tastes satirised (Bulwer and Disraeli did it with a beguiling lightness of touch) but Shelley all too frequently talked down to her readers, a point politely made by a reviewer in *The Sun*: 'her tone is a little too elevated' (L 547).

Villiers takes lodgings with a Mrs Derham, and Ethel joins him there. News of Villiers's impending arrest for debt coincides with the arrival of Mrs Derham's daughter. When Ethel once more meets Fanny she finds her reading a Greek text: '"You have not forgotten your old pursuits," said Ethel, smiling. "Say rather I am more wedded to them than ever. I need them to give light and glory to a dingy world ..."'

(L 307). The shade of Mary Wollstonecraft arrives to set the fortunes of the abandoned Ethel on an upward path.

The final volume of *Lodore* tells how the plight of Ethel and Villiers deteriorates until Villiers is imprisoned, at which point, with Fanny's help, Cornelia is made aware of the catastrophe. Cornelia's character then embarks on a steady upward curve of redemption. She discovers the horrors of her daughter's circumstances, at the same time recognising how much more deeply fulfilled she is than herself. The death of Saville's Italian wife enables Shelley, using another backward narrative loop, to reflect on Saville's fraught domestic history, resolving it through his renewed friendship with and eventual marriage to Cornelia. But we shall never know how truly successful Shelley was in writing the final volume because, in the process of sending and receiving copy to and from her publisher, a part of the manuscript was lost. There was no alternative but to set about rewriting the missing sections; she was already at work on a time-consuming series of biographical essays for Lardner, as well as moving steadily forward with her editing of Percy's poetry and prose.

The spell cast by Lodore in Volume I is broken in the course of Volume III primarily by Cornelia, who ends up, much to the amazement of old Aunt Elizabeth, humbly ministering to the poor and needy prior to her marriage to Saville. The bridge between the worlds of affluence and penury is Fanny Derham, but Shelley makes very little of Fanny's scholarly commitment. An early speech expounds the beliefs of her parents:

> It was my father's lesson ... to penetrate, to anatomize, to purify my motives; but once assured of my own integrity, to be afraid of nothing. Words have more power than anyone can guess.... People are so afraid to speak ... their voice fails them, when that alone is wanting to make the tyrant quail. (L 316)

But in the event Fanny achieves the reconciliation of mother and daughter through her natural friendliness, not through the delivery of Godwinian sermons on political justice. The resolution of the novel turns on Fanny as a perfect type of human being rather than as an intellectual warrior in the political arena. In the Conclusion Shelley describes her as a person who has only gone on to engage fully with the world after the action of the novel has ceased. Her story is therefore yet to be told; precisely who she is and what she can hope to achieve remain unclear. Far from looking forward through Fanny Derham, Shelley looked back to a mother for whom she could imagine no place in her own anxious life except as a symbol of the love and affection she continued to crave and failed to find.

In 1837, two years after the publication of *Lodore*, Shelley's final novel, *Falkner*, appeared. She was encouraged to persevere with *Falkner* in no small measure by the positive critical response to *Lodore*. Her reputation had recently been boosted by the reappearance of *Frankenstein*, and several reviews of *Lodore* refer to it as an indicator of Shelley's originality and promise:

> we think, moreover, that even the aforementioned little blue-stocking coteries can no longer doubt Mrs. Shelley's power of producing 'Frankenstein', or any other work of the highly imaginative class, after they peruse 'Lodore'. (L 545)

To Mary, depressed and pessimistic about her future, this comment from the *New Monthly Magazine* will have been particularly welcome. But embedded in the critical acclaim is the recurring suggestion that *Lodore* is not a contender for widespread public popularity: 'The work is very unlike the generality of our modern novels', was the reviewer's comment in *Fraser's Magazine*, who then delivered a long satirical description of contemporary sensationalist fiction (L 536). 'We think', *The Athenaeum* announced (on a similar tack), 'that all who can appreciate what is refined, and breathes of the affections rather than the passions, will share our pleasure' (L 532). *Fraser's* picks up the Byron/Lodore reading, while *The Examiner* clearly, if circumspectly, suggests the importance of a link between Lodore's rank and his behaviour. Nowhere is any mention made of Shelley's use of irony, and no reviewer was tempted to discuss the role of Fanny Derham.[13]

Whatever readers of later generations may make of the 1835 reviews, Shelley must have basked in their almost universal good opinion, and hoped for a pecuniary return that in the event never materialised. In 1837, on the eve of the publication of *Falkner*, she wrote hopefully to Charles Ollier, 'You said a New Novel might cause the remainder of Lodore to be sold.... Are you sure 700 are not sold & that £50 is not due to me?' (L II 280) *Lodore* had failed to catch the mass reading public, and the same fate awaited *Falkner*.

Shelley wrote *Falkner* during a period of particular difficulty. Her literary life was not unhealthy; she had reason to hope for great things
from *Lodore*, she felt confident about her new novel, and work
commissioned by Lardner for the *Cabinet Cyclopedia*   promised a
steady financial return for several years. The first batch of Lardner
essays appeared in 1835 in *Lives of the Most Eminent Literary and
Scientific Men of Italy, Spain and Portugal*, just one month before *Lodore*.
But this fact in itself reminds us of the pressure she was under. Her
health declined through 1835 partly for this reason, and also because
of the hours spent with her father, whose health had begun to fail.
Godwin died, aged 80, in April 1836. Earlier in the same year another
link with the past had gone when John and Maria Gisborne died. The
Journal (June 1836) provides a vivid insight into how Shelley set
herself to cope:

> But I! O my God – what a lot is mine – marked by tragedy &
> death – tracked by disappointment & unutterable wretched-
> ness – blow after blow – my heart dies within me – I say
> 'would I might die.' That is wicked – but life is a struggle & a
> burthen beyond my strength. My health is irremediably shat-
> tered – my hopes entirely low ...
>
> I have lost my dear darling Father – What I then went
> through – watching alone his dying hours! ...
>
> Thus is it – we struggle & storm but return to our task
> Master full soon. (J 548–9)

The 'task Master' is her writing, and in 1838 the next set of Lardner
essays appeared in Volume I of *Lives of the Most Eminent Men of
France*. Equally deleterious to her health was the continuing prepa-
ration of Shelley's *Poetical Works*. This appeared in January 1839, to
be followed by more Lardner essays. The death of her father not
only left Mary emotionally exhausted, it brought about a situation
which added a new threat to her precarious financial situation. She
was terrified that Godwin's life would now become the subject of
reminiscences that would stir up memories of his notoriety, not
least the relationship with Mary Wollstonecraft, and that there
would be a reaction from Sir Timothy. Trelawney, with an oppor-
tunist's eye for a reading public on the look-out for scandal, gossip
and tales of radical political drama, was eager to get started. Mary
knew exactly what kind of a book he would produce, and responded
with evident panic:

With regard to my Father's life – I certainly could not answer it to my conscience to give it up – I shall therefore do it – but I must wait. This year I have to fight my poor Percy's battle ... that this should be undertaken at a moment when a cry was raised against his Mother & that not on the question of *politics* but *religion*, would mar all – I must see him fairly launched, before I commit myself to the fury of the waves. (L II 280–1)

The writing of *Falkner* helped Shelley work her way through this fearful time. She moved back to London from Harrow, settling at 41d Park Street, Grosvenor Square, in 1837, and with the novel completed, had the satisfaction of seeing Percy Florence enter Trinity College Cambridge. Like *Lodore*, *Falkner* claims affinity with the silver-fork genre, the eponymous hero once more appearing in the guise of a tortured Byronic wanderer. But as his name suggests, Shelley is also addressing the memory of her father. The name of the principal aristocratic character in Godwin's first novel, *Caleb Williams*, was Falkland.

The heroine is Elizabeth Raby, who as an orphan child inadvertently saves Falkner from suicide, and is duly adopted by him. They travel across Europe: 'Outwardly', we are told, he might appear 'unemployed and tranquil', but inwardly he was 'torn by throes of the most tempestuous and agonising feelings' (FN I 40). He is eventually moved to join the fight for Greek independence:

> He was born to be a soldier; not the military man of modern days, but the hero who exposed his life without fear, and found joy in battle and hard earned victory, when these were sought and won for a good cause, from the cruel oppressor. (FN I 174)

Contemporary readers, remembering Byron's fate at Missolonghi, would have enjoyed reading how Falkner comes near to death in the campaign, only to be nursed back to health by his devoted foster-daughter. Elizabeth then falls in love with Gerard Neville; eventually we learn that he is the son of a woman wronged by Falkner in the past. The novel thus develops into a drama that sets Elizabeth's feeling of love for Neville against her deeply rooted sense of loyalty to Falkner. All the ingredients for a highly successful work of fiction are there: emotions run high, there are climactic moments of anger and sorrow, there are unsolved mysteries and moments of Gothic horror, not least when the body of Neville's mother is exhumed to establish who was truly guilty of her death. There is the *roman à clef* to play with, not just in the Falkner/Byron link, but in the portrait of Percy Shelley that shines through the young enthusiast for poetry and justice, Gerard Neville, 'essentially a dreamer and poet' (FN I 277): 'Gerard was young. He aspired to happiness with all the ardour of youth. While we are young, we feel as if happiness were the birthright of humanity ...' (FN III 14–15). But despite the possibilities of a plot that promised greater cohesion and momentum of action than *Lodore*, Shelley's tendency to lengthy introspective passages resulted in a novel where the narrative sinks beneath the weight of self-indulgent character analysis.

Shelley used the triangular relationship between Elizabeth Raby, Falkner and Neville to examine yet again the fraught history of her relationship with her father, her stepmother and her husband. Through her depiction of Elizabeth, and of Neville's mother, Alithea, she turned her attention to women's education and more generally to the position of women in society. But here more than ever we sense her looking back to the story of her own education, while the death of her father now left her agonisingly indecisive, as she hovered between her loyalty to Godwin (should she now memorialise his life, challenging a largely sceptical public?) and her love of Shelley. It was all written remorselessly into the novel:

> 'I am afraid,' she said, 'I suppose indeed that I am some-thing of a savage – unable to bend to the laws of civilization. I did not know this – I thought I was much like other girls – attached to their home and parents – fulfilling their daily duties, as the necessities of these parents demand.' (FN III 113)

'I thought I was much like other girls' is as telling a phrase as Shelley was to write. Towards the end of the book we quite literally witness the unearthing of a mother wronged not only by Falkner, but by others who were all too eager to believe the worst of her in life, and then to perpetuate their condemnation after her death.

Falkner, it emerges, abducted Alithea Neville believing her to be in love with him rather than her husband. He soon relents and attempts to release her from captivity. Before he is able to do so, however, she escapes, and is drowned in the course of her attempted flight. Shelley uses the plot to engage with two themes dear to her father's heart: the inadequacies of the legal system, and the evils of religious bigotry. The tragedy of Alithea's death is made all the worse by assumptions about her conduct based on the narrow religious beliefs of Alithea's former husband, Sir Boyvill; his closed, opinionated mind, the way he bullies and threatens his children (particularly Gerard), and his determination to think the worst of everyone, is presented as an inevitable consequence of what he likes to think of as his religious principles. Sir Boyvill is manifestly Mary letting off steam over her continuing harassment by Sir Timothy Shelley. As Gerard Neville reflects on the fate of his mother, on the father that Elizabeth feels she must be loyal to, and on the behaviour of his father, 'he began also to wonder by what strange coincidence they should both be doomed to sorrow, through the disasters of their parents' (FN III 97). It is Sir Boyvill's pleasure 'to despise everybody':

> to contradict everybody with marks of sarcasm and contempt, and to set himself up for an idol, and yet to scorn his worship-pers.... He had been a man of fashion, and retained as much good breeding as was compatible with a tetchy and revenge-ful temper.... (FN I 278–9)

Falkner was no more of a success than *Lodore*, but equally it did nothing to diminish the respect in which Shelley was now held as an author; but Sir Boyvill in fiction (if not in Shelley's reality) was already an outworn, dated trope, and it is likely that when Bulwer came to describe a recalcitrant aristocrat in his novel *Alice* (published the year after *Falkner*), his decision to call him Lord Raby might have been an invitation to compare him with Boyvill by way of suggesting that the days of bullying aristocrats are past; the modern magnate (though still pernicious) is a wholly different beast:

> A great man never loses so much as when he exhibits intoler-ance, or parades the right of persecution. 'My tenants shall vote exactly as they please,' said Lord Raby; and he was never known to have a tenant vote against his wishes![14]

Shelley's chief concern now became the task of negotiating terms with a 'tetchy and revengeful' Sir Timothy for the publication of her husband's poetry. In the four volumes of poetry and accompanying notes that were taking shape, she was reassembling her husband's life, reanimating him through his poetry and through her commentary upon it. From somewhere she found the stamina to see it through to a conclusion. 'The great work of life goes on', she wrote in October 1838, knowing it was nearing completion, but not knowing at that point whether or not her health would hold up long enough to allow her to complete it.

9
The Editor of Shelley, 1838–39

The sparseness of *Journal* entries for 1835–36 are a reminder of Shelley's poor health during this time. In November 1836 she went to Brighton, where she wrote of recovering 'slowly and painfully' (J 549). It was from Brighton in January 1837 that she wrote to Trelawney to say that she intended to write a life of her father, at the same time telling him that 'My happiness, my health, my fortunes are all wrecked ...' (L II 280). Trelawney visited her, and Claire was back in England, but these were not the friends she needed. If she did not know the detail, she knew well enough that both Claire and Trelawney were being less than complimentary about her behind her back. In February 1837 Trelawney was urging Claire to write a review of *Falkner* for *The Westminster Review*: 'will you do it,' he asked, adding, 'or failing that will you write me one of your long flighty fanciful letters commenting on the peculiarities and individuality of the Godwin school in which Mary is saturated... '.[1]

The publication in 1837 of Bulwer's *Ernest Maltravers* marked the cooling of another friendship. The one-time devotee of Percy Shelley's poetry was now changing tack, and doing so in his own authorial voice from the pages of his new novel:

> When Shelley, in one of his prefaces, boasts of being familiar with Alps and glaciers, and Heaven knows what, the critical artist cannot help wishing that he had been rather familiar with Fleet Street or the Strand. Perhaps, then, that remarkable genius might have been more capable of realizing characters of flesh and blood, and have composed corporeal and consummate wholes, not confused and glittering fragments.[2]

For Mary, this was yet one more betrayal in a long, wearisome sequence. Jane Williams Hogg, who had recently survived a difficult pregnancy, declined Shelley's invitation to join her for convalescence in Brighton: 'No! I have no friend – She who was once such is too absorbed in the disagreeableness of her own lot ...' (J 549). Working on the Shelley manuscripts did not help her sense of isolation, but she was writing to Julia Robinson who was staying in Ireland, and by the end of the year (1837), largely as a result of that correspondence, she was able to write, 'I am happier than I have been for years.... Tho' still too much alone, I am loved by some & that thought is peace to my heart' (J 551).

The move back into London from Harrow was good for her, and the reference to being 'loved by some' no doubt refers also to Samuel Rogers. Rogers (born in 1763) was a banker who had also enjoyed considerable success as a poet; he had admired and helped Godwin, and now acted as host to many of the leading literary and scientific celebrities of the day at his home in St James's Place. Throughout the 1830s and 1840s, Mary was a regular guest at Rogers's renowned breakfast parties. Besides her being an author of some repute, known also for her pending edition of Percy Shelley's poetry, there remained considerable interest in what the daughter of Godwin and Wollstonecraft was making of the volatile political state of affairs – hence her *Journal* note of 1838 that 'pretended friends' were inclined to criticise her 'lukewarmness in the "Good Cause"' (J 553). Few among those who met her can have long remained unaware of the influence of Sir Timothy Shelley on her conduct in this respect. In 1838, the year after the Chartists began to articulate working-class demands for the kind of sweeping political reforms that Percy Shelley would have endorsed, she continued to resist those who were urging her to come out publicly in favour of the 'People's Charter'. The risk such an act would constitute to the chances of seeing Percy's poems in print was simply too great; she believed the poems would liberate a force for good immeasurably greater than any public statement of her own views could ever be. Reflecting on the problem in her *Journal* for October 1838, she had recourse to the phrase used by Peacock in *Nightmare Abbey* (1818) to describe the aspirations of her parents and her husband, a phrase used satirically then ('a passion for reforming the world'), and certainly not without some irony by her now, twenty years on:

> In the first place with regard to the 'good Cause' – the right of
> the advancement of freedom and knowledge – of the Rights of

> Women &c – I am not a person of Opinions. I have said else-
> where that human beings differ greatly in this – some have a
> passion for reforming the world: others do not cling to partic-
> ular opinions. That my Parents & Shelley were of the former
> class, makes me respect it – I respect such when joined to real
> disinterestedness toleration & a clear understanding.... (J 553)

She was satisfied that the radicals who pressed her now lacked 'disinterestedness toleration & a clear understanding'. 'I am not for violent
extremes', she continued, adding that she had no confidence in her
'argumentative powers ... I feel the counter arguments too strongly'.
Chartism could well encourage a degree of unjustifiable lawlessness:
'it is not by taking away all restraining law that our improvement is to
be achieved' (J 554). She returns to the point some paragraphs later,
by which time her bitterness over the loss of Percy is flowing freely
and fuelling her candour:

> since I lost Shelley I have no wish to ally myself to the
> Radicals – they are full of repulsion to me. Violent without
> any sense of justice – selfish in the extreme – talking without
> knowledge – rude, envious & insolent – I wish to have
> nothing to do with them. (J 555)

She then goes on to admit to an uncertainty on her position over the
rights of women already illustrated in her treatment of Fanny Derham
in *Lodore*; she fears a hostile press; she feels guilt at her indecisiveness,
and in the process provides an oblique reflection on the way she has
become a victim of the egocentricity of her husband and her father.
'Victim' is not, of course, her own word for it, but it is a legacy that
when described sees both her father and husband as having abandoned her, the first of a long line of people to do so:

> To hang back, as I do, brings a penalty. I was nursed and fed
> with a love of glory. To be something great and good was the
> precept given me by my father: Shelley reiterated it. Alone &
> poor, I could only be something by joining a party – & there
> was much in me – the woman's love of looking up & being
> guided, & being willing to do any thing if any one supported
> & brought me forward, which would have made me a good
> partizan – but Shelley died & I was alone – my father from age
> & domestic circumstances & other things could not *me fair*

valoir – none else noticed me – had I been french I had been courted and flattered – & sympathized with. The solitude in which I lived with Shelley – my total friendlessness & want of connection – my first step in life (which except for that it was wrong I never repent on my own account – what ever may have been its effects) my being poor – my horror of pushing – & inability to put myself forward unless led, cherished & supported, all this has sunk me in a state of loneliness no other human being ever before I believe endured – Except Robinson Crusoe. How many tears & spasms of anguish this solitude has cost me lies buried in my memory – formed to feel pleasure in society – in intercourse with persons of wit & genius & the busy scene of life – how against the hair has fortune ever stroked me! (J 554–5)

Shelley's justification for her silence on radical reform comes to rest on a comparison between the social injustice complained of by the radicals, and the personal injustices she herself has suffered. She has her own personal bone to pick with her country: 'the usage I have suffered at her hands of neglect & loneliness would have been my dower nowhere else' (J 556).

Her final words are a desperate cry to be recognised for the person she is, not the one her contemporary 'accusers' would wish to make her: 'I am not all to blame – nor merit the heavy accusations cast on me for not putting myself forward – I *cannot* do that – it is against my nature – as well cast me from a precipice & rail at me for not flying' (J 559). Shelley, working on her husband's poems and preparing to write the life of her father, continues to reassert her right to be different from them. The message of *Lodore* regarding the control the dead can exercise over the living had indeed proved as true for her as it had for Ethel Villiers.

On 4 August 1838, through the good offices of John Gregson (Whitton's replacement as the Shelley family solicitor), Sir Timothy finally agreed to the publication of his son's *Poetical Works*. When the publisher Edward Moxon offered Mary £500 for the copyright, she was prompted to point out to Sir Timothy that despite his ban, pirated editions were being produced (the Galigni edition of 1828 and a two-volume *Shelley* in 1834 attributed to John Ascham), and pleaded her desperate need for the income. Sir Timothy's interest in his grandson (a young man who now clearly bore no resemblance to the character of his wayward father) had its part to play in his decision; Gregson also advanced the argument that sufficient time had elapsed to render Shelley's poetry no longer the threat to law and order it might once have been. Sir Timothy remained adamant that his son's life was not to be celebrated by a formal biographical tribute. Mary could agree to this since the biographical content was supplied through the medium of the notes she was writing to accompany the chronologically arranged contents.

The four-volume edition of *The Poetical Works of Percy Bysshe Shelley* appeared between January and May 1839. In August a second volume of Lardner's *Lives of the most Eminent Literary and Scientific Men of France* was published, to be followed in November by a one-volume *Poetical Works*. In December Shelley's *Essays, Letters from Abroad, Translations and Fragments* appeared. It is a list that looks like a triumphant culmination to Mary Shelley's career; the cherished Shelley memorial, born of immense effort and well-nigh intolerable heartache, had finally been completed. In the event, that was not how it turned out. An antagonistic response to the first volume of poems – notably from Trelawney and Hogg – left Mary with little time to savour the moment. Moxon had objected to the more overtly radical stanzas of *Queen Mab*, and Mary gave way, fearing that the whole project might be put in jeopardy. Trelawney and Hogg professed themselves outraged by her timidity; in her *Journal* Mary wrote: 'I feel that the great disappointment of my life is renewing itself & spreading desolation over those feelings which I too well know to be pregnant with moments of ineffable bliss' (J 562–3).

Julia Robinson nursed Shelley through a period of nervous exhaustion in March, after which work for Moxon continued. By the end of the month she had moved to a house near Putney. In November she was making coded jottings of a possible new romance. The object of her affections was probably Major Aubrey Beauclerk, a recently widowed reforming Member of Parliament. He remarried in 1841, but not to Mary Shelley (J 601–2). Around June 1840 a marked change of tone enters the *Journal*, and is sustained. Following all the difficulties of a year spent publishing her husband's work, Shelley now began preparations to spend the long vacation in Italy with Percy Florence and two of his Cambridge friends; the prospect of leaving England worked wonders, 'who on such a night must not feel the weight of sorrow lessened – For myself I repose in gentle & grateful reverie – & hope for others – & am content for myself.' (J 565)

It is all too easy to forget that while Shelley was suffering the mental anguish occasioned by work on her husband's poetry and prose, there was a part of her mind being called on to function in a very different way. She could not afford to be completely overwhelmed by her memories, nor by the physical symptoms of illness from which she was suffering. Much could be channelled in a controlled way into the novels *Lodore* and *Falkner*, but she also had an extensive programme of research and writing for Lardner. Lardner no doubt agreed to Mary Shelley as a contributor to the *Cabinet Cyclopedia* because of her reputation as a writer and researcher; but when his own history is considered, it also becomes clear that he may well have recognised a kindred spirit.

Lardner's background marks him out as a reader perfectly placed to appreciate to the full the intellectual matter that is woven into the plot of *Frankenstein*. Born in 1793, he developed an enthusiasm for science and its practical application that resulted in his rejection of a career in Law, directing him instead towards the study of logic, metaphysics, ethics, mathematics and physics, all of which he excelled at during his time at Trinity College, Dublin. He became involved in two encyclopaedic ventures, the *Encyclopaedia Edinensis* and the *Encyclopaedia Metropolitana*, and in 1827 he was elected to the Chair of natural philosophy at London University (now University College), where he initiated his own encyclopaedic project, the *Cabinet Cyclopedia*. The calibre of writers who agreed to contribute reflect the respect in which Lardner was generally held: Sir James Mackintosh wrote on English history, Sir Walter Scott on Scotland, and Thomas Moore on Ireland; Thirlwall wrote on Ancient Greece, Sismondi on Italy and Greece. Lardner himself contributed extensively on scientific subjects. The *Cabinet Cyclopedia* ran to 133 volumes and was completed in 1849. A second series, the *Cabinet Library*, was launched in 1830. This was wound up just two years later after a series of historical studies had been published.

Lardner maintained a high and sometimes controversial profile in the world of scientific debate, contributing articles across a wide range of journals and giving many lectures. He also attracted a degree of notoriety by conducting a protracted affair with the wife of Captain Richard Heaviside which culminated in an elopement in 1840. Lardner had separated from his first wife in 1820, though a formal divorce was not achieved until 1849. Heaviside went to court and was awarded £8000 damages. Lardner more than covered the debt by undertaking a lecture tour of the United States and Cuba. He settled in Paris in 1845 where he continued to lecture and publish; the list of his affiliations is remarkable, including the Royal Societies of London and

Edinburgh, the Royal Astronomical Society, the Linnaean Society, the Zoological Society, the Cambridge Philosophical Society, the Statistical Society of Paris, the Royal Irish Academy and the Society for Promoting Useful Arts in Scotland.

Lardner's politics were broadly in line with the radical French encyclopaedic tradition of the eighteenth-century *philosophes*. One of his most telling commissions in this respect was to engage Sir James Mackintosh to write *The History of England*. Mackintosh had been a member of Godwin's circle, and his name appears repeatedly on the roll-call of radical intellectuals in the 1790s. In 1792, along with other major dissenting figures including Paine, Priestley and Price, he had been made an honorary French citizen. He had written a less populist but no less radical riposte to Burke's *Reflections on the French Revolution* in 1791, the *Vindiciae Gallicae*. He died in 1832 before completing his contribution to the *Cyclopedia*. As his successor, Lardner chose W. Wallace, a man prepared to perpetuate the veteran historian's jaundiced view of eighteenth-century British history. In Volume VI, Chapter 3, the execution of Charles I prompted the following reflection on the British Constitution from Wallace:

> That popular delusion, called the ancient British constitution, is but an echo, propagated partly by English pride, partly as a device to prevent the improvement of civil polity from keeping its natural pace with popular reason and political science.[3]

The Revolution of 1688 is described as ushering in an age of cynical kingship and political manoeuvring, culminating in the Hanoverian succession. In Volume X Wallace wrote of George II:

> His predominant passions were Hanover and money; Pitt curbed the one, his mistresses made some successful assaults upon the other.... He was utterly destitute of all taste for literature or the arts; choleric in temper, obstinate in opinion; the slave of inveterate prejudices. It was not surprising to find strong superstition grafted upon such qualities; and it is confidently affirmed that he believed in Vampires.[4]

Wallace wrote in complete sympathy with Mackintosh's dislike of war, his scornful rejection of the irrational side of human nature, his commitment to common sense and the progress of science; he wrote also from a firm belief in the ideal of domestic love and virtue.

Though Shelley was not awarded the authorship of a 'History', her role was only marginally less prestigious. She would certainly have been expected to display her biographical subjects in a manner in keeping with the Lardner model, and this was frequently achieved through summoning up an idealised image of Percy Shelley. Not all the essays in Volumes I and II of *Eminent Literary and Scientific Men of Italy, Spain, and Portugal* are by her; one clue to her authorship in these circumstances is the glimpse we seem to get of Percy in some cases, while not in others. The essay on Boccaccio tells of how the poet had been tempted 'by superstitious zeal' to give up letters. He was then advised by Plutarch that 'learning was of small avail to its possessor, unless combined with moral principle and virtuous habits'.[5] The people of whom Shelley approves will be found to combine 'moral principles and virtuous habits', and to reject 'superstitious zeal'; they are Enlightenment radicals who, like Machiavelli and Galileo, were misunderstood and abused in their time, and who have been misrepresented ever since. It is surely the editor of Percy Shelley's *Poetical Works* who writes of Machiavelli, 'There is no more delightful literary task than the justifying a hero or writer, who has been misrepresented and reviled.'[6] Galileo was the victim of 'the presumptuous priest pronouncing infallible the decrees of his own erring judgement.'[7]

A number of the essays were brief sketches, but the sixteenth-century poet Tasso inspired a lengthy study. He was a man who suffered the fate of a true poet, his 'self-tormenting mind' eventually collapsing into madness.[8] There are echoes here of Shelley's poem *Julian and Maddalo*, and Mary will no doubt have reached once more for Byron's *The Lament of Tasso*:

> The wretched are the faithful; 'tis their fate
> To have all feeling, save the one, decay,
> And every passion into one dilate,
> As rapid rivers into ocean pour;
> But ours is fathomless, and hath no shore.[9]

The essays of 1835 and 1838 exhibit Shelley's thoroughness as a researcher. Much of the writing is detailed and unimpassioned, and displays an authoritative – and at times sleep-inducing – command of the minutiae. The essays tend to come alive when she enters more anecdotal waters, at which point her own personality begins to find its way through an otherwise frequently turgid prose. The essay on Rabelais in Volume I of *Eminent Literary and Scientific Men of France* is a characteristic mix of detail and anecdotal entertainment. Again, it is hard not to believe that this is Shelley's work when we read how Rabelais was brave enough to attack the 'wickedness and vices of popes, the lazy luxurious lives and griping avarice of the prelates, the debauchery, knavery and ignorance of the monastic orders, the barbarous and absurd theology of the Sorbonne, and the no less barbarous and absurd jurisprudence of the high tribunals of the kingdom'. Rabelais was an honest man who suffered from 'impertinent fictions' put about by an establishment determined to blacken his character.[10] Having castigated 'The purveyors of anecdotes', Shelley proceeds to use anecdotal evidence on behalf of her subject. Rabelais is said to have requested excommunication. His reason was that when a heretic was burned, any piece of wood not catching alight was excommunicated by the Pope. With his own likely fate in mind, therefore, Rabelais explained that 'he wished to be rendered incombustible by the same process.'[11]

The religious Establishment and the aristocracy at their worst were constantly in Shelley's sights. In the midst of much that is worthy but pedestrian in her essay on La Rochefoucauld, the following passage glows with controlled anger:

> To detail the conduct of a nobility emancipated from all legal as well as all moral and religious constraint, – bent only on the acquisition of power, – influenced by hatred and selfishness, – is no interesting task. It may be instructive; for we see what an aristocracy may become, when it throws off the control of a court, whose interest it is to enforce order, – and of the people, who spontaneously love and admire virtue, – and at once tramples on religion and law.[12]

The general point becomes, perhaps, even more obviously a personal one when she turns to Molière. *Tartuffe*, she writes, 'is a play which showed up the hypocrisy of those who cloaked the worst designs, and brought discord and hatred into families, under the guise of piety'.[13] It is a short step from this to Sir Boyvill in *Falkner*, and from Sir Boyvill to her father-in-law.

It is important to survey Shelley's work for Lardner if only to be reminded of her extraordinary ability to continue producing copy while under such extreme pressure during these years. It is hardly surprising that her work continued to reveal her habitual engagement with the past; Claire's attack on her for idolising Byron effectively made the same point:

> I stick to *Frankenstein*, merely because that vile spirit [Byron]
> does not haunt its pages as it does in all your other novels, now
> as Castruccio, now as Raymond, now as Lodore. Good God! To
> think a person of your genius, whose moral tact ought to be
> proportionately exalted, should think it a task befitting its
> powers to gild and embellish and pass off as beautiful what was
> the merest compound of vanity, folly, and every miserable
> weakness that ever met together in one human being!... You
> could write upon metaphysics, politics, jurisprudence, astron-
> omy, mathematics – all those highest subjects which they taunt
> us with being incapable of treating, and surpass them; and what
> a consolation it would be, when they begin some of their prosy,
> lying, but plausible attacks upon female inferiority, to stop their
> mouths in a moment with your name, and then to add, 'and if
> women, while suffering the heaviest slavery, could out-do you,
> what would they not achieve were they free?'[14]

Claire comes across as far more a true disciple of Godwin, Wollstonecraft
and Percy Shelley than Mary (in word at least). Yet it was Mary who had
continued to pursue a literary life. Against Claire's clarion call we have
Mary's eloquent, weary letter of June 1835 to Maria Gisborne:

> You talk about my poetry – & about the encouragement I am
> to find from Jane and my Father. When they read all the fine
> things you said they thought it right to attack me....
>   You speak of women's intellect ... I know that however clever
> I may be there is in me a vacillation, a weakness, a want of 'eagle
> winged' resolution that appertains to my intellect as well as my
> moral character.... In short my belief is ... that the sex of our
> material mechanism makes us quite different creatures – better
> though weaker but wanting in the higher grades of intellect....
>   ... I have been so barbarously handled both by fortune & my
> fellow creatures – that I am no longer the same as when you
> knew me – I have no hope – In a few years when I get over my
> present feelings & live wholly in Percy I shall be happier....

Shelley wrote this while she was ill, yet she remains the author of
Lodore and *Falkner*, the seemingly indefatigable member of Lardner's
team, the dogged editor of her husband's poetry and prose. The poem
she refers to was called 'A Dirge' and she transcribed it at the end of
the letter; that and the postscript are evidence enough of the extent to

which Shelley was still 'the author of *Frankenstein*', the prisoner of her past. The attitude of her father could not be ignored, nor indeed could that of Jane Williams Hogg:

> Papa loves not the memory of S – because – he feels he injured him; – and Jane – Do you not understand enough of her to unwind the thoughts that make it distasteful to her that I should feel – & above all be thought of by others to feel & have a right to feel – O the human heart – it is a strange juggle. –

A Dirge

1

This morn thy gallant bark, Love,
   Sailed on a sunny sea;
'Tis noon, & tempests dark, Love,
   Have wrecked it on the lee –

Ah Woe – ah woe, ah woe
   By spirits of the deep
   He's cradled on the billow,
   To his unwaking sleep!

2

Thou liest upon the shore, Love,
   Beside the knelling surge;
But sea-nymphs ever more, Love,
   Shall sadly chaunt thy dirge.

O come, O come – O come!
   Ye spirits of the deep!
   While near his sea-weed pillow
   My lonely watch I keep.

3

From far across the sea, Love,
   I hear a wild lament,
By Echo's voice for thee, Love,
   From Ocean's cavern's sent

   O list! O list! O list!
The Spirits of the deep –
Loud sounds their wail of sorrow –
While I for ever weep!

(L II 27–9)

With the publication of Percy Shelley's poetry and prose in 1839–40, the main vehicle by which Mary strove to establish her husband as a virtuous man and a poet of genius was completed. *The Poetical Works* are to be considered here primarily for the part they played in Mary Shelley's literary career. First of all we should consider the magnitude of the task, particularly when it came to reconstructing a virtuous Percy Shelley. In December 1838, Shelley wrote to Hogg to request the loan of his first edition of *Queen Mab* to help her in her editorial labours. Hogg replied that he had lent it to someone else who had not returned it. Though it is difficult, once immersed in Shelley's letters and the *Journal*, not to share her mistrust of Hogg, on this occasion his story could well have been true. *Queen Mab* had become a highly desirable text. Its appearance in 1813 had marked Percy Shelley down in the public eye as a blasphemous libertine, a view that had become entrenched by the time of Mary's first attempt to put the record straight with *Posthumous Poems* in 1824. George Cannon, a man profoundly disliked by Mary and Percy, published extracts from the poem in the *Theological Enquirer* of 1815, and in 1821 there was a pirated edition by William Clark, an American edition appearing at the same time. Clark was prosecuted by the Society for the Suppression of Vice and spent four months in prison. Many of the individuals involved in the *Queen Mab* piracy (Clark, Cannon and Thomas Moses) were also active in the clandestine publication of pornography.

There was nothing Percy Shelley could do after *Queen Mab* to redeem himself in the eyes of the critics even had he wished to. Lockhart, reviewing *Alastor* in *Blackwood's Magazine* in 1819 alluded to the charges of 'immorality and wickedness' against the poet, insisting that 'we do not think he believes his own creed'.[15] Shelley, he declared, was capable of being a great poet, but he must first clean up his life and opinions. The *British Review* was more straightforward when it came to assessing *The Cenci* in 1821: 'Such blasphemous ravings cannot be poetry, for they are neither sense nor nature.'[16]

One way to try and set the record straight was to publish all the poetry, thus setting *Queen Mab* in context as the poem of a still young, impetuous lover. Another was to compose a revisionary biography. In her letter of December 1838 to Hogg requesting his *Queen Mab*, Mary had written, 'Sir Timothy forbids biography – but I mean to write a few notes appertaining to the history of the poems ...' (L II 301). She knew she was never going to be able to write Percy's life in the way she might a Galileo, Machiavelli or a Rabelais, even had Sir Timothy allowed it; what she could do was use a Preface, and the editorial machinery of extensive notes, to produce a vindication of his character and a critique of his work that would display him as one of the greatest poets and thinkers of his age.

In the opening paragraph of the Preface to the 1839 *Poetical Works* she set out her intentions with characteristic clarity. The contrast between the authoritative public voice of Mary Shelley and the woman riddled by self-doubt and regret who had written to Maria Gisborne in 1835 is remarkable. While she bows to Sir Timothy's demands, 'I abstain from any remark on the occurrences of his private life ...', she takes him to the very edge of that proscription, 'except inasmuch as the passions which they engendered inspired his poetry':

> Obstacles have long existed to my presenting the public with a perfect edition of Shelley's poems. These being at last happily removed, I hasten to fulfil an important duty, – that of giving the productions of a sublime genius to the world ... and ... at the same time, detailing the history of those productions, as they sprang, living and warm, from his heart and brain. I abstain from any remark on the occurrences of his private life.... No account of these events has ever been given at all approaching reality in their details, either as regards himself or others.... Shelley may ... be fearlessly avowed by those who loved him, in the firm conviction that ... his character would stand in fairer and brighter light than that of any contemporary. (PW xxi)

The 1839 *Poetical Works* constitute another biographical work by Mary Shelley, albeit in a unique form; there is a quite distinct discussion to be had about Shelley's editorship. The proliferation of textual errors and of various omissions do not place her achievement significantly below the work of many other nineteenth-century editors. The fact that she used the Galigny edition and Ascham as copy for Moxon where possible rather than sending valuable originals to the printer by post was hardly surprising. In the case of Galigny, it was a publication she had encouraged and assisted, and therefore had good reason for confidence in its accuracy.[17] Anyone who has seen samples of Percy Shelley's original manuscripts must be left wondering how any definitive reading – then or ever – might be arrived at. The awkwardness of the following sentence serves as a reminder that late-twentieth-century editors confront a task every bit as difficult as that which faced their predecessors: 'Broadly speaking, the criterion has been to arrive at that copy text which, given what the author's intentions may be supposed to have been, requires the least editorial disturbance.'[18] In that circumlocutory 'may be supposed to have been' we have the crux of a much larger problem than mere legibility. Shelley felt confident that she knew not 'what the author's intentions may be supposed to have been'; as the man's wife she was satisfied she knew *precisely* what they were, and that knowledge was informed by her personal need to repair their interrupted relationship. Hence the 1839 Preface claimed a character for the poet in open defiance of existing perceptions. If outrage over Shelley as a libertine atheist had cooled somewhat, the notion of him as a seriously flawed character responsible for a school of poetry at best superficial in its fancifulness, at worst harmful to the nation's cultural and moral health, lived on. In his review of the *Posthumous Poems* of 1824 Hazlitt wrote:

> Whatever was new, untried, unheard of, unauthorized, exerted a kind of fascination over his mind.... The worst of it however was, that he thus gave great encouragement to those who believed in all received absurdities, and are wedded to all existing abuses: his extravagance seeming to sanction their grossness and selfishness, as theirs were a full justification of his folly and eccentricity.[19]

Against this Mary Shelley asserted her husband's essential goodness, 'a gentle and cordial goodness that animated his intercourse with warm affection and helpful sympathy'. He clothed that goodness in 'the fervent eloquence with which he discussed such subjects', in order to bring about 'human happiness and improvement' in the world at large. The Shelley who expressed his 'genuine and unforced inspiration' in poetry is the Shelley who still lives: 'his influence over mankind, though slow in growth, is fast augmenting ... ' (PW xxi-xxii). The political Shelley is not ignored, but is treated as already something of an anachronism. To a readership for whom the political battles of the 1830s constituted the context for politically oriented poetry, Mary concedes that Shelley's work will be hard to understand. 'He looked on political freedom as the direct agent to effect the happiness of mankind', she wrote, but in this he might be expected to be misunderstood by the 'younger generation rising around' on at least two counts (PW xxi). Firstly, few will share Shelley's ability to feel passionately 'on general and unselfish subjects'; passion, yes, but the focus of passion these days is increasingly selfish. Secondly, politically, Shelley's is now a voice from the past; the new generation 'cannot remember the scorn and hatred with which the partisans and reformers were regarded some few years ago, nor the persecutions to which they were exposed'. It will also therefore be difficult to understand the truth about what Shelley's beliefs were when it comes to love. Put all scandalous gossip to one side: 'Shelley's conception of love was exalted, absorbing, allied to all that is purest and noblest in our nature, and warmed by earnest passion ...' (PW xxi–xxii).

As well as correcting the misinformed reader on Shelley, Mary makes a case for her own behaviour towards him in the years immediately before his death. Her 'accusers', as she calls them, should be reminded that:

> A wise friend once wrote to Shelley: 'You are still very young, and in certain essential respects you do not yet sufficiently perceive that you are so.' ... time was not given to him to attain this knowledge.... The calm of middle life did not add the seal of the virtues which adorn maturity to those generated by the vehement spirit of youth. (PW xxiii)

Written at a time when the Romantic Movement in England was perceived to have died with Shelley's ill-fated generation, and when the few survivors were busy reconstructing themselves, this statement lays the coping-stone upon the edifice of the Romantic Poet constructed over previous decades by many hands. He is in possession of an imagination that renders him at once great and unfathomable, he is working beyond the limits of most mortals, 'few of us understand or sympathize with the endeavour to ally the love of abstract beauty, and adoration of abstract good ... with our sympathies with our kind' (PW xxii), yet he dies short of his maturity, having suffered the pain of physical illness, and the pain of rejection by his fellow beings:

> The weight of thought and feeling burdened him heavily; you read his sufferings in his attenuated frame, while you perceived the mastery he held over them in his animated countenance and brilliant eyes. (PW xxiii)

Though a passage such as this suggests that the *Poetical Works* helped set the seal on the image of the Romantic Poet, Shelley described her work as only 'the first stone of a monument due to Shelley's genius, his sufferings, and his virtues' (PW xxiv). It was certainly early days when it came to replacing the public perception of Shelley as an atheist with the image of a man patiently waiting for his wife to join him in Heaven:

> It is our best consolation to know that such a pure-minded and exalted being was once among us, and now exists where we hope one day to join him; – although the intolerant, in their blindness, poured down anathemas, the Spirit of Good, who can judge the heart, never rejected him. (PW xxiii)

Compared to present-day editions of Shelley's complete poetical works, the layout of the 1839 contents pages has an uncluttered look that emphasises the way the poetry charts the chronology of the life. Volumes One and Two contain the longer poems from *Queen Mab* through to *Hellas*; Volumes Two and Three group the shorter poems year by year (with a note on each group), going from 'Early Poems' to 'Poems of 1816', and then on year by year to 1822. At this point Mary reprinted her Preface to the *Posthumous Poems* of 1824.

The note to *Queen Mab* begins with a reminder that Shelley wrote the poem when he was just 18. Mary emphasises the poet's inexperience, and hence what she suggests is the uncharacteristic nature of the work. It is indeed remarkable, but remarkable 'as the production of a boy of eighteen', and having already been 'frequently reprinted, the omission would be vain'. Percy Shelley's own notes to *Queen Mab* are reprinted 'not because they are models of reasoning or lessons of truth' (they contain some of Shelley's most radical pronouncements) 'but because ... all that a man at once so distinguished and so excellent ever did deserves to be preserved'. She adds at once that, 'The alterations his opinions underwent' must also be made clear, 'for they form his history' (PW 835).

The 'history' begins with Shelley at Eton, and elaborates the image of the young ingenuous idealist that no biographer has been able wholly to resist ever since:

> It was the cardinal article of his faith that, if men were but taught and induced to treat their fellows with love, charity, and equal rights, this earth would realize paradise. He looked upon religion, as it is professed, and above all practised, as hostile instead of friendly to the cultivation of those virtues which would make men brothers.

> Can this be wondered at? At the age of seventeen, fragile in health and frame, of the purest habits in morals ... he was treated as a reprobate, cast forth as a criminal.
>
> The cause was that he was sincere; that he believed the opinions which he entertained to be true. And he loved with a Martyr's love; he was ready to sacrifice station and fortune, and his dearest affections, at its shrine. The sacrifice was demanded from, and made by, a youth of seventeen. (PW 836)

As the essay continues, we witness an intriguing reversal of roles brought about by the passage of time. Shelley no longer tutors the 16-year-old daughter of Godwin and Wollstonecraft; it is now her turn to lecture him:

> His readings were not always well chosen; among them were the works of the French philosophers.... He was a lover of the wonderful and wild in literature, but had not fostered these tastes at their genuine sources – the romances and chivalry of the middle ages – but in the perusal of such German works as were current in those days. (PW 836–7)

The poet of *Alastor* has grown up, his youthful enthusiasm tempered by 'the sad realities of life' (PW 30). There can of course be no specific mention of Harriet, and indeed Mary writes herself out of the European adventures of 1814–15; only Percy is described as visiting Switzerland and the Rhine. A 'few friends' join him on his excursions up the Thames in 1815, and once written, the contrast between *Queen Mab* and *Alastor* is profound:

> None of Shelley's poems is more characteristic than this. The solemn spirit that reigns throughout, the worship of the majesty of nature, the broodings of a poet's heart in solitude ... it was the outpourings of his own emotions, embodied in the purest form he could conceive.... (PW 31)

The Revolt of Islam is described as the result of time spent once more in Switzerland in 1816, when 'his genius was checked by association with another poet whose nature was utterly dissimilar to his own', and influenced by the difficulties he encountered on his return home. Byron is to be disapproved of; Shelley is the bereaved husband of Harriet whose grief dare not be told:

> such was his fear to wound the feelings of others that he
> never expressed the anguish he felt, and seldom gave vent to
> the indignation roused by the persecution he underwent....
> (PW 156)

This implies that Shelley's response to Harriet's suicide was not
cynical indifference; he behaved as he did out of concern for Mary's
feelings. The true Shelley will be found in the character of Laon, the
hero of *The Revolt*, 'animated throughout by an ardent love of virtue,
and a resolution to confer the boons of political and intellectual
freedom on his fellow-creatures' (PW 156). This is followed by a
description of the wretched state of the inhabitants of Marlow where
the couple were living in 1817, an experience that played a major part
in the political agenda of the poem. The countryside was beautiful,
but the wealth of nature was in the 'form of gentlemen's parks or soil
dedicated to agriculture'. A wretched harvest coupled with the Poor
Laws 'ground to the dust not only the paupers, but those who had
risen just above that state' (PW 157). The condition of most of the
inhabitants of Marlow 'stamps with reality his pleadings for the
human race'. In an interesting aside she adds '(I hope it is altered
now)'; if there is irony intended here, the general intention is clearly
to distance Shelley's postwar politics from the very different world of
the late 1830s.

The note concludes with a letter from Shelley to Godwin in reply to
the latter's criticism of *The Revolt* and other writings. It is well chosen;
Shelley comes out of it with considerable credit, since it is evident that
Godwin had been characteristically trenchant in his criticism.
Deference is delivered through rhetorically clenched teeth; Shelley is
a patient man, willing to learn from his mistakes, whatever the cost to
his pride might be: 'I cannot but be conscious, in much of what I
write, of an absence of that tranquillity which is the attribute and
accompaniment of power' (PW 158). This statement encapsulates a
central theme of Mary Shelley's fiction; she explored it primarily
through the restlessness of her heroes and the contrasting 'tranquillity' of her heroines.

The Shelleys' departure for Europe in March 1818 is described at the
beginning of the note to *Prometheus Unbound*. While never denying
the importance for the poetry of political opinion, Mary continues to
nudge the image of her husband towards that of a nature poet. The
main reason for travelling to Italy was for the good of Shelley's delicate health; as long as he stayed in England 'His dearest pleasure, the

free enjoyment of scenes of Nature, was marred by the same circum-stance.' (PW 270) She continues also to set his beliefs within the context of orthodox Christianity. Shelley believed that evil was 'not inherent in the system of creation, but an accident that might be expelled. This also forms a portion of Christianity: God made earth and man perfect, till he, by his fall, "Brought death into the world and all our woe."' (PW 271). Shelley believed that 'mankind had only to will that there should be no evil, and there would be none'. In fact it becomes clear that Mary understood the nature of her husband's thinking only too well, saw how it informed his poetry, and knew that she could never wholly embrace the consequences. Her strategy for dealing with this is to claim greatness for the poetry, while apologis-ing for some of the less palatable implications of the ideas involved by way of reference to the peculiar circumstances in which he worked:

> Shelley adapted the catastrophe of this story [*Prometheus*] to his peculiar views. The son greater than his father…was to dethrone evil…. England had been rendered a painful residence to Shelley, as much by the sort of persecution with which in those days all men of liberal opinions were visited. (PW 272)

The distancing effect of 'in those days' confirms the qualifying tone. He had come to believe 'that the majority of his countrymen regarded him with sentiments of aversion as his own heart could experience towards none' (PW 274). This alludes, at least in part, to his separation from the children of his first marriage.

In her note on the Poems of 1817, Mary had more to say about the Chancery ruling. 'No words can express the anguish he felt', she wrote; his response had been anger coupled with 'all the tenderness of a father's love', and she describes the fear which grew in him of having his children by Mary taken away (PW 551–2). To understand this poet properly, she maintains, you must see him as 'a man who brooded over his wrongs and woes, and was impelled to shed the grace of his genius over the uncontrollable emotions of his heart' (PW 552). There are clear echoes here of the fate of Tasso, the poet she was researching and writing on for Lardner at the time. Percy Shelley could scarcely have asked for a more eloquent writer to plead his cause, and passages such as this continue to influence even the most determinedly objective biographers.

Mary Shelley claimed that *The Cenci* of 1819 was Shelley's finest work. Set in Italy in 1599, it is a play about paternal tyranny, and it is not difficult to see why it came to have such a strong hold over Mary's imagination. She tells us that Shelley had first urged her to write a play around the story, but she convinced him that he should do it. She was then given a rare opportunity to influence its composition: 'This tragedy is the only one of his works that he communicated to me during its progress. We talked over the arrangements of the scenes together...' (PW 335). Later she claims, 'The Fifth Act is a masterpiece. It is the finest thing he ever wrote, and may claim proud comparison not only with any contemporary, but preceding poetry.' (PW 337) The main theme of the story reflected in many ways the drama of Mary's own domestic life with Percy. Beatrice, daughter of Count Francesco Cenci, loves Orsino; but Orsino becomes a priest and must therefore deny his true passion. Beatrice has this to deal with as well as the tyrannous behaviour of her father towards his family. Mary makes much of the accuracy with which Shelley describes the turbulent feelings in the 'noble heart' of Beatrice, evidently reading it as a portrait of herself. In Act I Scene 2, she sternly explains to her former lover (Orsino) why she can only 'swear a cold fidelity' to him; her family (her brother Bernard and her mother) must come first. Her love for Orsino is now 'turned to bitter pain':

> Alas, Orsino! All the love that once
> I felt for you is turned to bitter pain.
> Ours was a youthful contract, which you first
> Broke, by assuming vows no Pope will loose.
> And thus I love you still, but holily;
> Even as a sister or a spirit might;
> And so I swear a cold fidelity.
> (PW 282–3 ll. 20–6)

The death of Clara in September 1818 is recorded in the note to *Julian and Maddalo*, and Shelley is portrayed as having done all he could to save the child; the death of William in Rome, and their subsequent removal to the Villa Valsovana near Leghorn is described in the note to *The Cenci*. Her image of Shelley writing poetry in his 'airy cell' at the top of the villa, observing both land and sea, the vagaries of the weather, the storms, 'the dazzling sunlight and the heat', has again stamped itself indelibly on subsequent biography. Mary's description of intense creativity linked to an unimpeded experience of the natural world, 'the dark lurid clouds...waterspouts that churned up the waters beneath...the dazzling sunlight and heat...' is writing that has come to epitomise the inspirational quality of Romantic poetry (PW 336).

Mary used her note on *The Mask of Anarchy* to try to bring Shelley's views within sight of her own in the 1830s. 'Shelley's first eager desire to excite his countrymen to resist openly... had faded with early youth.' He was, she insists, 'a republican, and loved democracy', but her approach to this poem – as it is to Shelley's political views elsewhere – is to reiterate her 'in those days' reminder. These are matters of past history: 'Days of outrage have passed away, and with them the exasperation that would cause such an appeal to the many to be injurious.' (PW 345). What is left is the poetry, and it is on that that Percy Shelley's reputation must ultimately stand or fall.

The commentary on *The Witch of Atlas* contains a note of self-justification aimed at those she knows still think of her as an unsympathetic wife. She admits that she wished Shelley to follow *The Cenci* with something similarly accessible in plot and theme; instead he wrote a poem 'wildly fanciful, full of brilliant imagery, and discarding human interest and passion'. She had no wish for Shelley to seek popularity for its own sake: 'but I believed that he would obtain a greater mastery over his own powers.... Even now I believe that I was in the right.' Ultimately to blame is the English public, far too busy cooking up scandalous stories about him and revelling in 'flagitious calumnies and insulting abuse' to realise that they had a poetic genius in their midst (PW 388). Shelley was driven to think and write as he did by the attentions of a philistine readership and the insensitivity of reactionary reviewers.

The notes for the Poems of 1821 and 1822 focus primarily on Shelley's way of life, in particular his love of boats; the public persona and the politics are replaced by domestic detail as the narrative winds its way painfully towards his death. When the time comes, she tells the final chapter with a characteristic blend of precision and passion that confirms just how immediate and distressing the tragedy still was for her as she sat in her house in Putney in May 1839. Yet in the measured expression of her grief, the essay reveals too the manner in which she was able to write herself through it. The experience partook of a spiritual quality, 'lifting it from everyday life', and this ultimately sanctified the death of a poet who only now – after 17 years – was rewarded with a worthy monument, the *Poetical Works*:

> Not long before, talking of presentiment, he said that the only one he ever found infallible was the certain advent of some evil fortune when he felt particularly joyous. Yet, if ever

fate whispered of coming disaster, such inaudible but not unfelt prognostics hovered around us. The beauty of the place seemed unearthly in its excess: the distance we were at from all signs of civilization, the sea at our feet, its murmurs or its roaring for ever in our ears, – all these things led the mind to brood over strange thoughts, and, lifting it from everyday life, caused it to be familiar with the unreal. A sort of spell surrounded us; and each day, as the voyagers did not return, we grew restless and disquieted, and yet, strange to say, we were not fearful of the most apparent danger.

The spell snapped; it was all over; an interval of agonizing doubt – of days passed in miserable journeys to gain tidings, of hopes that took firmer root even as they were more baseless – was changed to the certainty of the death that eclipsed all happiness for the survivors for ever more. (PW 678)

This narrative of Mary Shelley's literary life has tended to resemble her own fictional storylines. *The Poetical Works* has pulled us back from 1839 to re-examine the years from 1814 to 1822. Throughout her published and unpublished writing the dividing line between reality and fiction is forever dissolving and reappearing, as she worked her way from present to past and back once more to what was left of the present. *The Poetical Works*, along with the prose published in December 1839, was to be Mary Shelley's last major publication. In August a second volume of Lardner's *Lives of the Most Eminent Literary and Scientific Men of France* appeared, and in 1844 she was to publish an account of her summer tour on the continent undertaken with Percy Florence in 1842. The final decade of her life proved no less eventful for its relative lack of literary activity, however, and there was no shortage of ghosts from the past waiting to dog her footsteps to the grave.

10
'Ten years which have made me old'[1]

With Mary Shelley's publications of 1839 and 1840, English readers now had before them a reconstituted Percy Shelley, a poet who would in due course even repent of his atheism.[2] In an essay of 1952, 'The Case of Shelley', Frederick A. Pottle provided a comprehensive survey of Shelley's posthumous career, at the centre of which stands the *Poetical Works* of 1839.[3] For all her persuasive rhetoric, Mary and her succeeding apologists were never able to dispel entirely the opprobrium attached to Percy Shelley's atheism, and his life of apparent moral laxity. But as the nineteenth century entered its latter decades, Pottle observes that if Shelley were to be criticised, it was as a poet of 'unreality and unsubstantiality' rather than a libertine.[4] When, in 1875, Swinburne declared that Shelley was 'supreme and without a second to his race', his enthusiasm was typical of his generation.[5]

Mary Shelley had always insisted on the need to assess Shelley first and foremost as a poet; and well before the end of the century, Pottle argues, in America as well as England, Shelley had come to be regarded as 'one of the greatest English poets'.[6] E. Rhys's 1886 edition of Shelley's prose illustrates how influential the critical approach established by Mary Shelley had become. Rhys argues that the poet's claim to fame rests on the beauty of his style and manifest sincerity. He was seeking to combat an attack on Shelley by John Cordy Jeaffreson in his book *The Real Shelley*, published in 1885. Jeaffreson's 'New View of the Poetic Life' of Shelley is a reminder that the dissenters by no means abandoned the field of conflict in the nineteenth century, though by the early 1900s Thomas Hardy and George Bernard Shaw were responsible, with W. B. Yeats, for confirming Shelley's reputation as one of England's finest poets and thinkers.

Mary Shelley's contribution to this narrative of critical reception was seminal, but after her death in 1851, Jane St John, who married Percy Florence Shelley in 1848, was scarcely less important. Lady Jane (as she became) willingly took on the role of keeper of the flame, exercising – with her husband – complete control over the Shelley archive, perpetuating and embellishing Mary's poet of the 1839 editions. Richard Holmes has described how Lady Jane 'made it her life work to establish an unimpeachable feminine and Victorian idealization of the poet.... a misunderstood man more sinned against than sinning'. This was achieved through 'Suppression, alteration and even destruction of certain journals, letters and papers', and by maintaining a firm hold over Shelley scholarship.[7] She called in particular on the services of Richard Garnett and Edward Dowden. Garnett, keeper of printed books at the British Museum, advised on documents that might be advantageously lost; he was a man whose 'preference for reputation over virtue was excessive even by Victorian standards.'[8] Dowden's adulatory two-volume *Shelley* appeared in 1886.

Given what Mary Shelley's intentions for her husband were, it is interesting to note that the quotation from Schiller with which the 1840 edition of the *Prose* begins suggests – at the very least – an unwillingness to compromise. The poet is 'the son of his time; but pity for him if he is its pupil, or even its favourite!'. He should grow to manhood elsewhere, and return (as Mary Shelley was now 'returning' Percy) 'a foreign shape, into his century; not however to delight it by its presence, but dreadful like the son of Agamemnon, to purify it'.[9] In her Preface, however, Mary insists that the public needs a knowledge of the poet as a man, rather than as a political thinker:

> I do not conceal that I am far from satisfied with the tone in which the criticisms on Shelley are written. Some among these writers praise the poetry with enthusiasm and even discrimination; but none understand the man. (S xxi)

Percy Shelley's prose writing is an important body of work 'whence those who did not know him may form a juster estimate of his virtues and his genius than has hitherto been done' (S v). His dubious record on morality will be put in the context of a man whose 'aspirations for a brotherhood of love' could result in 'tender bewailings springing from a too sensitive spirit'; what will invariably emerge from his pages, she argues, is his undoubted 'sincerity', and an unerring beauty of style (S vi).

In discussing one of the most potentially problematic texts, the translation of Plato's *Symposium*, which considers free love, she concentrates almost entirely on her husband's 'splendid and melodious' command of the language (S viii). She uses the unfinished novel, *The Assassins*, to correct the idea that he had no time for orthodox domesticity. It was written, she suggests, in a style 'warmed by the fire of youth', but a sensitive reader will appreciate that 'it breathes that spirit of domestic peace and general brotherhood founded on love' (S ix). Throughout her Preface, Mary leads Percy towards Christian redemption. No matter what his political and religious views may have been while he was alive, his eventual salvation is ensured by the beauty of his art:

> For myself, no religious doctrine, nor philosophical precept, can shake the faith that a mind so original, so delicately and beautifully moulded, as Shelley's ... would never be shattered and dispersed by the Creator; but that the qualities and consciousness that formed him, are not only indestructible in themselves, were united here, and that to become worthy of him is to assure the bliss of a reunion. (S xiii)

Volume I of the *Prose* contained philosophical and speculative pieces, while Volume II brought together material of a more domestic nature, including a selection of letters and essays, and a reprint of the *History of a Six Weeks' Tour*. While the *Journal* reveals that Shelley continued privately to suffer from acute self-doubt, as a publicist she remained as sure-footed as ever. The *Six Weeks' Tour* reinforced her theme that Percy's work constituted a glimpse of infinite beauty, in stark contrast to the plague of war and injustice that ravaged the world beneath. From France, 'a country wasted and pillaged by this plague, which in his pride, man inflicts upon his fellow', they had travelled to the Alps, whose 'immensity ... so far surpasses all conception, that it requires an effort of the understanding to believe that they indeed formed a part of the earth'.[10]

It was now 18 years since Percy Shelley's death; only now, it seemed, with her husband's work published, with his biography written (albeit in clandestine form), was Mary able to loosen her hold on the intensity of her grief. As she did so, her own literary life began to wind down. In 1840 she returned to Italy, accompanying her son and two college friends to Germany, travelling from thence, via Geneva, to

Lake Como. After Percy had graduated, she went with him again in 1842 to Germany, Venice, Florence, Rome and Paris, returning in 1843. From her *Journal* and her published account of these trips, *Rambles in Germany and Italy* (1844), it is clear that this long-delayed experience of returning to Italy moved Shelley on in her protracted process of grieving.

When it came to writing up the two excursions in book form, she was ready once more to challenge those who still misrepresented her relationship to Shelley:

> Can it, indeed, be true, that I am about to revisit Italy? How many years are gone since I quitted that country! There I left the mortal remains of those beloved – my husband and my children, whose loss changed my whole existence, substituting for happy peace and the interchange of deep-rooted affections, years of desolate solitude.... (R I 1)

She describes her own trepidation on approaching Italy in a way that might put the reader in mind of a plot dreamed up by Ann Radcliffe:

> With regard to the feelings that hold my wishes in check when I think of Italy, – these are all founded on fear. Those I loved had died there – would it again prove fatal, and do I only please my fancy to destroy my last hope? (R I 37–8)

She certainly shows that she has lost none of her powers of description (or irony) as she recalls their journey down the Rhine:

> We sped speedily down the rapid river, and at one point a little apprehension of danger, just enough to make the heart beat, was excited. We approached the Falls, we were hurrying towards the ledge of rocks; it seemed as if we must go right on, when, by a dexterous use of the oars, we found ourselves with one stroke in the calm water of a little cove; the moment was just agreeably fearful; and at the crisis, an eagle had soared majestically above our heads. It is always satisfactory to get a picturesque adjunct or two to add interest when, with toil and time, one has reached a picturesque spot! (R I 49–50)

Rambles in Germany and Italy illustrates the way Shelley's literary life had developed as a fictional rewriting of her actual experiences, as a balancing-act between an evolving Romantic persona for the 'artist' fed by works of fiction, and her own very specific – and very difficult – experiences living with a prime instigator of this powerful myth. The trip down the Rhine from Schaffhausen to the Falls of Terni serves as an analogy for the way Shelley had negotiated her literary career since the death of her husband. The Falls provide a perfect image of what is publicly picturesque, and privately (should we wish to 'read' further) an analogy for her own experience of life: 'It stirs, like passion, the very depths of our being; like love allied to ruin, yet happy in possession, it fills the soul with mingled agitation and calm' (R I 51).

At the beginning of the book, Shelley (ever her father's daughter) suggests it will have a practical use as a handbook for travellers; while readers learn about the history of Italy, and while they gain a few firsthand tips about how best to organise their travelling, they are also offered reflections of a more personal nature on the journey through life. In this respect, the influence on *Rambles* of the recently reprinted *Six Weeks' Tour* seems clear. The report of the young woman's emotions on first seeing the Alps – their 'immensity staggers the imagination' – is now complemented by her mature reflection:

> I always feel renewed and extreme delight as I watch the shadows of evening climb the huge mountains, till the granite peaks alone shine forth glad and bright, and a holy stillness gathers over the landscape. With what serious yet quick joy do such sights fill me; and dearer still is the aspiring thought that seeks the Creator in his works, as the soul yearns to throw off the chains of flesh that hold it in.... (R I 93)

The elegiac tone of 1844 clearly signals the distance between the first and the last chapters of her progress. When she finally sees Geneva again, 1816 seems a very long time ago, and the Maison Chapuis and the Villa Diodati are still, in some respects, a very, very long way away:

> At length I caught a glimpse of the scenes among which I had lived, when first I stepped out from childhood into life. There, on the shores of Bellerive, stood Diodati; and our humble dwelling, Maison Chapuis, nestled close to the lake below. There were the terraces, the vineyards, the upward path threading them, the little port where our boat lay moored; I could mark and recognise a thousand slight peculiarities, familiar objects then – forgotten since – now replete

with recollections and associations. Was I the same person who had lived there, the companion of the dead? For all were gone: even my young child, whom I had looked upon as the joy of future years, had died in infancy – not one hope, then in fair bud, had opened into maturity; storm, and blight, and death, had passed over, and destroyed all.... (R I 139–40)

Shelley is both burying the past, and rewriting it. All had been destroyed by 'storm, and blight, and death'; yet now the long-overdue pilgrimage had been made, she was reconciled to what was left.

Rambles in Germany and Italy has a solid political framework. Shelley writes as an expert on the history of Europe, explaining that England prides itself on being the home of liberty, a situation likely to breed an unhealthy degree of complacency. Italy undeniably lags behind in its political maturity, the most harmful effect of the oppression it suffers being a tendency to indulge in the proliferation of secret societies. True liberty cannot be gained by such means:

> While thus every passion, bad and good, ferments – a touch is given, and up springs armed revolt. This must be put down or the peace of Europe will be disturbed. (R I x)

The evils of war had been a major preoccupation in the *Six Weeks' Tour*:

> the distress of the inhabitants [of France], whose houses had been burned, their cattle killed, and all their wealth destroyed, had given a sting to my detestation of war....[11]

Volume I of *Rambles* ends with a call for enlightened political change, but Shelley insists that her vision of liberty is one where people are raised to new heights of prosperity and civic virtue, recognising that many still fear liberty as an incitement to revolutionary action destined to destroy rather than enhance the quality of life.

Parts Two and Three of *Rambles* refer to the second trip of 1842–43. There is much here of poignant, personal reminiscence, but though her time spent in Italy tends therefore to be firmly located in the past, it is also represented as part of an historical process from which no life (literary or otherwise) can escape. There is much here that explains why a visionary poet embraced radical political ideas: the shameful history of the Hessian mercenaries, the evils of the Papacy, the ravages of the Napoleonic armies as they hacked their way through Europe, and the inspiring tales of resistance that are still told; 'Every portion of the route we traversed had been the scene of victory or defeat, and rendered illustrious by the struggle for liberty' (R II 202–10; III 44). There is much that complacent, insular, middle-class Englishmen have never understood about the struggles for freedom that continue to punctuate European history, and she is determined to rectify that:

> An English person, accustomed to the gigantic fortunes and well-ordered luxury, – to the squalid penury, hard labour and famine, – which mark the opposite orders of society in his own country, is struck by the appearance of ease and equality that reigns in Tuscany, and especially at Florence. (R III 181–2)

Beneath the surface the 'ease and equality' of Tuscany is by no means all it seems, but for all that, as she no doubt recalled some of the political discussions that had gone on around her in comfortable, dark-brown London dining-rooms, she suggests that Italy can teach England some valuable lessons. For one thing, we have lacked great poets whose work will inspire our leaders with the necessary vision; in this respect Manzoni is implicitly compared to Shelley, the latter having been rejected and ridiculed by his countrymen. Manzoni's work still counts for something in the destiny of his nation: 'His soul is filled with love of the beautiful, the elevated, and the pure' (R III 201). The greatest writers are those who write for the needs of their time, which is to say not with 'the scepticism of Lord Byron', but with a determination to affirm the beauties of liberty as the sacred right of all peoples (R III 201).

Where Percy Shelley's vision and sense of beauty and truth had shown a way forward, Mary now saw only cynicism. William Hazlitt, for example, lined up with many others in the late 1830s, only too ready to damn political reform with faint praise:

> it plainly proves, that the Reform, for which we are indebted to Lord Grey and the Whigs, is so far from a *real* one, that it seems to have increased Knavery, folly, and every base, mischievous, and detestable passion ten-fold.[12]

No doubt behind Mary's comments on Manzoni lay her memory of Bulwer's criticism of Shelley in *Ernest Maltravers*. Bulwer's novel contains a satirical caricature of an Italian poet, Castruccio Cesarini (a name not without Shelleyan associations) who does indeed exhibit all the Shelleyan vices of self-absorption coupled to an over-heated imagination.

The *Rambles* is a fluent, energetic attack on the kind of middle- and upper-class complacency about the condition of England that continued to exercise the minds and imaginations of nineteenth-century novelists, philanthropists and social commentators. For example, readers of the *Edinburgh Review* in 1809 were assured that 'honour ... morality and justice' flourished uniquely in England, and that this fact set England, Church and State, for ever apart from any possible rival:

> perhaps the ecclesiastic, like the civil polity of England, possesses a racy flavour of its native soil, which, by nations of different temperament and prejudices, may rather be admired than imitated.[13]

By way of contrast, *Rambles* contains frequent panegyrics on the beauties of Italian art and poetry that invariably revert to direct commentary on the degenerate political state of England: 'I used to pride myself on English humanity; but the boast is quenched in shame, since I read, last winter, the accounts of the cruelties practised in the Afghan war' (R III 229).

Shelley's determination to nail English arrogance does not blind her to shortcomings in Italian society; but what she does do is exploit with great skill what has already become the mythical narrative of her time with Percy Shelley in Italy, using it to help her convey a quality of mysterious beauty unknown in the squalid streets of London and along the damp lanes of the English country-side:

> Often, when here before, I looked on this scene, at this hour, or later, for often I expected Shelley's return from Palazzo Mocinego, till two or three in the morning; I watched the glancing of the oars of the gondolas, and heard the far song, and saw the palaces sleeping in the light of the moon, which veils by its deep shadows all that grieved the eye and heart in the decaying palaces of Venice. Then I saw, as now I see, the bridge of the Rialto spanning the canal. All, all is the same; but as the poet says – 'The difference to me!' (R III 81)

She concludes the book with a tribute to her husband's visionary powers that transforms her from a cold and unfeeling moon to a moon of 'silver fire'. It is an invitation to look, with Percy Shelley, beyond the mundane:

> to breathe the fragrance of the orange flowers – to see the calm sea spread out at our feet, as we look over the bay to Naples – while above us bends a sky – in whose pure depths ship-like clouds glide – and the moon hangs luminous, a pendant sphere of silver fire. (R III 296)

The tour of 1842–43 followed important developments in the Shelley household. Percy had attained his majority in 1840, and graduated in 1841. Visits to Field Place began, and an allowance of £400 a year was secured from Sir Timothy. On a sadder note, shortly before her departure, there was a falling-out with the Robinson family, while in June 1841, Mary's stepmother died.

The travellers of 1842 were Percy Florence, Mary, and Alexander Knox, a Cambridge friend of Percy. At Dresden they were joined by Henry Pearson, a musician who in 1839–40 had published *Characteristic Songs of Shelley*. Pearson soon proved a difficult travelling companion, and, after some necessary encouragement, left them at Florence. The main part of their tour completed, the party returned in late summer to Paris where Mary stayed with Claire for a few weeks, while Percy and Knox returned to England. Paris at this time was home for a group of Italian refugees, and Shelley became friendly with one in particular, Ferdinand Gatteschi. She loaned him money, intending to make over the profit from *Rambles* to him, believing he would use it to further the cause. She also wrote him letters that betrayed a degree of affection that Gatteschi later used in an attempt to blackmail her.

In April 1844, Sir Timothy, aged 91, died, and the vexed process of sorting out the estate began. It was a mess, and though saddened by the consequent bickering among those she wanted to think of as friends, at least the irony of the shifting alliances now evident at Field Place provided her with a source of wry amusement:

> We are at this moment returned from Field Place where we were invited – They were all immensely civil – & Lady Shelley

> told Percy she was sorry she did not know me before – Why then did she not?... John Shelley has quarrelled with his Mother because Sir Tim left her so much. This of course renders her more enclined to be civil to us. (To Claire, June 1844, L III 134–5)

Claire was staying with Lady Sussex (otherwise Lady Lennox) when she received this, and it was, ironically, to Lady Sussex that Gatteschi had turned after Mary for funds and affection. In response to his threat to publish Mary's letters, Alexander Knox was dispatched to Paris where he dealt with Gatteschi with admirable efficiency, using details of the latter's questionable political activities as grounds for having the French police raid his home. In the course of the raid the offending letters were carried off and duly destroyed.

Just two weeks after Gatteschi had been silenced, a more serious blackmail threat materialised. G. Byron, a man who claimed to be an illegitimate son of the poet, contacted Mary, stating that he possessed love-letters written by Shelley to Mary dating back to the time of their first meetings. He also claimed to have letters from Harriet, Percy's first wife. Publishing letters from the abandoned Harriet would threaten the reputation that Mary was so painstakingly constructing for her husband. In years to come, Percy Florence and his wife were to preside over a campaign aimed at progressively blackening Harriet's character in order to justify Shelley's desertion of her. At this point, however, it was mainly a matter of ensuring that people were given the opportunity to forget her. Fortunately, Byron's motive was pecuniary; he had no special interest in blackening Shelley's name, and was therefore open to negotiation. A number of letters were bought; then possibly because an alternative source of funds presented itself, he ceased his activities, only to reappear with more manuscripts in 1847. With the help of Hookham, Mary managed to trick Byron into parting with some of these letters, after which there were no more serious threats.

The sanitising of Percy Shelley's memory tempted at least one more hopeful beneficiary to try his hand at blackmail. Thomas Medwin, a cousin of Shelley who had been at Syon House School with him, and later became part of the Pisan circle, now wrote to Mary in 1846 to say he intended publishing a life of Shelley. Writing to him (probably from her new home in Chester Square),

Mary turned down Medwin's demand for £250, and sought to shame him into silence:

> Your letter has surprised and pained me – I had no idea that you contemplated the work you mention.
>
> ... the time has not yet come to recount the events of my husband's life. I have done all that can be done with propriety at present. I vindicated the memory of my Shelley and spoke of him as he was – an angel among his fellow mortals.... In modern society there is no injury so great as dragging private names and private life before the world. It is one from which every honourable and upright mind shrinks.... In these publishing, inquisitive, scandal-mongering days, one feels called upon for a double exercise of delicacy, forbearance – and reserve.... (May 1846, L III 284)

Medwin was unmoved; but when his book did appear in the following year, public indifference to its revelations suggests that, where people were reading Shelley, they did so without concern for either his personal details or the political implications of his poetry.

Against the insults, blackmail and bickering that followed Sir Timothy Shelley's death, Mary could set the friendship of Jane St John, who married Percy Florence in 1848. She devoted herself to Mary's comfort and to the task of promoting Percy Shelley as 'an angel among his fellow mortals'. Jane's health had given some cause for alarm, and in 1849, with her husband and Mary, she travelled to Italy to escape the English winter. Jane recovered; Mary, diagnosed as having 'rheumatism of the nerves', did not fare so well. It is good to imagine her, on one of her better days, sitting in the May sunshine on the shores of Lake Como, taking up her pen to write to Isabel Baxter Booth, the friend she had first met in Scotland before meeting Percy Shelley. Since those early years they had by no means always seen eye to eye; but now she was at peace, and wanted to share the moment:

> I long to be at home – tho just now feeling pretty well – with the sun shining the blue lake at my feet & the Mountains in all their Majesty & beauty around & my beloved children happy & well, I must mark this as a peaceful & happy hour. (L III 378)

Jane's health was a deciding factor in the abandonment of Field Place for the kinder climate of Boscombe Manor, near Bournemouth, and Mary moved between London and Hampshire until a series of strokes confined her to Chester Square. She died there on 1 February 1851.

Ten years earlier, almost to the day, Shelley had written a characteristically despairing – at times scarcely coherent – entry in her *Journal*:

> I injured my health – I gave thought, passion, care, toil – I gave all the treasure of my heart; all was accepted readily – & more & more asked – & when more I could not give – behold me betrayed, deserted; fearfully betrayed so that I would rather die than any of them more.... (J 573)

This is her bleak summary of life after her husband's death, but the biographer is bound to reflect on the appropriateness of such an outburst as a description also of the life she had lived with her husband. Of one thing at least we may be reasonably sure: in the course of the ten years since writing those despairing words in the *Journal*, for all the continuing difficulties, Mary Shelley's final years were spent with people she could once more unreservedly love and trust. Everything she wrote, however, reflects the fractured, complex world she was forced to inhabit all her life. Her novels are a commentary on the way she was constantly being challenged to think and act by different people who had their own memories of her past, and whose voices were for ever jostling for dominance over her own. The narratives she produced in these circumstances are forced continually to turn back and look again at situations from which there can be no clearly discernible way forward.

The ironies and contradictions of her literary life, never truly hers to call her own, are apparent in the memorial of 1854 intended for St Peter's Church, Bournemouth. It was designed by H. Weeks in the form of a Neo-classical *Pietà*, and depicts Mary cradling the drowned Shelley on the sea shore as though he were Christ just lowered from the cross. Weeks finally granted the atheist Shelley the Christ-like status Mary had long been claiming for him. Mary herself, though, becomes by the same token a broken-hearted mother, rather than the wife of this saintly victim. It was all too much for the Christians of Bournemouth however, who refused the monument because they knew Shelley to have been an unrepentant atheist. Christchurch Priory agreed to take it, and it is the case that visitors to the Priory in the late twentieth century generally recognise the female figure as Mary, but only because they tend to assume it to be Mary the mother of Christ, not Mary Shelley.

In his play, *Bloody Poetry*, Howard Brenton has Byron playfully challenging Mary to a duel; they have to choose their weapons. Byron suggests rhyming couplets, Mary opts for 'Home truths', to which Byron replies, 'I – am dead.'[14] Mary Shelley had played an influential part in establishing a mythology of Romanticism centred on the personalities of Byron and Shelley, but as Brenton seems to suggest, her literary life (not just her published work) was equally about destabilising that mythology, and we have yet to appreciate to the full the contribution of her 'home truths' in that respect.

Notes

1 Introduction

1 Mrs Julian Marshall, *The Life & Letters of Mary Wollstonecraft Shelley*, 2 vols (London 1889), vol. 1, p. 2.
2 Jane Dunn, *Moon in Eclipse* (London 1978); Muriel Spark, *Mary Shelley: a Biography* (New York 1987).
3 Emily Sunstein, *Mary Shelley: Romance and Reality* (Boston 1989).
4 Audrey A. Fisch, Anne K. Mellor, Esther H. Schor, *The Other Mary Shelley* (Oxford 1993).
5 Johanna M. Smith, *Mary Shelley Revisited* (New York 1996); quotations are from the Preface, p. ix.
6 Mrs Julian Marshall, op. cit., vol. 2, p. 316.
7 Sylva Norman, *Mary Shelley: Novelist and Dramatist* (Oxford 1938), pp. 57 and 61.

2 Parents

1 Mary Wollstonecraft, *A Short Residence in Sweden,* ed. Richard Holmes (London 1987), p. 153.
2 Thomas Jefferson Hogg, *The Life of Percy Bysshe Shelley* (London 1858).
3 Thomas Love Peacock, 'Memoir of Percy Bysshe Shelley', in *The Works of Thomas Love Peacock*, ed. H. F. B. Brett-Smith and C. E. Jones (London 1934), vol. 8, pp. 134 and 232. Richard Holmes, *Shelley: the Pursuit* (London 1974), p. 232. On the Peacock 'Memoir', see also Marilyn Butler, *Peacock Displayed: a Satirist in Context* (London 1979), p. 315, notes 8 and 11.
4 Quoted in Anne K. Mellor, *Mary Shelley: Her Life, Her Fiction, Her Monsters* (New York and London 1988), p. 194.
5 *The Letters of Percy Bysshe Shelley*, ed. Frederick L. Jones, 2 vols (Oxford 1964), vol. 2, pp. 109 and 435.
6 Mellor, op. cit. p. 255.
7 Peter H. Marshall, *William Godwin* (New Haven and London 1984), p. 331.
8 Maria Edgeworth, *Ennui*, ed. Marilyn Butler (London 1992), p.143.
9 Helen Maria Williams, *Letters Written in France: 1790* (Oxford 1989), pp. 126–7.
10 Charles Brockden Brown, *Edgar Huntly, or Memoirs of a Sleepwalker* (Kent and London 1987), p. 49.
11 William Godwin, *Memoirs of the Author of 'The Rights of Women'*, ed. Richard Holmes (London 1987), pp. 266 and 271.
12 Ibid., pp. 272–3.
13 William Godwin, *St. Leon*, ed. Pamela Clemit (Oxford 1994), pp. 292–4.
14 Claire Tomalin, *The Life and Death of Mary Wollstonecraft* (London 1977), p. 224.
15 *European Magazine and London Review*, XXXIII (1798), p. 251.
16 Richard Holmes, op. cit., p. 101.

17   William Godwin, *Memoirs of the Author of 'The Rights of Women'*, op. cit., p. 206.
18   Mary Wollstonecraft, *Mary*, ed. Janet Todd (London 1992), p. 39.
19   Claire Tomalin, op. cit., p. 89.
20   *A Short Residence in Sweden*, op. cit., p. 131.
21   William Godwin, *Enquiry Concerning Political Justice* (Harmondsworth 1985), p. 170. See also William St Clair, *The Godwins and the Shelleys* (London 1989), p. 197.
22   *A Short Residence in Sweden*, op. cit., pp. 152–3.

3   Early Years, 1797–1814

1   Mary Shelley, 'Introduction' to *Frankenstein* for the third edition of 1831 (New York and London 1996), ed. J. Paul Hunter, p. 169.
2   Aaron Burr, quoted in Robert Gittings and Jo Manton, *Claire Clairmont and the Shelleys* (Oxford 1992), pp. 8–9. Jane (Claire Clairmont) quoted from a letter to Edward Trelawney written in 1871, quoted in Gittings and Manton, op. cit., p. 8.
3   Tolstoy, *Anna Karenin*, trans. Rosemary Edmonds (Harmondsworth 1956), p. 13.
4   Holmes, op. cit., p. 170.
5   Quoted in *The Journals of Claire Clairmont*, ed. Marion Kingston-Stocking (Cambridge, Mass. 1968), p. 15, and in Holmes, op. cit., p. 171.
6   See William St Clair, *The Godwins and the Shelleys* (London 1990), p. 250.
7   Ibid., p. 254.
8   Richard Polwhele, *The Unsex'd Females: a Poem* (London 1798), p. 16 note. He adds: 'the crimsoning blush of modesty, will be always more attractive than the sparkle of confident intelligence'.
9   Mary Wollstonecraft, *Mary*, op. cit., pp. 7–8.
10   Helen Maria Williams, op. cit., p. 37.
11   Mary Wollstonecraft, *An Historical and Moral View of the Origin and Progress of the French Revolution and the Effect it has Produced in Europe* (London 1794), p. 222.
12   Richard Polwhele, op. cit., pp. 13, 15, 9 and 30.
13   Stuart Curran, 'Women Readers, Women Writers', in *The Cambridge Companion to British Romanticism* (Cambridge 1993), pp. 177–95.
14   Mary Hays, *The Victim of Prejudice*, ed. Eleanor Ty (Peterborough, Ontario 1994), p. 30.
15   Sydney Owenson, *Woman, or Ida of Athens* (London 1809), p. 68.
16   Charlotte Smith, *Desmond* (London 1792), p. ix.
17   Ibid., p. 109.
18   Mary Robinson, *Perdita: the Memoirs of Mary Robinson*, ed. M. J. Levy (London 1994), pp. 17–18.
19   Mary Wollstonecraft, *A Vindication of the Rights of Woman*, ed. Miriam Brody (London 1992), pp. 300–1.
20   Mellor, op. cit., pp. 15 and 194.
21   St Clair, op. cit., p. 17.
22   Godwin, *Memoirs*, op. cit., p. 213.

23   Wollstonecraft, *A Vindication*, op. cit., p. 279.
24   Mellor, op. cit., pp. 8–9.
25   Ibid., p. 10.
26   Ibid., p. 4.
27   Quoted in Gittings and Manton, op. cit., pp. 9–10. See also Mellor, op. cit., p. 13.
28   Wollstonecraft, *A Short Residence in Sweden*, op. cit., p. 69.
29   Mellor, op. cit., p. 13.
30   Godwin to Booth, 6 September 1809, in *Shelley and His Circle*, ed. Kenneth Neill Cameron (Oxford 1961), vol. 2, p. 558.
31   Mellor, op. cit., pp. 15–16.
32   Mary Wollstonecraft, *Maria*, ed. Janet Todd (London 1992), p. 67.
33   Mary Hays, op. cit., p. 3.
34   *The Poems of Shelley*, ed. Geoffrey Matthews and Kelvin Everest, vol. 1 (London 1989), p. 397.
35   Ibid., p. 444,
36   Ibid., p. 444.
37   Gittings and Manton, op. cit., p. 12.
38   Mellor, op. cit., p. 23.
39   Mary Shelley, 'The English in Italy', in *Westminster Review*, October 1826. See Appendix A in *Journals of Claire Clairmont*, op. cit.

4   The Author of *Frankenstein*, 1814–20

1   *Political Justice*, op. cit., p. 763.
2   *The Poems of Shelley*, op. cit., p. 368.
3   Jane Austen, *Love and Freindship*, in *The Works of Jane Austen*, 6 vols (London 1954), vol. 6, pp.80 and 81.
4   Holmes, op. cit., p. 16.
5   Ibid., p. 37.
6   *The Poems of Shelley*, op. cit., p. 275, l.134.
7   Mrs Julian Marshall, op. cit., vol. 2, p. 317.
8   Mary Shelley, *History of a Six Weeks' Tour through a part of France, Germany, and Holland, descriptive of a sail round the Lake of Geneva, and of the glaciers of Chamouni* (London 1817), p. 38. See also *Journal* pp. 16–17.
9   *The Journals of Claire Clairmont*, op. cit., p. 31.
10   *The Poems of Shelley*, op. cit., pp. 462–3.
11   Ibid., p. 463.
12   Quoted in Leslie A. Marchand, *Byron: a Portrait* (London 1970), p. 233.
13   *The Journals of Claire Clairmont*, op. cit., p. 59.
14   Thomas Love Peacock, *Nightmare Abbey*, ed. Raymond Wright (London 1986), pp. 47 and 95–6.
15   Holmes, op. cit., p. 221.
16   Charles Brockden Brown, *Wieland; or the Transformation*, ed. Emory Elliott (Oxford 1994), pp. 19–20.
17   Ibid., p. 49.
18   Ibid., p. 142.
19   Ibid,. p. 17.

20 *The Poems of Shelley*, op. cit., p. 488 ll. 681–7.
21 The original title of the poem, *Laon and Cythna; or, The Revolution of the Golden City: a Vision of the Nineteenth Century*, was abandoned as potentially too inflammatory. The poem was published in January 1818 as *The Revolt of Islam*. In *Shelley: Complete Poetical Works*, ed. Hutchinson and Matthews (Oxford 1971), p. 38 ll. 55–63, pp. 155–6, ll. 4810–15.
22 *Six Weeks' Tour*, op. cit., p. 174.
23 *Laon and Cythna*, op. cit., p. 37, ll. 19–20.
24 *The Poems of Shelley*, ed. Matthews and Everest, op. cit., p. 407.
25 *St. Leon*, op. cit., p. 415.
26 Bodleian Library Abinger deposit c.477. Quoted in Jane Blumberg, 'A Question of Radicalism: Mary Shelley's Manuscript "History of the Jews", in *Revolution and English Romanticism*, ed. Hanley and Selden (Hemel Hempstead 1990), p. 136.
27 'Valerius: the Reanimated Roman', in *Mary Shelley: Collected Tales and Stories*, ed. Charles E. Robinson (Baltimore 1976), p. 337.
28 *The Letters of Percy Bysshe Shelley*, op. cit., vol. 2, p. 373.

5 The Wife of Shelley, 1820–22

1 Holmes, op. cit., pp. 481–4.
2 Quoted in Holmes, op. cit., from drafts of Shelley's letters, p. 629.
3 See Editor's Note to *Epipsychidion* in *Shelley's Poetry and Prose*, selected and edited by Donald H. Reiman and Sharon B. Powers (New York and London 1977), pp. 371–2.
4 *Shelley: Complete Poetical Works*, op. cit., p. 413, ll. 41–4.
5 Ibid., p. 415, ll. 149–53.
6 Ibid., p. 419, ll. 368–72.
7 Ibid., p. 412, l. 5 and 21, p. 413, ll. 75–6.
8 Ibid., p. 418, ll. 295–300.
9 Ibid., p. 419, ll. 360–1.
10 *Mary Shelley: Collected Tales*, op. cit., p. 42.
11 *Shelley's Prose*, ed. David Lee Clarke, New Preface by Harold Bloom (New York 1988), p. 256.
12 Denis Mack Smith, *The Making of Italy* (London 1968), p. 36.
13 *Letters of Shelley*, op. cit., vol. II, p. 279. See Holmes, op. cit., p. 655.
14 Ibid., vol. II, p. 245.
15 Ibid., vol. II, pp. 353–4.
16 Mellor, op. cit., p. 209.
17 See Johanna M. Smith, op. cit., p. 73.
18 *Mary Shelley: Collected Tales*, op. cit., p. 13.
19 Edward John Trelawney, *Records of Shelley, Byron, and the Author*, ed. David Wright (Harmondsworth 1973), pp. 161–2.

6 The Widow of Shelley, 1822–26

1 *Posthumous Poems of Percy Bysshe Shelley*, ed. Mary Shelley (London 1824), pp. iii–viii.

2 Ibid., pp. iii–iv.
3 Ibid., p. iv.
4 Ibid., p. v.
5 Ibid., p. v.
6 Ibid., p. vi.
7 Ibid., p. vi.
8 Ibid., pp. vi–vii.
9 *The Journals of Claire Clairmont,* op. cit., p. 285.
10 *Blackwoods,* XIII (1823), p. 284, quoted in Walling, op. cit., p. 55.
11 Byron, 'Darkness', in *Complete Poetical Works,* ed. Frederick Page, revised by John Jump (Oxford 1970), p. 95 ll. 2–5.
12 Quoted in Fiona J. Stafford, *The Last of the Race* (Oxford 1994), p. 161.
13 William Hazlitt, *The Spirit of the Age,* in *The Complete Works of William Hazlitt,* ed. P. P. Howe (New York 1967), vol. 11, p. 42.
14 Quoted Stafford, op. cit., p. 186.
15 Byron, *Heaven and Earth,* op. cit., p. 559 ll. 925–9.
16 *The Quarterly Review,* vol. 26, October 1821, p. 149.
17 Byron, *Don Juan,* Canto IX, stanza 27, op. cit., p. 773.
18 Ibid., Stanza 27, p. 773.
19 Shelley, *Posthumous Poems,* op. cit., pp. iv–v.

7   Writing to Live, 1826–34

1 *Mary Shelley: Collected Tales,* op. cit., p. 60.
2 Ibid., p. 91.
3 Pamela Horn, *The Rural World 1780–1850* (London 1980), p. 93.
4 Edward Bulwer-Lytton, *The Disowned* (London 1852), p. 475.
5 E. P. Thompson, *The Making of the English Working Class* (London 1965), p. 228.
6 See Allan Conrad Christensen, *Edward Bulwer-Lytton* (Athens 1976), p. 72.
7 *The Disowned,* op. cit., p. 96.
8 Ibid., p. 15.
9 Ibid., p. 172.
10 Ibid., pp. 306–7.
11 Ibid., p. 94.
12 Ibid., pp. 457–8.
13 Johanna M. Smith, op. cit., p. 82.
14 Elizabeth Nitchie, *Mary Shelley: Author of 'Frankenstein'* (New Brunswick 1953), p. 173.
15 H. M. Milner, *Frankenstein; or, The Man and the Monster,* reproduced in *The Hour of One: Six Gothic Melodramas,* ed. Stephen Wischhusen (London 1975), p. 11. Page number refers to the text of this particular play.
16 Quotations from the 1831 edition of *Frankenstein* are taken from the Oxford University Press edition of the novel, edited by Marilyn Butler (Oxford 1994), Appendix B, pp. 198–228, which gives substantive changes. The full 1831 text is reproduced in the Penguin edition of the novel, edited by Maurice Hindle (London 1992). The above quotation is on p. 210.
17 Ibid., p. 212.

18   Ibid., pp. 202–3.
19   Ibid., p. 219.
20   *Mary Shelley: Collected Tales*, op. cit., pp. 121 and 128.
21   *Frankenstein*, Oxford University Press, op. cit., p. 222.
22   Edward Bulwer-Lytton, *Paul Clifford* (London 1855), p. 202.
23   Ibid. pp. 240–1.
24   Ibid. p. 244.

8   Fiction and the Marketplace: *Lodore* and *Falkner*, 1834–38

1   James Barry, *The Birth of Pandora*, in the Manchester City Art Gallery.
2   Percy Shelley, 'Song to the Men of England' ll. 1–8, in *Complete Poetical Works*, op. cit., p. 572.
3   Gary Kelly, 'Romantic Fiction', in *The Cambridge Companion to British Romanticism*, ed.   Stuart Curran (Cambridge 1993), p. 202. Samuel Richardson, *Pamela: or Virtue Rewarded*, ed. William Sale Jr (London 1993), pp. 270–1.
4   Edmund Burke, *A Philosophical Enquiry into the Origin of our Ideas of the Sublime and Beautiful*, ed. Adam Phillips (Oxford 1990), Section Headings beginning p. 53.
5   Elizabeth Inchbald, *Nature and Art*, 2 vols (London 1791) i. p. 78. Quoted in Gary Kelly, *The English Jacobin Novel* (Oxford 1976), pp. 104–5.
6   Jane Austen, *Sense and Sensibility* (Oxford 1933), p. 47.
7   Lady Caroline Lamb, *Glenarvon*, ed. Frances Wilson (London 1995), p. 142.
8   William St Clair, *The Godwins and the Shelleys; the Biography of a Family* (London 1989), p. 139.
9   Benjamin Disraeli, *Henrietta Temple* (London 1837), reprinted in *Novels of High Society from the Victorian Age* (London 1947), p. 4.
10   Walling, op. cit., p. 107.
11   Fiona Stafford, 'Lodore: a Tale of the Present Time', in *Romanticism* 3.2 (1997), pp. 213–14.
12   Thomas Paine, *Rights of Man*, ed. Henry Collins (Harmondsworth 1969), pp. 63–4.
13   Reviews referred to here are to be found in: *The Athenaeum* No. 387 (28 March 1835), pp. 238–9; *The Examiner*, No. 1425 (24 May 1835), pp. 323–4; *Fraser's Magazine for Town and Country* 11 (May 1835), pp. 600–5; *New Monthly Magazine* 44 (June 1835), pp. 236–37; *The Sun* (15 April 1835), p. 2, col. 5.
14   Edward Bulwer-Lytton, *Alice or The Mysteries* (London 1875), pp. 185–6.

9   The Editor of Shelley, 1838–39

1   Quoted in Gittings and Manton, *Claire Clairmont*, op. cit., pp. 171–2.
2   Edward Bulwer-Lytton, *Ernest Maltravers* (London 1840), p. 124.
3   *The Cabinet Cyclopedia* (London 1830–49) vol. 6, p. 127.
4   Ibid., vol.10 p. 382.

5 *Eminent Literary and Scientific Men of Italy, Spain and Portugal* (London 1835) vol. 1, p. 138.
6 Ibid., vol. 1, p. 256.
7 Ibid., vol. 2, p. 49.
8 Ibid., vol. 2, p. 151.
9 Byron, *Complete Poetical Works*, op. cit., p. 367, ll. 60–4.
10 *Eminent Literary and Scientific Men of France* (London 1838), vol.1, pp. 31–2.
11 Ibid., p. 29.
12 Ibid., p. 74.
13 Ibid., p. 129.
14 Quoted in Mrs Julian Marshall, op. cit., pp. 265–7.
15 Quoted in *Romantic Bards and British Reviewers*, ed. John O. Hayden (London 1971), p. 384.
16 Ibid., p. 390.
17 For further discussion of Shelley as editor, see Michael O'Neill, "Trying to Make It as Good as I Can": Mary Shelley's Editing of Shelley's Poetry and Prose', in *Romanticism*, 3.2 (1997), pp. 185–97.
18 *The Poems of Shelley*, ed. Matthews and Everest, op. cit., p. xiv.
19 *Edinburgh Review* XL (July 1824), in Hayden, op. cit., p. 420.

10 'Ten years which have made me old'

1 Letter to Isabella Baxter Booth, 26 May 1850, op. cit., III, 378.
2 St Clair, op. cit., p. 493.
3 Frederick A. Pottle, 'The Case of Shelley', in *English Romantic Poets*, ed. M. H. Abrams (Oxford 1975), pp. 366–83.
4 Pottle, op. cit., p. 366.
5 Quoted in Walter Peck, *Shelley*, 2 vols (Boston 1927), vol. 1, p. ix.
6 Pottle, op. cit., p. 367.
7 Holmes, op. cit., p. xv.
8 St Clair, op. cit., p. 494.
9 Percy Bysshe Shelley, *Essays, Letters from Abroad, Translations and Fragments*, ed. Mary Shelley, 2 vols, New Edition (London 1852). The quotation from Schiller is printed before Mary Shelley's Preface, p. i. (Hereafter, S in text.)
10 *History of a Six Weeks' Tour*, op. cit., p. 40.
11 Ibid., p. 19.
12 William Hazlitt, *Hazlitt's Sketches and Essays*, reviewed in *The Gentleman's Magazine*, July 1839 p. 53.
13 *Edinburgh Review*, XXVI (Jan 1809), p. 493; XVI (July 1806), p. 314. See John Clive, *Scotch Reviewers: the 'Edinburgh Review' 1802–1815* (London 1957), pp. 170–1.
14 Howard Brenton, *Bloody Poetry*, in *Plays 2* (London 1989), Act One, Scene 4, p. 261.

Further Reading

Primary Texts

A comprehensive collection of Mary Shelley's writings was published in 1996 by Pickering and Chatto in eight volumes as *The Novels and Selected Works of Mary Shelley*, General Editor Nora Crook, with Pamela Clemit, and Consulting Editor Betty T. Bennett. Included are the novels, dramas, reviews, prefaces, and travel-writing. The editors have brought our knowledge of what Mary Shelley wrote up to date, although a number of uncertainties remain, particularly around the essays written for Lardner's publications in the 1830s, and new discoveries are always a possibility. In November 1997, several English newspapers deemed the discovery of an unpublished story by Shelley written in 1820 worthy of front-page treatment. *The Novels and Selected Works* are available only as an eight-volume set. This leaves the following novels available in affordable modern editions: *Frankenstein, or the Modern Prometheus*, for which there are two editions of the 1818 text: the Norton Critical Edition edited by J. Paul Hunter (1996), and one edited with an introduction and notes by Marilyn Butler (Oxford 1993); the 1831 text, edited with an introduction by Maurice Hindle is published by Penguin (1992); *Matilda*, in *Mary Wollstonecraft, Mary and Maria: Mary Shelley, Matilda*, edited with an introduction by Janet Todd (Harmondsworth 1991); *Valperga*, edited with an introduction by Stuart Curran (Oxford 1997); *The Last Man*, edited with an introduction by Morton D. Paley (Oxford 1994); *Lodore*, edited with an introduction by Lisa Vargo (Peterborough, Ontario 1997).

Betty T. Bennett has published *The Letters of Mary Wollstonecraft Shelley* in three volumes (Baltimore 1980–88); Bennett subsequently produced a single-volume edition through the same publishers in 1995. *The Journals of Mary Shelley: 1814–1822* were published by the Clarendon Press in 1987 in two volumes, edited by Paula R. Feldman and Diana Scott-Kilvert.

In 1976 Charles E. Robinson published *Mary Shelley: Collected Tales and Stories* (Baltimore).

Mention should also be made here of *The Journals of Claire Clairmont*, edited by Marion Kingston-Stocking (Cambridge 1968).

For further details of primary texts, I recommend the bibliography in Johanna M. Smith's *Mary Shelley Revisited* (New York 1996), pp. 186–7.

Biography:

Chapter 1 of this book gives a brief account of Mary Shelley biography. The scholarly apparatus of Feldman and Scott-Kilvert's edition of Mary Shelley's *Journal* is an invaluable source in this respect; a comprehensive picture of the life can be constructed by setting the chronological tables contained in the *Journal* alongside that in Bennett's single-volume *Letters*, and in Anne K. Mellor's *Mary Shelley: Her Life, Her Fiction, Her Monsters* (New York and London 1988). In 1992, Bennett published 'Finding Mary Shelley in her Letters' in *Romantic Revisions*, edited by Robert Brinkley and Keith Hanley (Cambridge), and in the same year Johanna M. Smith edited a series of essays, *Mary Shelley: 'Frankenstein'* (Boston), several of which contain biographical material on the early years. In 1998 the Johns Hopkins University Press published an extended version of Betty T. Bennett's Introduction to the Pickering and Chatto *Novels and Selected Works* as *Mary Wollstonecraft Shelley: an Introduction*. In addition to what has already been said in Chapter 1, it is worth suggesting that Florence A. Marshall's two-volume biography of 1889, *The Life & Letters of Mary Wollstonecraft Shelley*, is well worth another look as a perceptive and provocative account (facsimile edition by Haskell House, New York, 1970). It is Marshall who begins to extract her subject from the male-centred strands of literary mythology that dominate the Romantic Movement.

William St Clair's *The Godwins and the Shelleys* (London 1989) is a very readable and informative general biography, beginning now to slip off bibliographies primarily because of its vintage. It is interesting to compare St Clair's treatment of Mary Shelley with Richard Holmes in his biography of Percy Shelley, *Shelley: the Pursuit* (London 1974).

Criticism

Most work on Mary Shelley continues to remain more or less wedded to her early period, and in particular to *Frankenstein*. The *Novels and Selected Works* will inevitably contribute significantly towards an already broadening frame of critical reference; but given the nature of the impact of her first novel on cultural production since its first appearance, we should expect no diminution of interest in *Frankenstein*.

This short selection of recent critical work is arranged in reverse chronological order: *Romanticism: Mary Shelley Bicentenary Issue*,

Volume 3.2, (1997); The Norton Critical Edition of *Frankenstein*, edited by Paul J. Hunter (1997), includes a selection of secondary material divided into 'Nineteenth-Century Responses' and 'Modern Criticism'; Judith Halberstam, *Skin Shows: Gothic Horror and the Technologies of Monsters* (Durham 1995); Katherine Hill-Miller, *'My Hideous Progeny': Mary Shelley, William Godwin, and the Father–Daughter Relationship* (Newark 1995); Stephen Bann ed., *Frankenstein, Creation and Monstrosity* (London 1994); Tilottama Rajan, 'Mary Shelley's *Mathilda*: Melancholy and the Political Economy of Romanticism', in *Studies in the Novel*, 26 (1994); Pamela Clemit, *The Godwinian Novel: the Rational Fictions of Godwin, Brockden Brown, Mary Shelley* (Oxford 1993); Jane Blumberg, *Mary Shelley's Early Novels* (Iowa 1993); Robert Gittings and Jo Manton, *Claire Clairmont and the Shelleys* (Oxford 1992); Anne McWhir,'Teaching the Monster to Read: Mary Shelley, Education, and *Frankenstein*', in *The Educational Legacy of Romanticism,* edited by John Willinsky (Waterloo, Canada 1990); Emily Sunstein, *Mary Shelley: Romance and Reality* (Baltimore 1989); Anne K. Mellor, *Mary Shelley: Her Life, Her Fiction, Her Monsters* (New York 1988); Chris Baldick, *In Frankenstein's Shadow: Myth, Monstrosity and Nineteenth Century Writing* (Oxford 1987); Mary Poovey, *The Proper Lady and the Woman Writer: Ideology as Style in the Works of Mary Wollstonecraft, Mary Shelley, and Jane Austen* (Chicago 1984); Paul A. Cantor, *Creature and Creator* (Cambridge 1984); George Levine and U.C. Knoepflmacher eds., *The Endurance of Frankenstein: Essays on Mary Shelley's Novel* (Berkeley 1979); Sandra M. Gilbert and Susan Gubar, *The Madwoman in the Attic: the Woman Writer and the Nineteenth Century Literary Imagination* (New Haven 1979); Elizabeth Nitchie, *Mary Shelley: Author of 'Frankenstein'* (New Jersey 1953). This last text would be equally appropriately listed as an early example of biography.

Index